Ontology and Ethics

Ontology and Ethics

Bonhoeffer and Contemporary Scholarship

Edited by
Adam C. Clark
and Michael Mawson

Foreword By
Clifford J. Green

◒PICKWICK *Publications* · Eugene, Oregon

ONTOLOGY AND ETHICS
Bonhoeffer and Contemporary Scholarship

Copyright © 2013 Wipf and Stock Publishers. All rights reserved. Except for brief quotations in critical publications or reviews, no part of this book may be reproduced in any manner without prior written permission from the publisher. Write: Permissions. Wipf and Stock Publishers, 199 W. 8th Ave., Suite 3, Eugene, OR 97401.

Pickwick Publications
An Imprint of Wipf and Stock Publishers
199 W. 8th Ave., Suite 3
Eugene, OR 97401

www.wipfandstock.com

ISBN 13: 978-1-62032-530-8

Cataloguing-in-Publication Data

Ontology and ethics : Bonhoeffer and contemporary scholarship / edited by Adam C. Clark and Michael Mawson ; foreword by Clifford J. Green.

xviii + 216 p. ; 23 cm. Includes bibliographical references.

ISBN 13: 978-1-62032-530-8

1. Bonhoeffer, Dietrich, 1906–1945. 2. Bonhoeffer, Dietrich, 1906–1945—Criticism and interpretation. 3. Dialectical theology. I. Clark, Adam C. II. Mawson, Michael. III. Green, Clifford J.

BX4827.B57 O58 2013

Manufactured in the U.S.A.

Contents

Foreword by Clifford J. Green / vii
List of Contributors / xi
Acknowledgments / xv
Abbreviations / xvi

1 Introduction: Ontology and Ethics in Bonhoeffer Scholarship / 1
—ADAM C. CLARK and MICHAEL MAWSON

2 The Mandates in an Age of Globalization / 19
—ROBIN W. LOVIN

3 Bonhoeffer on the Ontological Structure of the Church / 32
—CHRISTIANE TIETZ

4 Hegel, Bonhoeffer, and Objective *Geist*
An Architectonic Exegesis of Sanctorum Communio / 47
—JEFF NOWERS

5 Dispossessed Science, Dispossessed Self
Dilthey and Bonhoeffer's Christology Lectures of 1933 / 57
—JACOB PHILLIPS

6 Shame and the Other
Bonhoeffer and Levinas on Human Dignity and Ethical Responsibility / 72
—BRIAN GREGOR

7 Bonhoeffer, Kierkegaard, and the Teleological Suspension of the Ethical
The Beginning or End of Ethics? / 86
—MATTHEW D. KIRKPATRICK

8 Bonhoeffer on Law-Breaking
A Reassessment of the Ethical Exception to the Divine Command / 102
—JEREMY K. KESSLER

9 Liturgy, Kenosis, and Creation
Bonhoeffer and Lacoste on Being before God without God in the World / 118
—Kendall Walser Cox

10 The Conversion of Social Life
Bonhoeffer's Mandates as Theological Dispositifs / 133
—Markus Franz

11 Ethics beyond Biopower
Bonhoeffer, Foucault, and the Problem of Race / 150
—Brandy Daniels

Endnotes / 163
Bibliography / 209

Foreword

Clifford J. Green

One measure of health in a field of studies is the dissertations it generates. Numbers aren't everything, of course, but when two graduate students sent their peers a call for papers for a Bonhoeffer conference, about fifty proposals were received from other doctoral students and newly-minted PhD's, not only from North America but also from Britain and Germany. The conference was held in April 2011 at the University of Notre Dame. This book is mainly a selection of the papers by members of what the editors call the "third generation" of Bonhoeffer scholars. While several members of previous generations of Bonhoeffer scholars—Robin Lovin, Christiane Tietz, Bernd Wannenwetsch—made presentations, and two of these are published here, most of the papers in this volume reveal the interests of relative newcomers to Bonhoeffer scholarship.

While popular interest focuses on Bonhoeffer the historical actor, frequently in heroizing simplifications, the contributors to this volume realize that, even sixty-five years after his death, essential work is still needed before we fully understand Bonhoeffer the theologian, the thinker. Two observations are pertinent to this point. First, Bonhoeffer's theology is not an epiphenomenon of his resistance to National Socialism. It cannot be deduced from his work in the Church Struggle and his role in the resistance conspiracy to overthrow the Third Reich. Much as Bonhoeffer's theology informed these activities, that theology is not a mere by-product of his historical agency. Second, formative developments in Bonhoeffer's theology had occurred between 1927 and 1932, from his doctoral dissertation to the key ideas of *Discipleship*, in other words, before Hitler came to power in 1933. A basic concern underlying a volume such as this, therefore, is Bonhoeffer the theologian.

Essential to the work of better understanding Bonhoeffer the theological thinker is clarifying the meaning of his individual writings. Consistent with this, close readings of individual texts are to be found in the following chapters. Among these are Bonhoeffer's doctoral dissertation, *Sanctorum Communio*, his 1933 lectures on Christology, and his lectures on Genesis 1–3 in the book *Creation and Fall*. Closely related to studies of specific texts is analysis of a central dimension of Bonhoeffer's theology, namely ethics, by exploring the *Ethics* volume in relation to other texts dealing with ethical topics. Prominent in several chapters is special attention to Bonhoeffer's doctrine of mandates.

Another very prominent feature of this book is pairing Bonhoeffer with an interlocutor, and exploring how Bonhoeffer's thought engages issues raised by our contemporaries many decades later. Such dialogue also highlights distinctive aspects of Bonhoeffer's theology, and can stimulate detailed insight into his texts. This is a familiar strategy in Bonhoeffer studies. As one who commented over forty years ago on what can be described as comparative studies of Bonhoeffer, it is interesting to contrast the names paired with Bonhoeffer then and now. In those days it was Bonhoeffer and . . . Friedrich Gogarten, Emil Brunner, Werner Elert, Reinhold Niebuhr, Karl Barth, Paul Tillich, Carl Jung, Harry Stack Sullivan, and others. Recently it has been Levinas, Foucault, Agamben, and Lacoste, with a look back to Hegel, Dilthey, and Kierkegaard. This reveals how readings of Bonhoeffer are significantly driven by theories and problems from the era of his interpreters, and not necessarily by the issues that Bonhoeffer himself raised.

If studies of particular texts and the relationships between them, as well as dialogue between Bonhoeffer and older or more recent interlocutors, can contribute to our deeper understanding of Bonhoeffer the theologian, there remains a fundamental question begging for attention. This question is intensified by the completion of the seventeen-volume Dietrich Bonhoeffer Works English Edition. Given that the complete Bonhoeffer corpus is now before us in English as well as German, the pressing question is this: what is the distinctive contribution of Bonhoeffer's theology *read as a whole*? Is there an intelligible trajectory from "a theological study of the sociology of the church" to the "worldly, non-religious interpretation of Christianity" of the *Letters and Papers from Prison*? Is Bonhoeffer, as Karl Barth once said, "an impulsive, visionary thinker"? Or is there, in the diversity of his writings, a coherent theological project which is pertinent to the future of theology, the church, and Christian life?

Confronting the challenge to read Bonhoeffer's theology *as a whole*, one might be tempted to take refuge in the story of the wise librarian at Harvard Divinity School many years ago who counseled a student struggling to finish a dissertation that was threatening to run out of bounds: "Take a piece of text about the size of a tram ticket," she advised, "and write a commentary on it." But once the dissertation is written, it is time for a different agenda. When we ask regarding Barth, Bultmann, Tillich, or Niebuhr—Bonhoeffer's older contemporaries—what is the meaning and import of their theologies *read as a whole*, we know what the answers are. The challenge of this question now confronts the newest generation of Bonhoeffer scholars.

Contributors

Adam C. Clark is a doctoral candidate in Christian Ethics at the University of Notre Dame. His dissertation addresses the contribution of the Christian grammars of creation and salvation history to the formation of public reason as it pursues social justice. His wider interests include continental philosophy and disability studies.

Kendall Walser Cox is a doctoral candidate in Philosophical Theology at The University of Virginia. She is currently writing a dissertation on the parable of the prodigal son in the theologies of Julian of Norwich and Karl Barth.

Brandy Daniels is a doctoral student in Theological Studies at Vanderbilt University, where she focuses on the intersections between twentieth-century systematic theology, critical theory, race, gender, and sexuality.

Markus Franz is a doctoral candidate in Christian Ethics at the University of Leipzig. He is working on a dissertation on Luther's discourse of the "three estates," which explores its implications for a theory of contemporary evangelical/theological ethics. The dissertation also includes in its line of analysis other theologians who draw on Luther's concept for their construction of theological ethics (e.g., Bonhoeffer).

Clifford J. Green is the Executive Director of the Dietrich Bonhoeffer Works, English Edition and Professor of Theology Emeritus, Hartford Seminary, Connecticut. He holds a Th.D. (distinction) from Union Theological Seminary, New York, and taught at Wellesley College, Goucher College, and Hartford Seminary. He is the author of *Bonhoeffer: A Theology of Sociality* (1975, 2nd ed. Eerdmans, 1999), co-editor of *Ethik* (DBW

6), *Jugend und Studium* (DBW 9), and *The Young Bonhoeffer* (DBWE 9), and editor of *Sanctorum Communio* (DBWE 1), *Ethics* (DBWE 6), *Fiction from Tegel Prison* (DBWE 7), and *Barcelona, Berlin, New York: 1928-1931* (DBWE 10)."

Brian Gregor is Assistant Professor of Philosophy at California State University, Dominguez Hills. He is the author of *A Philosophical Anthropology of the Cross: The Cruciform Self* (Indiana University Press, 2013), and coeditor of two volumes of essays on Bonhoeffer, *Bonhoeffer and Continental Thought: Cruciform Philosophy*, and *Being Human, Becoming Human: Dietrich Bonhoeffer and Social Thought*.

Jeremy K. Kessler is David Berg Foundation Scholar at N.Y.U. Law School. A graduate of Yale Law School, he is currently completing his Ph.D. on the legal history of conscientious objection at Yale. Kessler's research focuses on the relationship between civil liberty and state power, particularly how the growth of the administrative state in the twentieth century has changed the way we think about freedom of conscience and expression. He has subsidiary interests in international human rights law, constitutional theory, and administrative law.

Matthew D. Kirkpatrick is Lecturer in Ethics and Doctrine at Wycliffe Hall, University of Oxford. He is the author of *Attacks on Christendom in a World Come of Age: Kierkegaard, Bonhoeffer, and the Question of Religionless Christianity* (Pickwick, 2011), *Bonhoeffer's Ethics: Between Pacifism and Assassination* (Grove, 2011), and editor of the forthcoming *Engaging Bonhoeffer: The Impact and Influence of Dietrich Bonhoeffer's Life and Thought* (Fortress Press, forthcoming).

Robin W. Lovin is Director of Research at the Center of Theological Inquiry in Princeton, NJ, and Cary M. Maguire University Professor of Ethics emeritus at Southern Methodist University. He has engaged Bonhoeffer extensively in several of his books, including *Christian Faith and Public Choices: The Social Ethics of Barth, Brunner and Bonhoeffer* (1984) and *Christian Realism and the New Realities* (2008).

Michael Mawson is Lecturer of Theological Ethics at the University of Aberdeen. His doctoral dissertation focused on Bonhoeffer's ecclesiology and social ethics. His broader interests are in modern German theology and theology and disability studies. He has published articles on issues in political theology, Christian ethics, and human rights.

Jeff Nowers is a pastoral associate at St. James Cathedral, Toronto, and adjunct lecturer in the Toronto School of Theology consortium at the University of Toronto, where he is finishing a PhD dissertation that treats Hegel's impact on Bonhoeffer's early theology. He has coedited *Theology and the Crisis of Engagement: Essays on the Relationship of Theology and the Social Sciences* (Pickwick, 2013). His other research interests include the religious dimensions of hip hop culture and the politics and spirituality of North American indigeneity.

Jacob Phillips is a doctoral candidate at King's College London. His work focuses on Bonhoeffer and philosophical hermeneutics, in particular the influence of Wilhelm Dilthey on Bonhoeffer during the 1930s. He has broader interests in the thought of John Henry Newman, the German intellectual tradition and various aspects of continental philosophy.

Christiane Tietz is Professor of Systematic Theology at the University of Zurich. She is the President of the German section of the International Bonhoeffer Society, and has written and edited several books and articles on Bonhoeffer in English and German, including *Mysteries in the Theology of Dietrich Bonhoeffer* (co-editor) and *Dietrich Bonhoeffer's Theology Today* (co-editor). She is co-editor of the Dietrich Bonhoeffer Yearbook and has also worked extensively on Bonhoeffer's philosophical engagements in his early theology, in particular in his Habilitation thesis *Act and Being*.

Acknowledgments

WE ARE APPRECIATIVE OF the many people who have had a hand in this project. We thank especially Gerald McKenny and Randall Zachman, who provided invaluable advice and made themselves available to comment on drafts during the editorial process. Thank you also to Clifford Green, Bridget O'Brien, and Josh Kaiser for editorial comments on the Introduction. And special thanks are due to the team at Pickwick Publications for their helpful and patient collaboration in bringing the volume to fruition.

We also would like to thank those who contributed to the original conference at Notre Dame, *New Conversations on Bonhoeffer's Theology*. Thank you to the Nanovic Institute for European Studies, the Graduate School, and the Department of Theology at Notre Dame for believing in and funding the conference. Thank you also to all those who contributed either at the conference or behind the scenes to making it a success: Bernd Wannenwetsch, Clifford Green, David Congdon, Marie-Theres Igrec, Matthew Puffer, Krista Duttenhaver, Matthew Ashley, Cyril O'Regan, Michael Driessen, Brian Hamilton, Kevin McCabe, Bridget O'Brien, Emily Stetler, Harriet Baldwin, Monica Caro and Jennifer Lechtanski.

Finally, we would like to thank the Institute for Scholarship in the Liberal Arts at Notre Dame, which not only supported the conference but also underwrote the costs of the present publication.

Abbreviations

Dietrich Bonhoeffer Werke

DBW 1	*Sanctorum Communio*
DBW 2	*Akt und Sein*
DBW 3	*Schöpfung und Fall*
DBW 4	*Nachfolge*
DBW 5	*Gemeinsames Leben; Gebetbuch der Bibel*
DBW 6	*Ethik*
DBW 7	*Fragmente aus Tegel*
DBW 8	*Widerstand und Ergebung*
DBW 9	*Jugend und Studium: 1918–1928*
DBW 10	*Barcelona, Berlin, Amerika: 1928–1931*
DBW 11	*Ökumene, Universität, Pfarramt: 1931–1932*
DBW 12	*Berlin: 1932–1933*
DBW 13	*London: 1933–1935*
DBW 14	*Illegale Theologenausbildung: 1935–1937*
DBW 15	*Illegale Theologenausbildung: 1937–1939*
DBW 16	*Konspiration und Haft: 1939–1945*
DBW 17	*Register und Ergänzungen*

Dietrich Bonhoeffer Works (English)

DBWE 1	*Sanctorum Communio*
DBWE 2	*Act and Being*
DBWE 3	*Creation and Fall*
DBWE 4	*Discipleship*
DBWE 5	*Life Together and Prayerbook of the Bible*
DBWE 6	*Ethics*
DBWE 7	*Fiction from Tegel Prison*
DBWE 8	*Letters and Papers from Prison*
DBWE 9	*The Young Bonhoeffer: 1918–1927*
DBWE 10	*Barcelona, Berlin, New York: 1928–1931*
DBWE 12	*Berlin: 1932–1933*
DBWE 13	*London: 1933–1935*
DBWE 14	*Theological Education at Finkenwalde: 1935–1937*
DBWE 15	*Theological Education Underground: 1937–1940*
DBWE 16	*Conspiracy and Imprisonment: 1940–1945*

1

Introduction

Ontology and Ethics in Bonhoeffer Scholarship

ADAM C. CLARK and MICHAEL MAWSON

Introducing the Volume

THIS VOLUME MAKES TWO related contributions to current scholarly discussions. First, it provides a snapshot of recent scholarship on Dietrich Bonhoeffer. On the one hand, its contributors come from universities across Germany, the United Kingdom, and North America and engage a range of topics, approaches, and interlocutors. Thus, they broadly represent the diverse kinds of work being done around the world on Bonhoeffer today. On the other hand, they also disclose a trajectory of Bonhoeffer scholarship that has now developed across three generations.[1] As we will indicate further below, each of these generations introduced distinctive contributions that have transformed and extended the purview of Bonhoeffer studies. In this volume, Robin Lovin's essay exemplifies the contribution of the early second generation; Christiane Tietz's, that of the late second generation. The remainder of the essays are by an emerging, third generation of scholars. These contributors are all either advanced graduate students or junior scholars in their first academic positions, many having just published their first books.² The first generation, comprised of scholars working shortly after Bonhoeffer's death in 1945 (among whom were many of his former students and political and ecumenical contacts), obviously could not be included directly in the volume. However, as we shall detail further below, these scholars established a hermeneutical and conceptual framework for articulating Bonhoeffer's core theological concerns that appears in the present essays and provides their basic context. Thus, taken as a whole, the volume allows the reader to survey the development of Bonhoeffer studies from its beginnings to the present day.

Importantly however, from its inception Bonhoeffer scholarship has centered on a common theme with broad social and intellectual relevance: the conceptualization of "being" (ontology) and its relationship to ethics. Tracing the development of Bonhoeffer studies thus naturally leads to the second aim of this volume, which is to indicate what the study of Bonhoeffer's theology might have to offer interdisciplinary discussions on these themes. To take but one prominent example: recent critical and deconstructive philosophies have posed the question of whether inherited forms of ontological language do justice to existence itself, and especially to the Other.³ Either implicitly or directly, several contributors to this volume argue that Bonhoeffer provides a critical ontology that is in fact ethically fruitful. While other contributors may not address this particular question, they too indicate that Bonhoeffer's ontology provides central insights needed to advance intellectual, social, and ethical life today.⁴

In this introduction, then, we will provide an overview of the development of Bonhoeffer scholarship and of the essays in this volume. To be clear, we cannot offer a synopsis of existing Bonhoeffer scholarship in all its detail. Instead, we will provide a basic narrative that highlights many of the important methodological and conceptual contributions of the first three generations of Bonhoeffer scholars, especially as these bear on the theme of ontology and ethics.

Bonhoeffer Scholarship: A Narrative

Eberhard Bethge and the First Generation

Dietrich Bonhoeffer (1906–45) first became widely known for his 1937 *Discipleship*, a work valued primarily for its pastoral and devotional insights—even if these were presented with a rather unusual degree of theological rigor. A small circle within and beyond Germany, however, knew him already at this time for his role in the German resistance to National Socialism. Since the early 1930s, he had been a central figure in the Confessing Church struggle against Hitler and the German *Volkstheologie* that provided an ecclesial legitimization of the National Socialist program. Bonhoeffer led the Confessing Church's underground seminary at Finkenwalde from 1935–37. Subsequently, he served in the *Abwehr* as a double agent and was eventually arrested, imprisoned, and then executed for his subversive actions, and especially for his role in the failed "July 20th" plot to assassinate Hitler.[5] After the war, many more came to know this side of "Pastor Bonhoeffer." Bonhoeffer's commitment to live the theology he preached, even at the cost of his life, led some already in the late 1940s to venerate him as a kind of Protestant martyr. This is the Bonhoeffer that most continue to encounter today—at least initially.[6]

The first wave of widespread scholarly interest in Bonhoeffer, however, emerged in response to the posthumous publication of his *Ethics* (1940–44) and *Letters and Papers from Prison* (1944–45) in the late 1940s and early 1950s.[7] As Ernst Feil later reflected, *Letters and Papers* was particularly important in stimulating first German and then international attention to Bonhoeffer: "all texts [by Bonhoeffer] lead again and again to those last letters from prison which stimulated all the interest in Bonhoeffer and without which little notice would be paid to the earlier writings."[8] Both texts were published by Eberhard Bethge, who had been his pupil at Finkenwalde, his closest friend during the prison years, and ultimately his literary executor.[9]

These texts, however, were highly fragmentary, in part due to the nature of their composition during the period of Bonhoeffer's resistance to Hitler and subsequent imprisonment. For similar reasons, they also contained a number of potentially seminal yet largely inchoate ideas, like Bonhoeffer's recommendation that a "world come of age" now required a "religionless Christianity." The seemingly radical cast of these ideas proved quite shocking to many post-war readers, who had only known the ostensibly more traditional, "Pastor Bonhoeffer."[10] The conceptual underdevelopment of Bonhoeffer's mature theology, coupled with the fragmentariness of his corpus as a whole, rendered it in turn especially open to contradictory interpretation and constructive development. In the 1960s, a number of thinkers began to emphasize precisely its radical potential. Though disagreeing on many specifics, these thinkers generally held that Bonhoeffer's apt identification of a world "come of age" demanded the recognition of the "autonomy" of contemporary humanity—and thus an agenda of aggressive "secularization."[11] No longer did human beings need Scriptural and creedal Christianity to provide a normative framework for the life that is good and just. Instead, they were finding this framework emerging organically from within their cultural milieu (which paradoxically was already oriented toward God *in* its rejection of God).

Put in terms of our central theme, these thinkers understood Bonhoeffer to offer a fully historicized, substantially Hegelian ontology, which locates the emergence of intellectual and ethical truth, indeed of what is most properly "real," in immanent, cultural developments [the *Sittliche*]. According to such an ontology, theology is only a linguistic symbol, an outer garment, of this higher, inner truth. As cultural developments attain to the apex of this truth, the self-sufficiency of human thought as such, humanity reaches maturity and may shed the theological garment of its youth. This "secularist" account thus took Bonhoeffer's "religionless Christianity" to be a call to end any materially Christian formation of personal existence and public life. It was a call to the purely immanent self-confidence that already fueled so much late modern thought and praxis.

Galvanized by the secularists, what we are calling the first generation of Bonhoeffer scholars came together to debate their claims and offer a better, alternative interpretation.[12] These debates put in place a network of scholars with a common agenda that would soon crystalize into an organized forum for Bonhoeffer research. The claims of the secularists drew an especially strong reaction from Eberhard Bethge, who had first published the works in question.[13] This reaction appeared in three works, all published in 1967: Bethge's magisterial biography, and his articles, "Bonhoeffer's Christology and his Religionless Christianity" and "Turning Points in Bonhoeffer's Life and Thought."[14] Once Bonhoeffer's constant companion, later his literary executor, Bethge's staunch and rigorous responses carried an unparalleled weight. It is difficult, therefore, to overestimate Bethge's importance in bringing together this first generation of scholars, and in setting the tone for Bonhoeffer scholarship more broadly.

Bethge's response took three forms. First, he sought to clarify Bonhoeffer's thought by outlining his textual development and establishing its continuity as a multivalent depiction of a single, guiding christological ontology. He showed that the ontology implied in *Letters and Papers* did not equate Christ with certain cultural developments or self-perceptions. Rather, Bonhoeffer was asking what "a church, a community, a sermon, a liturgy, a Christian life mean in a religionless world."[15] That is, Bonhoeffer's concern was not how *Christianity* could become religionless, shedding the traditional elements by which it mediated a basic conformation of the world to Christ. Rather, he asked how that mediation could occur in a *world* that no longer looks to a "Christendom" focused on inwardness for guidance. As Bethge also showed in detail, similar questions of how to witness to Christ-reality (*Christuswirklichkeit*) as the most basic reality at work in the world clearly guided both the interests and method of Bonhoeffer's other major works.[16]

Second, Bethge pointed out that Bonhoeffer himself at least partially fills out some of his inchoate conceptions with specific content from the biblical narrative. Persons come of age and are conformed to Christ as they share Christ's suffering in Gethsemane, a suffering that consisted in Christ's "failure" (from a human standpoint) to "make something of himself." Thus, as we cease to desire to have our lives turn out well and instead "live unreservedly in life's duties, problems, successes and failures, experiences and perplexities . . .[like Christ,] we throw ourselves completely into the arms of God."[17] On this account, "religionless Christianity" does not designate a "secularized" ontology in which humanity is defined by its rejection of God. Rather, it indicates a paradigm in which, as Bonhoeffer states in related passages in *Letters and Papers*, "God" ceases to function as a "working hypothesis" and *deus ex machina*. "God" is no longer a "presence" that intervenes only sporadically to ensure our dreams of a "successful," progressive resolution to life's drama. Instead, God is the one that calls us to share God's abandonment of humanity in Christ to a world that is without such resolution and yet is still *good*.[18]

Third, Bethge used Bonhoeffer's life to clarify the impulses behind his theology. Bethge's central argument here was that common work in the resistance with non-Christians had led Bonhoeffer to acknowledge a wider social movement toward the good outside of "conscious Christianity." This movement nevertheless conformed to the *christologically-defined* human ontology proclaimed by the church. It therefore was best supported by similar proclamation, albeit in a grammar tailored to recognize the wide lordship Christ had already established beyond the church proper.[19] Bonhoeffer's aim, in other words, was to underscore and amplify the true depth of the world's ontological formation by a materially-Christian "spirit."

As demonstrated in the dissertations and books written on Bonhoeffer from the 1960s through the early 1980s, many scholars joined Bethge in his commitments, though important disagreements about the degree and forms of continuity in Bonhoeffer continued.[20] One might say that Bethge's commitment to resisting any notion of radical discontinuity eventually became the first mark of a developing, if minimal, Bonhoefferian "orthodoxy." Accordingly, these first generation thinkers increasingly came to perform a correlative "orthopraxy" for interpreting both Bonhoeffer's corpus and its relation to other thinkers and issues. Studies generally defined Bonhoeffer's conceptual insights by tracing their development from his earliest academic works (e.g., *Sanctorum Communio* or *Act and Being*) to his more pastoral writings (e.g., *Discipleship* or *Life Together*), and finally to his late works *(Ethics* or *Letters and Papers)*. Likewise, they sought to relate Bonhoeffer's insights to those of other thinkers and to current issues by beginning with his own basic question in *Letters and Papers*: Who is Christ for us, today? In doing so, they addressed both practical and intellectual interests as a way of articulating and fleshing out Bonhoeffer's commitment to a pervasive christological ontology.

A number of these scholars also began to ask questions about how the christology Bethge highlights relates to other central themes in Bonhoeffer's ontology: Christian "worldliness," the nature of ecclesiology and sociality, the concrete formation of the world by the divine "commandment."[21] Scholars also took up Bethge's emphasis on the importance of Bonhoeffer's biography. Several began to consider how the different stages of Bonhoeffer's political activities might help better order the manuscript fragments in the *Ethics* and clarify their conceptual development. Others began to try to understand the "breaks" in Bonhoeffer's intellectual development by considering his life and context.[22] Bonhoeffer himself speaks for example of a turn from "the phraseological to the real," which occurred for him around 1932. A number of first generation scholars thus considered how various aspects of Bonhoeffer's experiences might have affected the way the "academic" definitions of ontology that he had developed prior to 1932 carried over to the more "pastoral" subsequent works. Late in this period, however, Clifford Green made the case—successfully, in our view—that the fundamental shift was not from the academic to the pastoral, i.e., from the theoretical to the practical. Rather, Bonhoeffer was undergoing a conversion in his understanding of the basic form of human existence. He was moving from defining the person as a (romanticized) hero engaged in a glorious struggle to defining her as the humble disciple who simply obeys God.[23] Thus, the Bonhoefferian shift was at once theoretical and practical, since changes in the ontological picture had immediate implications for the kind of ethical action suggested to the reader.

Finally, many scholars in this first generation directly emphasized the social and political ramifications of Bonhoeffer's theology. Some members of this generation were themselves involved in important social and political causes; for instance, John de Gruchy pointed to Bonhoeffer's resistance to National Socialism, which ontologized race, as a model for Christians engaging South African government and society under apartheid. Jürgen Moltmann used Bonhoeffer to develop a political theology built on a creational ontology, eschatologically transformed through Christ's crucifixion. It was also Moltmann who first suggested that Bonhoeffer's *Ethics* intentionally broadened the social ontology of his first dissertation to include all created social forms, rather than just the church.[24] Dorothee Sölle similarly appealed to Bonhoeffer to support the *politisches Nachtgebet* (political night prayer) and other grassroots movements as the source of historical change. For all three, Bonhoeffer's "christology from below" made identification with the suffering and marginalized central to what it means to be human. In North America, Larry Rasmussen investigated how Bonhoeffer's christological identification with others affected questions of pacifism and resistance. In all these examples, scholars found Bonhoeffer's ontology to have profound implications for ethics and politics.

In summary, the first generation scholars set into motion a mutually implicating set of conceptual, ethical, and methodological commitments that continue to guide scholarship today. In addition, these first generation scholars also established many of the forums and tools now essential to ongoing Bonhoeffer research. Many were involved in founding the International Bonhoeffer Society, which remains the central institution promoting scholarship and debate on Bonhoeffer in Germany, North America and beyond.[25] Many were also integral to initiating and bringing to their recent completion the Dietrich Bonhoeffer Works series and its English translations. This series has provided critical editions of all of Bonhoeffer's major works as well as several volumes of his letters and occasional writings.[26] The Works series has provided scholars and students with unprecedented levels of access to the breadth of Bonhoeffer's theology.[27]

The Second Generation

During the second generation of Bonhoeffer studies, from roughly the 1980s to the early 2000s, a distinctive set of interests and approaches began to appear in several dissertations and monographs.[28] In these works, one finds comparatively less emphasis on Bonhoeffer's late theology and biography, and fewer attempts to translate his theology into a direct demand for a specific political action in a particular context (as in de Gruchy or Sölle).[29] Especially the first of these two changes testifies to the success of the first generation in establishing the basic continuity and moral and pastoral implications of Bonhoeffer's theology. Their success gave second generation scholars the space to step back from polemics and apologetics and to contemplate the more specific features of Bonhoeffer's concepts and intellectual context.

This of course does not mean that scholars ceased to focus on Bonhoeffer's ontology as deeply relevant to their own ethical and sociopolitical contexts. Rather, the success of the first generation led to a more systematic and precise approach to this task, especially in the early second generation. For instance, Robin Lovin's work in the early 1980s presented Bonhoeffer as providing intellectual resources for formulating a comprehensive paradigm for Christian engagement in society and politics.[30] Putting Bonhoeffer in dialogue with Barth and Brunner, Lovin drew from him conceptions of public reason and church-world cooperation that attempted to move beyond the impasse between critique and correlation many found in the latter thinkers. That is, Lovin used Bonhoeffer's polemical unification of church and "worldly" communities in a single, christological ontology to call late modern, Western societies to a specific form of shared life. Like many in the early second generation, Lovin thus solidified and extended the basic link between ontology and ethics discerned by the first generation.

Especially late in the second generation, the success of the first led to a stronger turn to the details and complexity of Bonhoeffer's thought. Scholars increasingly began to examine the insights of specific works on their own terms, especially Bonhoeffer's earlier and more academic writings, e.g., *Sanctorum Communio* (1929) and *Act and Being* (1931). They worked out conceptual developments within particular periods of Bonhoeffer's theology. And they began to consider individual relationships of dependence and influence between Bonhoeffer and other thinkers in a less polemical environment (and one that also admitted stronger criticisms of Bonhoeffer himself).[31] Treatments of Bonhoeffer's theology in this period thus became more conceptually robust.

Similarly, the turn to these early works meant that scholars began to confront and clarify the complex relationship these established between Bonhoeffer's theology and modern philosophy, social science, and the humanities. In *Act and Being,* for instance, Bonhoeffer had engaged a number of philosophers in detail, including Kant, Hegel, Husserl, Scheler and Heidegger. On the one hand, second-generation scholars claimed in Bonhoeffer a specifically theological response to these philosophers' limitations—especially their collective self-confidence in offering complete ontological descriptions. As Charles Marsh puts it, Bonhoeffer's "task involves the inner rethinking of this [modern] philosophical tradition so that otherness and plurivocity are not reduced to self-mediation."[32] On the other hand, scholars also asked how reflection on modern philosophical concepts—i.e., "ontology," "subjectivity," etc.—might lead to a more nuanced appreciation of Bonhoeffer's theology. Tietz's work, including the essay in this collection, exemplifies both elements of this late second-generational turn.[33]

These developments have made several lasting contributions to Bonhoeffer studies. Most basically, attention to the philosophical categories in Bonhoeffer's works led to a sustained examination of his direct statements about ontology. Likewise, this attention has made Bonhoeffer studies structurally interdisciplinary. Bonhoeffer scholarship today increasingly asks how his thought intersects with thinkers and debates that raise fundamental questions, whether or not they are directly or even broadly theological. At the same time, the rigorous investigation of Bonhoeffer's conceptuality in itself allows him to become a theoretical resource for other disciplines.

Perhaps most importantly, these developments have led to a greater appreciation of the way that the fine details of Bonhoeffer's ontology are themselves already ethical and political gestures. That is, they function both with and against the formation of social life by other discourses. Wayne Whitson Floyd, for instance, argues that Bonhoeffer develops a form of negative dialectics that can foster a more christologically-unified political public than the similar dialectics of Adorno and the Frankfurt school. Likewise, Charles Marsh argues that Bonhoeffer's ecclesiology transforms Hegel's communal ontology into a mode of life that is more deeply other-centered. The first generation had already appropriated many ethical and political insights from Bonhoeffer's ontology. Yet those appropriations often operated out of Bonhoeffer's most basic convictions or asked what basic demand Bonhoeffer's theological ontology might make of a specific political context. Since the developments in the late second generation, Bonhoeffer scholarship has increased its focus on drawing out the ethical and political demands made in the subtle nuances of that ontology.[34]

Finally, as in the first generation, scholars emerging in the second generation also have supported organized forums devoted to detailed and rigorous work on Bonhoeffer. Many of its scholars have made and continue to make substantial contributions to the International Bonhoeffer Society and the Dietrich Bonhoeffer Works series, especially through editing its more recent volumes. Some have also developed new forums, including the *Dietrich Bonhoeffer Jahrbuch* (since 2006) and the annual International Bonhoeffer Colloquium, which publishes a selection of its papers as the series *International Bonhoeffer Interpretations* (since 2007).[35]

An Emerging Third Generation[36]

Where then does this leave Bonhoeffer scholarship today? While it is difficult to identify emerging trends with any precision, some tentative observations are possible.

First, as is apparent from the essays in this collection, the third generation of scholarship continues to build on the conceptual and methodological commitments of the previous generations. Much scholarship today simply presupposes the first generation's emphasis on the general coherence of Bonhoeffer's corpus, moving freely between different works to develop a thicker account of key aspects of Bonhoeffer's ontology. Similarly, contemporary scholarship continues to value added, late second generation methods. For instance, the essays in this volume by Jeff Nowers and Jacob Phillips pursue a close investigation of the details of Bonhoeffer's early works and connect his ontological conceptions with those of his immediate interlocutors.[37] Further, the fact that several authors in this collection teach and write in disciplines other than theology demonstrates the thesis that the second generation opened Bonhoeffer to an interdisciplinary audience.[38] Finally, several essays also display a marked interest in developing the political nature of particular elements of Bonhoeffer's ontology.

However, two more distinctive forms of constructive engagement also appear in these essays. First, scholars today draw on Bonhoeffer's theology to engage specific contemporary issues and problems which, while not entirely foreign to Bonhoeffer, have at least developed significantly or taken on markedly different historical forms. Markus Franz and Brandy Daniels, for instance, use Bonhoeffer to address problems of managerialism and racism. As Franz and Daniels indicate, these problems are related to but not coterminous with the racist programs of social organization pursued by German National Socialism, which drew such a strong response from Bonhoeffer in his own day.[39] Similarly, they are related to but not precisely the same as the institutionalized form of racism de Gruchy dealt with in apartheid. Rather, Franz and Daniels show, they involve more pervasive "economizing" and "racializing" forces that are deeply embedded in Western politics as such, forces that no doubt also undergirded both the pogroms and apartheid. As the latter comment makes clear, one distinctive contribution of more recent generations is the attempt to move past this or that presenting issue toward a diagnosis of the underlying malaise. Clearly, it is the turn to Bonhoeffer's ontology as political *in se* that makes this contribution possible.

Second, several of the contributions to this volume exhibit a methodological turn to *bricolage*—that is, to an approach that works by creatively assembling elements from different approaches and thinkers without positing continuities and differences of a more basic kind. Notably, diverse forms of this methodology also appear in a diverse number of contemporary thinkers, from the pragmatic political theorist Jeffrey Stout to the Continental architects of deconstructive philosophy, Derrida, Deleuze, and Guattari, among others.[40] This constructive turn is particularly important, for it suggests that Bonhoeffer's ontology, which the early works explored in more "modern" terms and the late theology sought to express in a "religionless world," can and does continue its formative work in our late/post-modern sociopolitical and intellectual context.

Contributors to this collection operate as *bricoleurs* in several ways. First, they operate as ecumenical, theological *bricoleurs*. Jeff Nowers, for instance, concludes his reading of Bonhoeffer as a "*Geist* theologian" by drawing a parallel with notions of *theosis* typically associated with Orthodox theologies of personal and communal transformation. Similarly, Kendall Cox suggests that Bonhoeffer corrects aspects of Lacoste's theology of creation in ways resonant with traditional Catholic discussions, while Lacoste—who actually is Catholic!—takes further Bonhoeffer's late interpretation of salvation history, which forms the core of many Protestant approaches. However, in contrast to certain thinkers especially in the first generation of Bonhoeffer studies, neither of these contributors is interested in claiming or addressing more systematic, doctrinal convergences.[41] Rather, each highlights how *ad hoc* proximities allow theology as a whole to better address neuralgic and contemporary problems.

Second, a number of scholars also operate as intellectual bricoleurs more broadly.[42] In this volume, examples include Brian Gregor, as well as Daniels and Franz, who offer comparisons of Bonhoeffer to Levinas, Foucault and Agamben, respectively. These scholars suggest that such constructed dialogues might help us to appreciate related insights into the contemporary situation appearing in Bonhoeffer and such thinkers. Yet these authors also suggest that their investigations allow us to resolve certain limitations or aporiae into which Bonhoeffer and these interlocutors, each considered only on his own terms, might lead life and discourse today. Through this methodology, these authors also suggest, we come to understand better what are the most lasting and significant contributions of Bonhoeffer's theology.

Let us then close this section with a brief summary of the narrative of Bonhoeffer studies, highlighting its significance for questions of ontology and ethics. In its first generation, Bonhoeffer scholarship defended the thesis that his corpus has its center in a coherent theological ontology, which they found to have immediate ethical and political implications for their own contexts. The early second generation extended these efforts more systematically, while the late second generation worked to develop the significance of the details of Bonhoeffer's ontology more fully. The second generation thus was able to suggest with greater nuance and explicitness how Bonhoeffer's ontology already re-defines and redresses the intellectual, historical, and sociopolitical dimensions of contemporary ethical problems. The third generation continues to expand these efforts: by considering the whole of Bonhoeffer's corpus, which the first and second generations have now set so clearly before us; by placing Bonhoeffer in relation to a wider set of interlocutors and issues; by using the breadth of Bonhoeffer's ontological reflections to unearth the root of the modern malaise; and by doing all this with a method that performs the christological relation to the contemporary, "postmodern" world demanded by Bonhoeffer's ontological commitments.

The Essays

We turn, then, to providing an overview of the essays. The order in which we have placed them aims to accomplish several ends. First, the essays reflect the movement from the early second through the third generations, described above. Second, essays two through eight traverse the span of Bonhoeffer's corpus, each highlighting one or two of the major works along this textual chronology. Reading these in order provides an introduction to key themes and concerns at each stage of Bonhoeffer's development, while highlighting the significance of the whole. Third, the order also allows something of a movement from Bonhoeffer's most basic ontological determinations to an increasing specification of their contemporary ethical and political implications. The first four essays thus provide a fundamental grasp of Bonhoeffer's theories of history, community, the individual, and the act of knowing. The next four turn to more specific determinations of ethical responsibility and social life that Bonhoeffer builds on this foundation. The last two bring Bonhoeffer to bear on specific issues in the present context: the managerial commodification and racialization of social life. To turn, then, to the themes of each essay:

Robin Lovin opens the collection with an essay that highlights the importance of the ongoing development of Bonhoeffer scholarship. For Lovin, it is crucial that scholars today negotiate the distance that separates us from Bonhoeffer. He also suggests, however, that Bonhoeffer provides just the kind of historical ontology necessary to make this possible. Lovin then offers his own negotiation, asking what the current reality of globalization might mean for an appropriation of the "venture of free responsibility" and the "mandates" outlined in Bonhoeffer's *Ethics* and *Letters and Papers*. He claims that these works point to given, christological, and unifying wholeness at the center of created social forms (the mandates) that funds responsibility in them. This wholeness, he argues, is particularly important for fostering relationships between different, "relatively autonomous" social groups in the ever-expanding global community.[43] Lovin also highlights in the mandates something akin to notions of natural law, civic virtues, and political authority found in many earlier theologies. His comments on this score not only raise important questions about what forms the normative bounds of social life, they also signal possibilities for the constructive dialogue between Bonhoeffer, Niebuhrian "pragmatic naturalism," and Catholic Social Teaching that Lovin pursues elsewhere.[44]

Christiane Tietz argues in the second essay for the importance of the largely underappreciated ecclesiology of Bonhoeffer's earliest work, *Sanctorum Communio* (1929). She argues that parsing this ecclesiology with the explicitly philosophical language of Bonhoeffer's second dissertation, *Act and Being* (1931) firmly establishes the centrality of ecclesiology for Bonhoeffer's account of ontology. Tietz stresses that Bonhoeffer's account of the church moves from a theological core to exposition in terms of the categories of philosophy and social science. This movement is crucial, she argues, for it expresses Bonhoeffer's conviction that only the "act" of revelation produces a genuine ontology. Tietz highlights how this ontology preserves proper and fully personal relations between self and God and between human beings.

Jeff Nowers also offers a reading of the status of church and community in *Sanctorum Communio* but with different concerns. Whereas Tietz emphasizes Bonhoeffer's theological premise, Nowers examines how Bonhoeffer's account proceeds through a negotiation of Hegelian social theory. Nowers' claim is that Bonhoeffer centrally relies upon a reworked appropriation of Hegel's concept of "objective spirit." Insofar as this concept names the way that the mutual encounter forms a lasting historical community, it allows Bonhoeffer to show how the church can become a concrete and ongoing manifestation of God's revelatory presence. His conclusion, therefore, is that Bonhoeffer should be read as a "*Geist* theologian" of sorts, albeit one who has moved beyond Hegel, especially in regard to preserving God's transcendent influence on and in objective spirit. Nowers tentatively suggests that this reading of Bonhoeffer could contribute to the budding dialogue around Orthodox notions of the ontological "divinization" of human creatures.

Jacob Phillips advances the discussion chronologically by comparing the conceptions of subjectivity and the human sciences at work in Bonhoeffer's *Christology* lectures (1933) with those of Wilhelm Dilthey, whom Bonhoeffer had engaged at key points in *Act and Being* (1931). Phillips' thesis is that one can see in Bonhoeffer a subtle appropriation of Dilthey's framework for human knowing, as well as his criticisms of the scientific disciplines of his day. Nevertheless, Bonhoeffer simultaneously wields these criticisms against Dilthey himself and reconstitutes Dilthey's overarching framework christologically. In effect, Bonhoeffer's lectures perform a "dispossession" of the "self" and "sciences" in a thinker influential to the recent trajectory of continental thought. If Nowers offers one way of cashing out the implications for community of the ontology explicated in Tietz, Phillips suggests its implications for individual knowers and for the work of the Academy.

Brian Gregor's essay moves to Bonhoeffer's later work, correlating Bonhoeffer's *Creation and Fall* (1933) with his *Ethics* (1940–44). He also offers one of the strongest exhibitions of third generation method, placing these works into a dialogue with the continental philosopher Emmanuel Levinas that is wholly constructive. On the one hand, Gregor believes we have much to learn from both thinkers regarding the nature of shame as a given human reality, and the link between social disregard for shame and the destruction of human dignity. Yet on the other, Gregor uses Bonhoeffer to criticize Levinas's attempt to safeguard human dignity through a notion of radical responsibility. Moreover, he claims that Levinas's conflation of sensed phenomena with being ontologizes shame in problematic ways. Gregor then inquires into how the ontological relation of Christ to creation in Bonhoeffer can address these limitations.

Matthew Kirkpatrick's essay considers Bonhoeffer's theological ontology as an elaboration of Kierkegaard's "teleological suspension of the ethical," which emphasizes the individual standing in direct relationship to God apart from every valuation supplied by earthly communities. Kirkpatrick notes this concept leads many to charge Kierkegaard with an individualistic "acosmism" that loses the world, principled ethical thought, and the community of neighbors which ethics serves. However, Kirkpatrick suggests that Bonhoeffer provides an interpretation of Kierkegaard that indicates that the teleological suspension in fact avoids such problems. Kirkpatrick makes his case by demonstrating that Bonhoeffer's thought makes use of the teleological suspension in *Discipleship* (1937), but also throughout his corpus, in ways scholars of Bonhoeffer and Kierkegaard both have failed to recognize. For instance, Kirkpatrick claims that Kierkegaard plays a direct role in the development of Bonhoeffer's *communal* ontology in *Sanctorum Communio* and in the *Ethics*. Thus Bonhoeffer provides an interpretation through which we may reclaim Kierkegaard the "cosmic communitarian."

Jeremy K. Kessler also concentrates on the relation of human ethics to the work of the transcendent God; however his concern is to trace a certain development in Bonhoeffer's conception of this relationship, which occurs both within the *Ethics* manuscripts themselves and as Bonhoeffer moves toward the late theology of *Letters and Papers* (1944). Kessler's basic interest is to indicate how and why Bonhoeffer increasingly succeeds at integrating the ultimacy of God's interventions with the basic continuity of "penultimate," earthly forms of life possessing their own integrity. Kessler's provocative reading is that Bonhoeffer achieves this integration through a version of the concept of "autonomous life," taken from Wilhelm Dilthey, in *Letters and Papers*. He claims that some such integration is necessary to a coherent depiction of God's will for earthly communities and thus ethical and legal discernment within them.

Kendall Cox likewise takes up questions of revelation and ethics, rupture and continuity, and transcendence and creation in *Ethics* and *Letters and Papers*. However, Cox pursues these concerns by placing Bonhoeffer into dialogue with the contemporary French Catholic theologian and philosopher Jean-Yves Lacoste. On the one hand, Cox commends Lacoste's "liturgical reduction" for establishing human identity in the life of prayer. This reduction, she finds, resists "ontotheological" construals of being (Heidegger) that make "God" and others a function of the human demand for a range of identities fulfilled by and in history. Cox claims this liturgical reduction is a better development of Bonhoeffer's similar concern in *Letters and Papers*. Yet on the other hand, Cox also indicates that Lacoste's theology suffers from an "elliptical sidelining of creation" that Bonhoeffer's notions of "natural" and "autonomous, worldly" life can correct. Like previous authors, Cox emphasizes the necessity of a creational definition of being for ethics, particularly focusing on its necessity for the moral recognition of finitude.

As indicated above, the final two essays turn to particular problems in contemporary history addressed by Bonhoeffer's ontology. The first, by Markus Franz, begins with an exploration of Foucault's diagnosis that contemporary social relationships operate as self-perpetuating apparatuses. These "economizing, managerial" *dispositifs* of power subvert subjectivity, the vital source of social renewal. Franz then argues that Agamben takes Foucault's theory further, showing the distinctly theological roots of this problem, which lie in a split between ontology and economy in early Christian debates about the Trinity. Franz notes that these diagnoses tend to lend such historical developments the force of social fate. As a result, they likewise see conceptions of social power and authority as inextricably compromised. Franz turns then to Bonhoeffer's discussion in the *Ethics* of the social relationships of family, economy, government, and church as "mandates," developed over against National Socialist attempts to manage these relationships as fully immanent economies. His thesis is Bonhoeffer's "mandates" overcome the split between immanent social praxis and transcendent ontology by providing a social economy rooted in God's becoming human in Christ. He thus proposes that Bonhoeffer provides for the "conversion" of social life toward forms that support free subjectivity, thereby renewing the possibility not only for genuinely public politics but also for alternative operations of a reconstituted power and authority.

Brandy Daniels draws Bonhoeffer's resistance to National Socialist management of social reality into dialogue with a distinct but related set of Foucauldian analyses. First, she explores Foucault's claim that modern states often maintain themselves by creating a social stability predicated on certain "racial" divisions and exclusions within the body politic and then claiming that this stability must be defended. National Socialist eugenics, exercised by creating a stigmatized Jewish body, were the most extreme instance of this more pervasive tendency. For Foucault, Daniels points out, this tendency in turn is rooted in modern epistemologies that inscribe the necessity of securing one's identity through categorical mastery of the world. Drawing together Bonhoeffer's *Christology* lectures (1933) and his reflections on absolute, given human unity in *Life Together* (1935), Daniels argues that Bonhoeffer provided an alternative epistemology and ontology that overcomes racialization "at its core." Daniels traces how Bonhoeffer developed these conceptions in connection with a call to stand with "Christ's Jewish flesh." Noting that Bonhoeffer's overcoming of racial ontology remained problematic and incomplete, Daniels' essay calls us to bring his work to its full social and ethical completion.

Continuing the Conversation

Early on in Bonhoeffer studies, Heinrich Ott demonstrated that Bonhoeffer himself was aware that he was leaving behind a legacy both "fragmentary" and "experimental." Yet, Ott also wrote, the unsystematized nature of Bonhoeffer's insights is exactly the fertile ground and intellectual prod scholars need to develop the import of those insights for their own context.[45] Writing in 1966, Ott believed that the historical "horizons" of his own time were essentially the same as Bonhoeffer's. For Ott then, the task of developing Bonhoeffer's insights seemed fairly straightforward—if not entirely simple. In contrast, Robin Lovin reminds us that our historical horizons are not so nearly Bonhoeffer's own. Thus, the task of engaging Bonhoeffer today is more complex.

The essays in this volume offer one set of responses to Ott's and Lovin's common charge to develop Bonhoeffer's thought in service to the contemporary academy and world. As the foregoing survey makes clear, these essays draw the diverse range of Bonhoeffer's insights into conversation with a breadth of intellectual questions, practical issues, and significant interlocutors. In so doing, they also collectively address several central themes of perennial interest to Bonhoeffer studies and the wider academy. None of these scholars claim to have offered a full and definitive explication of either the broad themes or the specific insights. Instead, they offer what Ott saw Bonhoeffer himself as offering: initial steps of analysis and constructive response that can only prod us to further conversation and above all, mutual and responsible action.

2

The Mandates in an Age of Globalization

Robin W. Lovin

Like all Christian ethics, Dietrich Bonhoeffer's ethics is a response to the problems of his time. The Christian life must be lived in a particular place in the world and at a particular point in history, and ethics, as Bonhoeffer himself said, must be about the life as it is, and not about "how everything in the world ought to be, but unfortunately is not."[1] To understand what Bonhoeffer writes about ethics, then, we must know the world in which he lived. To understand what his ethics means *for us*, we must know how our world is different from his. His life inspires us with its adventures and its dedication and its hard decisions, and so we are always trying to project ourselves into Bonhoeffer's world, trying to imagine what it would be like to be there, facing his choices, thinking his thoughts. But projecting ourselves into that world is not quite ethics. In fact, if Bonhoeffer is to be a guide to our own moral lives, we have to put some distance between him and the world *we* live in, or rather, we have to recognize the distance that is already there, separating us from a man who was born over a century ago into a world very different from our own.

Ferdinand Schlingensiepen rightly notes at the beginning of his excellent biography that we need a new study of Bonhoeffer's life, not because we have new sources that Bethge and other biographers did not have, but because we ourselves are not in a position to understand the political events, the issues of church governance, and the ecumenical meetings that were part of the background experience of the first generation of Bonhoeffer's readers after the Second World War.[2] Much has to be clarified before we can fully understand what Bonhoeffer was doing. Other purely local events and incidental quarrels need to fade into the background, so that the big picture can emerge for new readers. Younger scholars writing at the beginning of the twenty-first century mark the transition from those who could speak of Bonhoeffer as a contemporary to those who see him as a historical figure of lasting significance, but if their aim is to make his theology and his ethics available to the future, they will have to help their readers see the distance that separates us from Bonhoeffer as well as the life that draws us to him.

For this essay, I will try to do both of those things. I want to describe the political context of Bonhoeffer's work in a way that makes it comprehensible to us, but I also want to see the differences that require us to read his work in somewhat different ways to grasp its implications for our own time. I will focus on what Bonhoeffer called the "Divine Mandates," the four spheres of family, culture, government, and church in which the commandment of God becomes concrete and specific as people take responsibility for the particular circumstances of their own lives. The idea is generally familiar from the history of Lutheran social thought, and more immediately in Bonhoeffer's theological context from the "orders of creation" that Emil Brunner posed as an alternative to Barth's direct, unlimited encounter with the divine command. Bonhoeffer wrote his most extended treatment of the subject in the chapter on "The Concrete Commandment and the Divine Mandates" that appears to be the last chapter he wrote on his ethics manuscript, shortly before his arrest in 1943.[3] By that time, however, he had integrated the idea thoroughly into the rest of his thinking about ethics, so that it bears little relation to Lutheran "estates," or to Brunner's orders of creation, or even to the "orders of preservation" which appear in his lectures on *Creation and Fall* from 1932–33.[4] The mandates are part of his ethics of responsibility, which runs through his the ethics manuscripts as a whole, and his distinctive way of thinking about them still has a great deal to teach us, provided that we take responsibility for our own lives and times, instead of simply trying to relive his.

Modern Politics and the Loss of Responsibility

Bonhoeffer was clear-sighted about the ways that his ethical thinking was shaped by the events of his time. Even the idea of "ethics as formation," which appears in one of the first manuscripts Bonhoeffer wrote as he began work on *Ethics*, reflects the politics of the Church Struggle. The specter of a national church conformed to the purposes of a totalitarian state required a new emphasis on Christian identity, conformed to the reality of Christ and acknowledging no other authority. Hitler's *Gleichschaltung*, which reorganized every social institution according to the new "leadership principle," had to be answered by the resistance of a separate community of disciples who would respond to the call of Jesus with single-minded obedience. But Bonhoeffer was aware that this was not some universal, a-historical church located in an ideal space separated from temporal concerns. "The body of Christ takes up physical space here on earth," Bonhoeffer said in *Discipleship*, and, "Thus the body of Jesus Christ can only be a visible body, or else it is not a body at all."[5] A church that could exist already in eternity would not need to compete with a totalitarian state for space on earth, but that would not be the church of Jesus Christ. In the same vein, Bonhoeffer wrote in "Ethics as Formation" that "we are placed objectively by our history in a particular context of experience, responsibility, and decision from which we cannot withdraw without ending up in abstraction. Whether or not we know about it in detail we actually live in this context."[6]

Thus, Bonhoeffer devoted much time as he began writing his *Ethics* to reading and reflecting on the situation of the human person living in the modern West. It would have been easy, and understandable given his immediate concerns, to focus narrowly the unique problems of German politics—on the relative immaturity of German democracy, for instance, or the burdens imposed by the Treaty of Versailles. It seems, in fact, that Bonhoeffer came to America in 1930 with a little notebook in which he had jotted down some of those explanations.[7] But a decade later, his vision had widened even as the vision of many of his fellow Germans narrowed. Hitler may have been uniquely evil, but he was also quintessentially modern. His rise to power had to be seen as part of a self-glorification of humanity that was not confined to any particular nation.

In the twentieth century, the modern world gave rise to a new form of government that was at once populist and authoritarian. This new totalitarian politics aligned itself with the people against the forms of privilege and tradition, but once it had claimed power, it clamped down on those same people with a merciless authority that reached deeper into their lives than kings and emperors had ever done. The Nazi regime was typical of these developments—an incongruous wedding of charismatic leadership and mechanized bureaucracy. The fearsome thing about it, from Bonhoeffer's point of view, was not that it was uniquely German, but that it was so clearly the result of a general loss of human dignity among the people of the modern West.

Lacking the sense of confidence and freedom that is rooted in a relationship to God, people sought success and security in other places, relying either on their own cunning or on a heroic leader who could provide them with a sense of worth and purpose. As a result, the steady work of those who sought a better world through practical engagement with social realities came to be despised. Christian discipleship and even ordinary civic goodness seemed foolish, for who wants to waste time on penultimate problems when the ultimate solution is available? Bonhoeffer summed it up in a chapter titled "Heritage and Decay": "What is neither Machiavellian nor heroic can be understood only as 'hypocrisy' by those who no longer comprehend the slow, hard struggle between knowing what is right and what is necessary at the time, that is, that kind of genuine Western politics, which is full of compromises and of really free responsibility."[8]

Compromise does not suit the heroic leader, any more than responsibility for others suits the Machiavellian. But the problem in 1940, as Bonhoeffer saw it, was not that responsibility had been taken away by a new, totalitarian power. The larger problem of Western history was that responsibility had already been rejected by people who could no longer see themselves working at penultimate tasks. "The hungry person needs bread," Bonhoeffer wrote, beginning a short inventory of the kind of work that responsible people do. "The homeless person needs shelter, he insisted, "the one deprived of rights needs justice, the lonely person needs community, the undisciplined one needs order, and the slave needs freedom."[9] Meeting those needs can be deeply satisfying to people who see their lives in relationship to God and who are prepared to risk action on behalf of others. They do not mind that this work has to be done and redone, over and over again, nor will they hold back from their efforts because their work is often tainted by guilt or limited by failure.

Penultimate tasks, however, do not provide ultimate meaning. Those who cannot see success and failure in relation to God's grace reject this ambiguous, endless responsibility and demand to see their efforts vindicated at once history. They will choose a leader who promises ultimate meaning in politics, and once that is done, the rest of the choices are obvious. Subsequent choices will in any case be made by the leader or by the party. The only thing required of the people is obedience.

So rejection of responsibility is the starting point for a totalitarian politics that then makes responsibility unavailable. Seen in purely historical terms, this loss is irreversible, which is precisely why the "thousand year Reich" and the various "People's Republics" that dotted the globe during the twentieth century were so easily convinced of their own permanence. It is probably also why most of them found ethics, theological or philosophical, to be a discipline not quite to their liking.

Venturing Responsibility

Responsibility cannot be restored by seizing it. That would just be another denial of history, exemplified by the typical coup d'état in which one totalitarian regime replaces another, perhaps interrupted briefly by an interval in which the new leader expounds on the virtues of democracy. Responsibility can only be restored by claiming it on the authority of the Christ who takes form in history. The incarnation creates a space of freedom within the constraints of law and necessity, where it is once again possible to engage in genuine Western politics, "full of compromises and really free political responsibility."

Only this venture of responsibility can restore the possibility of real politics in the modern world, and it would scarcely be worth beginning a book about ethics without that possibility. So the conspiracy against Hitler in which Bonhoeffer was engaged while he was writing his *Ethics* becomes the necessary precondition for the existence of the book—not in the narrowly instrumental sense that in a victorious Nazi state, Bonhoeffer's book would never have been published, but in the more basic sense that until the rejection of responsibility that leads to totalitarian politics is reversed, there is no reason to write a book about the kind of penultimate decisions that only responsible people will take seriously.

Bonhoeffer's Divine Mandates are integrally related to this ethics of responsibility. Family, culture, state, and church provide the structures within which responsible action is possible. We mistake the whole idea of the venture of responsibility if we think that they conspirators were saying to themselves, "Let's kill Hitler and see what happens then." They had confidence in the underlying structures of their society, and Bonhoeffer understood those structures as the framework of within which the command of God can be heard. Without the mandates, there is no framework of intelligibility to separate what God is saying to us from the mutterings of our own imaginations. Without the mandates, a venture of responsibility is nothing but a desperate gamble that order will somehow emerge from chaos.

Within the structure of the mandates, however, a venture of responsibility has some sense of goals and limits. That seems to be how the participants in the *Abwehr* conspiracy saw their purpose. They were not simply replacing the head of the state. They aimed at a restoration of a society whose institutions had been destroyed by the Nazi *Gleichschaltung*. Making peace with the Allied Powers would have been the first order of business if the assassination plot had succeeded, of course, but Bonhoeffer was thinking about the reconstruction of German life the whole time that he was involved in the conspiracy against Hitler and working on his *Ethics*.[10]

What the four mandates tell us is that God wills distinct kinds of human good that cannot simply be collapsed into one or traded off, one for another. Family, culture, state, and church offer different kinds of possibilities and require different forms of responsibility. No one of them can replace any of the others, nor should any one of them demand a person's attention to the exclusion of the others. Bonhoeffer sees family, culture, church, and state not as social structures, but as elements of a complete life: "God has placed human beings under all these mandates, not only each individual under one or another, but all people under all four. There can be no retreat, therefore, from a 'worldly' into a 'spiritual' 'realm.' The practice of the Christian life can be learned only under these four mandates of God."[11]

For the individual as for the society as a whole, then, responsibility is a matter of acting freely and thoughtfully within the structure provided by each of the mandates and at the same time maintaining the distinctions between them. Those who actually have experienced responsibility for business or law, for example, must be assumed to know what these institutions require better than those who want to impose an alien leadership structure on them, or use them to serve other purposes. "Provided that the term is not misunderstood," Bonhoeffer writes, "one might speak of a relative autonomy here."[12]

Bonhoeffer is understandably hesitant at this point. Set against the backdrop of his earlier theological work, "relative autonomy" threatens to undermine the comprehensive claims of the command of God, and the suggestion that those who work in the institutions of society are best equipped to discern the command of God in their places of responsibility veers dangerously in the direction of natural law. His insistence on the same page that he means nothing like that does not entirely put to rest the suspicion that he must mean *something* like that, if he means what he says about relative autonomy. Bonhoeffer is led in that direction, precisely by what he sees wrong in the National Socialist order that is being imposed on the society around him. His appreciation for natural law and civic virtues will grow in his later writings, at least insofar as he sees that these traditions were able to identify substantive flaws in Hitler's regime that the Protestant emphasis on order and obedience sometimes passed over in silence.[13]

What was wrong with National Socialism was that it destroyed this relative autonomy, imposing a single structure of command and obedience on things that should in their nature be ordered separately. The point is made indirectly, not in a political treatise, but in the little essay on "What Does It Mean to Tell the Truth?" Here, Bonhoeffer tells the simple story of a child from a dysfunctional home whose teacher asks, "Is it true that your father often comes home drunk?" He does, of course, but the child denies it.[14] Now, if there is one order of command and obedience that runs across all aspects of life, that is a lie. But what the child has intuitively understood is that the teacher's question violates the boundaries between family and culture, and the lie restores them.

The child here is a stand-in for the military officers in the circle of the conspiracy who were troubled by the duplicity and the violation of their military oath that their participation in the assassination plot required. Bonhoeffer's answer to their scruples was that the risk of guilt that is inherent in responsible action extends not only to actions within each of the mandates, but also to those actions that keep the distinctions between the mandates intact. For the military officers no less than for the schoolchild in the story, a power that presumes to draw everything and everyone under its authority is no longer entitled to obedience or to truth. The mandates are unified only in Christ.[15] Because that is so, we *must* speak of "a relative autonomy" that protects each of them from totalitarian claims, whether these originate in the state, or the church, or anywhere else.

Consciously or unconsciously, then, Bonhoeffer seems to have formulated his social ethics as an answer to the *Gleichschaltung* that threatened the church after Hitler came to power. Against the claim that the same order of command and obedience must apply everywhere, Bonhoeffer asserts the genuine differences between social institutions and the corresponding freedom of those who participate in these institutions to exercise responsibility in the particular ways that these different settings require. The freedom that the church claimed during the Church Struggle thus becomes a paradigm for other sorts of freedom, too. The church "takes up space," but so do family and culture, all of them alongside the state. To try to unify the four mandates by giving ultimate loyalty to any one of them is an evasion of the responsibility we have for penultimate politics and within the framework the mandates provide. When we ask the state, or the market, or even the church to provide the unity that is the work of Christ, we are also refusing the work we have been to do. We are saying that we will not feed the hungry, shelter the homeless, befriend the lonely, and do all the other penultimate tasks that God's commandment assigns us.

Bonhoeffer's Problems, and Ours

The divine ordering of history and society that Bonhoeffer envisions in his *Ethics* remains inspiring and challenging, even in the very different world that we live in today. Bonhoeffer was both deeply involved in the most important political events of his time and committed to theological reflection on them. For him, Theological understanding was an essential part of the process of change. The idea that a "venture of responsibility" is a blind leap into an unknown future, the idea that the person of faith acts now and reflects later is a misunderstanding of the secret agent who was writing a book about ethics the whole time he was engaged in the conspiracy. The venture involved great risks and required great faith at a personal level, but it was undertaken with full consideration of both the means and the ends sought.

What would it mean for us today to become part of such an effort to re-order our lives and our society in accordance with the Divine Mandates? It would be a more open conspiracy, no doubt—undertaken in the public square, rather than under cover of military intelligence, and it would require a much larger circle of conspirators. But what would these twenty-first century conspirators be trying to do?

They might think of themselves as engaged in a Christian critique of all politics, a movement that stands apart from the state and its coercive power as a witness to the peace of Christ. That, however, is too narrow a focus for Bonhoeffer's ethics. There may have been a time when Bonhoeffer was a pacifist or a time when he believed that faithful witness was the only form of Christian politics, but that was not what he believed when he wrote about the venture responsibility and the divine mandates. To be sure, the power of the totalitarian state was the most important political problem of his time. Probably it was the most important political problem of the twentieth century. But he looked forward to a time after the war, when "the West," as he called it, could be re-formed in an way more in keeping with its heritage. He did not foresee—no one saw it coming—the long Cold War that followed Hitler's war, but it does not miss the point by much to say that Bonhoeffer wanted to be and expected to be exactly where we find ourselves now: in a world where totalitarian ideologies have been decisively discredited and a united Europe could turn to the tasks of political reconstruction and durable peace. He would have wanted theologians to be in the middle of *that* conspiracy, too.

Sometimes, as in his reflections on "the successful man," we can see Bonhoeffer struggling to envision what the life of faith would be like in a world where Hitler was a permanent reality.[16] In a longer historical perspective, however, we see that regimes like those of Hitler and Stalin and their more recent imitators were the product of a particular set of historical circumstances that no longer obtain. The totalitarian systems that still exist—North Korea and Belarus and the like—are on the margins of the global system, not at its center in the way that Hitler's Reich and the Soviet Union were. Nor is it possible to imagine some new leader taking control of all of life in the way that was possible in the century and a half that runs from Napoleon through Stalin. The digital communications revolution has proved to be a political revolution as well. Twitter may have toppled some regimes. It certainly will prevent other would-be dictators from rising.

In our time, in fact, the power of the state is in retreat, especially in the most developed countries. The great danger to peace is not fascism or communism, but a clash between the forces of the market and the forces of religious fundamentalism, both of which are rushing in to fill the vacuum left by the declining power of the state. Conspirators thinking about a venture of responsibility today might well ask themselves whether the state is *powerful enough* to perform the essential functions of protecting its people from economic exploitation and from religious intolerance.

We might also ask about the freedom of the church, for which Bonhoeffer risked so much. We can still get a feeling that we are making an important witness when we repeat Bonhoeffer's claim that "the body of Christ takes up physical space here on earth," but what does this mean in a society that says to the church and to everybody else, "Take up as much space as you want"? It is cheap grace to think that we have paid the cost of discipleship by asserting the freedom of the church when no one is denying it.

Here again, we find that if we are just trying to repeat what Bonhoeffer said in his time, the message falls short of a genuine witness to the command of God, because the problems he faced are not our problems and the world he lived in is not our world. Our problem is not *Gleichschaltung*. It is fragmentation. We do not face a power that is trying to hold everything in a rigid order imposed without exception. Our problem is that we lack any sense of unity and identity that enables us to stand as whole persons over against the disparate powers that compete for our attention with their always promising—but always incomplete—rewards. Politics, culture, family, and church—each offers so many opportunities and promises us that we can have these opportunities without making choices.

In many ways, our political and social problems are thus a mirror image of the problems Bonhoeffer faced. We cannot be disciples of Jesus Christ by simply by saying what he said, not even by saying it and believing it. But what we do share with his time is the underlying theological problem of people in the modern age that he named so clearly: We refuse to take responsibility before God for the particular circumstances in which we find ourselves. Like the German people in the 1930s, North Americans and Europeans at the beginning of the twenty-first century find the penultimate problems we face overwhelming: We cannot integrate our cultures as fast as we have integrated our economies. We do not know how to care for an aging population. We do not know how to organize the world of work so that everyone who participates in it will have food and clothing, adequate shelter, and necessary health care. We want everyone to enjoy basic human rights, especially us, but we are afraid of what other people will do with those rights if we allow them to have them.

In Bonhoeffer's time, the evasion of responsibility took the form of a search for a heroic leader who would tell them what to do. Today, it takes the more Machiavellian form of a self-interested effort to get what we want out of each sphere of life without thinking about the future or about the other people who share it with us. The result, however, is the same: No one understands real politics, which looks hopelessly compromised because it always delivers less than what we wanted, less than what we think we deserve, or less than what we think God requires. At this more basic level, Bonhoeffer speaks directly to the problems of our day. "What is neither Machiavellian nor heroic can be understood only as 'hypocrisy' by those who no longer comprehend the slow, hard struggle between knowing what is right and what is necessary at the time, that is, that kind of genuine Western politics, which is full of compromises and of really free responsibility."[17]

Genuine Politics

While we do not exactly face the same problems that Bonhoeffer did, our "conspiracy" must nevertheless share the same goal with his. We are looking for a venture of responsibility that is not a flight from the present into some unknown future, but the restoration of the "genuine Western politics" within the framework of these diverse orders of family, culture, state, and church. The church today must take up space in the world by proclaiming that there is a unity to these diverse spheres of responsibility, even when that is inconvenient for our cunning efforts to exploit each of them separately as it suits our purposes for the moment.

Bonhoeffer had to insist that the mandates cannot be unified by any one of them alone. We must insist on his more fundamental truth that they are, nonetheless, united in Christ. The wholeness of human life that God took on in the incarnation now takes form in history in a unity of life that enables us to be responsible in all four of the mandates at the same time. Genuine freedom is not the Machiavellian cunning that allows us to get what we think we want by playing the mandates off against one another: "Now, I am making my contribution to culture, and family must wait its turn until I am finished writing my book on Bonhoeffer." Or, "The purpose of the corporation is to make profits for its shareholders, so questions about paying for health care and funding retirements are for someone else to solve." Or, "The state must fight its wars and balance its budget, so universities and hospitals and the homeless must unfortunately be left out of the calculation for the moment." These positions are not genuine Western politics. They are a flight from responsibility masquerading as politics. The church, too, would be in a better position to point out that irresponsibility if it were more accountable to the state and to the family for the ways that it deals with its finances and with the sexual misconduct of its clergy.

There is no escape, then, from the diversity and unity of the divine command that Bonhoeffer articulated in his explanation of the four mandates in which we encounter the concrete commandment of God: "God has placed human beings under all these mandates, not only each individual under one or another, but all people under all four." That is a truth which applies to each of us personally, and also to our life as a society. There are many people who lack freedom because the demands of work or family have overwhelmed the rest of their life. That is a problem to be solved not only by work and the family, but also by the church and the state. Much of our political discourse today is about what the family ought to do for itself or what the state cannot do because it lacks the resources, but this fragmentation evades the commandment that makes the mandates jointly responsible for the wholeness of human life. Where the freedom to participate in that wholeness is lacking, we must together bring it into being. Where that freedom exists, as it does for most of us in the democracies of the developed world, we must exercise it with genuine responsibility, not with self-interested cunning.

Dietrich Bonhoeffer was not primarily motivated to overthrow a dictator, nor even to liberate his church from its captivity to nationalism. He looked elsewhere, in England, America, and even India, for alternatives to the responsibilities that his vocation and his family connections thrust upon him. When he made his decisive choice to return to Germany in July 1939, it was not the resistance that drew him home, but another task that he could already see beyond the impending disaster: "I will have no right to participate in the reconstruction of Christian life in Germany after the war if I do not share the trials of this time with my people."[18] Already at the beginning of the war, he understood that the cultural forces that had brought Hitler to power were at work everywhere in the modern world, and his comprehension of what the task of reconstruction would involve deepened as he worked on his *Ethics*. If he had lived to the end of the war and if the reconstruction of Europe had begun in 1945 instead of 1989, he might have found himself at the center of a very different kind of conspiracy, unlike the one for which we remember him, but very much like the one we must form, if we are to reconstruct genuine politics in the world today. It is because we are now where he so much wanted to be that his words still speak clearly to us across the six decades that separate us; and because we have got a late start on what will surely be a long process, we can be confident that some version of these ideas will still be relevant, far into the future.

3

Bonhoeffer on the Ontological Structure of the Church

CHRISTIANE TIETZ

FROM THE BEGINNINGS OF Bonhoeffer scholarship there has been a debate about whether there is one basic topic in his thinking. Regardless of the many changes and different concerns of his work, is there one main topic that he dealt with throughout his life, one topic that could be called the "*cantus firmus*" of his whole thinking?

Since Ernst Feil's book on the theology of Dietrich Bonhoeffer,[1] there has been a consensus among Bonhoeffer scholars that Christology provides this *cantus firmus*. It can be discovered in Bonhoeffer's earliest writings with their formula "Christ existing as church-community,"[2] in the book from Finkenwalde in which he unfolds discipleship as following after Christ, and in his final prison writings in which he explores the question "who is Christ actually for us today?"[3]

Yet one could also argue that ecclesiology provides the *cantus firmus*. Ecclesiology is a constant concern for Bonhoeffer; it is central to his early dissertation on the sociological structure of the church, to his book on discipleship in which he unfolds the church as the community of those who follow Christ (and are distinct from the world), and to his latest writings in prison in which he describes the church as fundamentally being-there-for-others. This is of course not a different *cantus firmus*; ecclesiology and

Christology go hand in hand for Bonhoeffer. One aim of this essay, then, is to set out why this is the case by analyzing Bonhoeffer's early thoughts on the *ontological structure* of the church. Bonhoeffer initially developed these in his dissertation *Sanctorum Communio* and in his postdoctoral dissertation *Act and Being*; his goal in these was to understand what it means that there *is* the church. How is this *being there* of the church to be understood? What does it mean to say that the church *is*?

I will present Bonhoeffer's early ontological theory of the church, then, firstly by explaining the theological premise of Bonhoeffer's early concept of the church, secondly by analyzing his ideas on the premise of theology, thirdly by presenting the fundamental sociological theses of Bonhoeffer's concept of the church, and fourthly by unfolding the ontological relationship of Christ and the church. The fifth and final part of my lecture will present the ontological structure of the church directly. In this sense the first four parts present the foundation for this fifth part. While I do not begin my lecture with the ontological structure of the church, by the end it should have become apparent why it is that Bonhoeffer conceives of the church in this way.[4] Bonhoeffer's aim with this is to show that in the church God encounters human beings in a manner which has fundamental relevance for their whole existence.

The Theological Premise of Bonhoeffer's Early Concept of the Church

Bonhoeffer's dissertation *Sanctorum Communio* was one of the first sociological approaches to the church in Christian theology. When describing the essence of the church, Bonhoeffer uses insights from the fairly young disciplines of sociology and of social philosophy. Bonhoeffer nevertheless stresses that his dissertation belongs "not to the discipline of sociology of religion, but to theology."[5] In his analysis of the church, it is theology and not sociology that is given priority. Although sociology can assist with this analysis, this is only after theological premises have been accepted.

With this approach to the essence of the church, then, Bonhoeffer differs significantly from those contemporary uses of sociology in ecclesiological theory which describe how people feel connected with each other through religious communities, or which analyze how taking part in certain communal religious actions can help people to live their lives. Such uses are concerned solely with the anthropological function of communal religion, and neglect the question of truth; they explicitly avoid taking into account any theological or "dogmatic" perspective. Although Bonhoeffer was one of the first theologians who was open to sociology, he does not use sociology in this manner. What is fundamental for Bonhoeffer is theology and its premise. Sociology is useful only when describing the social dimensions of this premise.[6]

What then is Bonhoeffer's theological premise of the church? It is that "the church . . . is simultaneously a historical community and one established by God."[7] Let's begin with the second part of this premise. That the church is "established by God" (*gottgesetzt*)[8] means that the very essence of the church is characterized by "new basic-relations *established by God*."[9] (At a later point, we will consider the shape of these new relations. Here we need to note that God is the first and fundamental actor in the church.)[10] That these new relations are established by God cannot be seen because "every empirical formation is subject to the ambiguity of all human action."[11] You cannot see that God is the one acting behind human beings' activities in church. That the church is established by God is a real premise, which means that it has to be believed.[12]

This raises the question of whether it would be more accurate to maintain that the second part of the premise (if you will the "establishment clause") is theological in nature, whereas the first part (the church as a "historical community") is a sociological premise. This is not the case because the church is not a historical community by accident.[13] The main reason for the historical dimension of the church is that it is "God's will that all God's revelation, both in Christ and in the church, be concealed under the form of historical life."[14] While the church as a historical community is visible, this historicity is also grounded in God's will.

At a later point we will examine the relation of church and revelation and why specifically the historical dimension of revelation is essential. Here it is sufficient to summarize that both aspects—being established by God and being a historical community—belong to the theological premise of Bonhoeffer's concept of the church in that both refer to God's will and action. That the church essentially is "God's church"[15] means the "concept of the church . . . cannot be deduced."[16]

The Premise of Theology

The reason that a strictly sociological analysis as such cannot grasp the essence of the church, as Bonhoeffer explains in Sanctorum Communio, is that what the church is can only be understood through believing its premise. This is similar to how Bonhoeffer argues against the ability of philosophy to understand who human beings are in his habilitation thesis *Act and Being*.

Philosophical concepts attempt to understand the human self only out of itself. They always present "a system in which the I understands itself through itself and can place itself into the truth."[17] In this way they ignore the fact that who one is, from a theological perspective, can only be understood by beginning with revelation, with "an occurrence originating with God."[18]

What exactly is the structure of Bonhoeffer's theological critique of philosophy? Does he begin with philosophy and then prove that philosophy with its self-relatedness cannot reach the truth? Or does he instead begin with a certain theological concept of truth and then prove that philosophy cannot comprehend this truth? In other words, when he assesses the usefulness of philosophy, does he begin with philosophy, or does he begin with theology? I will argue that Bonhoeffer (in a way that parallels his use of sociology) begins with theology. He begins with the thesis that the human being as a sinner "refers everything to himself, puts himself in the center of the world, does violence to reality, makes himself God, and God and the other man his creatures."[19] In this way the human being misses his or her own reality entirely.

This self-enclosed structure is what defines the sinful human being and how this being uses his or her reason philosophically. Human reason after the fall is such that "[t]hrough the act of knowing, the known is put at the disposition of the I."[20] Every "[g]odless thought . . . remains self-enclosed."[21] In other words, philosophy cannot understand who human beings really are, simply because it is not theology. Insofar that it only deals with reason (without faith), it has the same sinful, self-enclosed structure as the sinner as such.[22]

Bonhoeffer is very much aware that this insight into the insufficiency of philosophy has been gained from a theological perspective: "Those who have been placed in the midst of such presuppositions [namely, that it is not possible for human beings to place themselves into the truth] must alone judge to be untruth Dasein's [that is: a human being's] attempts to understand itself out of its own possibilities . . . This means that nothing can justify this presupposition save God—which is to say, the presupposition justifies itself."[23] What this means, then, it that theology always begins with revelation. Furthermore faith is the only adequate relation to revelation. It is only through faith that one is able to acknowledge revelation and know of its truth: "Faith is acceptance of God's sovereign will, submission to the divine truth."[24] Consequently, "faith is the given prerequisite for positive theological knowledge."[25] In summary: the premise of theology is revelation and faith in this revelation.

This also means that it is important to conceive revelation correctly. In Bonhoeffer's judgment, many theological concepts fail to do this in a satisfactory way. Either they fail to understand the historical dimension of revelation, or they neglect its God-established dimension.

Karl Barth, for example, fails to understand the historical dimension of revelation. In Barth's theology (and Bonhoeffer is here referring to the theology of the second edition of his Letter to the Romans), God reveals himself in his historical word. In Bonhoeffer's assessment, however, "God is bound to nothing, not even the 'existing,' 'historical' Word."[26] His "real word [*eigentliches Wort*]" is free.[27] In this way Barth has too weak an understanding of the historical dimension of revelation and of how God through revelation has somehow bound himself to history. In Bonhoeffer's opinion, revelation "is a matter of God's *given* Word, the covenant in which God is bound by God's own action . . . God freely chose to be bound *to historical human beings* and to be placed at the disposal of human beings. God is free not from human beings but for them. Christ is the word of God's freedom."[28] In other words, God freely chose to be bound to historical human beings! This is therefore why revelation has such a strong historical dimension; revelation really has to be found in history, rather than always already in the past when human beings think they have encountered it. For Bonhoeffer, there has to be a continuity of revelation in history.

Rudolf Bultmann, by contrast, fails to adequately preserve the "God-established" dimension of revelation. According to Bonhoeffer, Bultmann correctly stresses the importance of the historicity or "*Geschichtlichkeit*" of human existence. This *Geschichtlichkeit* especially means for him that human beings must constantly and at every moment of history decide how they want to live, either authentically or inauthentically. Or, put theologically, they must decide whether they want to live as sinners or in faith. Even if Bultmann stresses that faith is not possible without grace, faith for him is an "ontological possibility" of human existence.[29] In Bonhoeffer's judgment, Bultmann therefore thinks of revelation "within the *static* possibilities of Dasein." He fails to see "that the essence of revelation lies in its *event-character* . . . it . . . has the essential character of an event, one that comes from God's freedom."[30] In other words, Bultmann neglects how revelation is comprehensively established by God. In this way Bultmann neglects the actuality of revelation.

Some theological concepts deny the historical character of revelation (Barth), whereas others deny how it is established by God (Bultmann). For Bonhoeffer, by contrast, revelation is both; it is something historical *and* something that is established by God.

In Bonhoeffer's theology, then, it is the church which meets both of these criteria of revelation: it has a historical dimension and it is established by God. But what about the aspect of community: "the church . . . is simultaneously a historical *community* and one established by God"[31]? Before identifying the church as the place where revelation takes place we need to understand why revelation requires this communal aspect. Why do we encounter revelation only in a community of human beings? On this basis we now turn to Bonhoeffer's interest in sociality.

The Sociality of Human Spirit and of the Christian Concept of Personhood

Bonhoeffer approaches the question of sociality of human beings from a twofold perspective. On the one hand, he discusses the sociality of the human spirit; on the other, he discusses the sociality of the Christian concept of personhood. The first is a discussion at the level of the characteristics of human mind; the second is a discussion at the level of ethics.

We turn first to the sociality of the human spirit. For Bonhoeffer, the basic capacities of human spirit—i.e., thinking, willing and feeling—all presuppose and require sociality. These capacities require a certain *structural openness* to other human beings.[32] At the same time, however, he also insists that they require a corresponding *structural closedness*. These capacities require an independent *I* who is both conscious of these capacities and determines him or herself in them.[33]

Of special interest for our concern is Bonhoeffer's description of the human will. What proves definitive for the human will? For Bonhoeffer, the human will becomes active only when it encounters resistance: "Will comes into being where there is 'resistance.'"[34] Bonhoeffer emphasizes that this resistance cannot be physical in nature, because something physical is a boundary only for human power, but not for human will. Let me give an example for this: If we *will* to go through a wall, then this wall is clearly a limit on a physical level. However, it still does not limit our willing to go through the wall; this is something we are still able to will. Only the will of another human mind that can provide real resistance: "Will itself experiences resistance only in the will of a person who wills something different."[35] In other words, when I encounter the will of another human being, either he submits to my will or I submit to his or her will. It is for this reason, then, that will as such only exists in sociality.

With both of these aspects in mind—the openness and closedness of the human spirit—Bonhoeffer concludes that "one cannot speak of the priority of either personal or social being."[36] This openness and closeness, then, or being open to another human being and yet still being a self-conscious and self-determined I, is the formal presupposition for becoming a person.

With this in mind we can now turn to Bonhoeffer's concept of personhood. If human beings are such that "[t]hrough the act of knowing, the known is put at the disposition of the I"[37] and that every "[g]odless thought . . . remains self-enclosed,"[38] then a decisive change for human existence only becomes possible when this power of the I encounters a real boundary, that is, something that cannot simply be put at the disposal of the I but which breaks open its self-enclosedness. Where can human beings experience a real encounter or boundary of this kind? Bonhoeffer argues that this becomes possible only "within the ethical sphere."[39] The ethical sphere is the place in which a human being stands "in the situation of responsibility."[40] Specifically, it is where he or she has to respond to the claim of the other.

Why is it that the other human being constitutes a real encounter for me? To be clear, this is not because he or she is different or occupies a place which I myself do not. Rather, it is because this other human being makes a claim that I *should* be responsible to him or her. It is through this claim that our wills encounter one another. The will of the other person presents a limit for me (as could be seen in the characteristics of the human spirit). By recognizing that there is another will that I cannot simply put under my disposal, then I recognize that there really is a "You"[41], that is, someone transcendent who comes from the outside.[42] What is also important here is that this is a *concrete* transcendence, a transcendence "experienced only by those facing a decision."[43] As Bonhoeffer insists, "it can never be demonstrated to someone on the outside."[44] This situation of decision, then, is the situation in which I become *a person*.[45]

In this sense, becoming a person is only possible when I recognize the *other* and answer to him or her (openness), and do so precisely as an *I* (closedness). In summary: spirit at one level requires social existence (i.e., as its formal presupposition). More importantly, however, becoming a person requires an encounter with others; personhood requires community.

This ethical concept of personhood *could* be understood as if Bonhoeffer is claiming that it is only in the ethical encounter with another human being that we encounter God; the ethical encounter of humans is the *mediator* for encountering God. Some sentences in *Sanctorum Communio* seem to suggest just this, and he writes, for example that the "you-character is in fact the essential form in which the divine is experienced."[46]

In *Act and Being*, however, Bonhoeffer clearly criticizes this understanding of an ethical concept of personhood: "Only *through* Christ does my neighbor meet me as one who claims me *in an absolute* way from a position outside my existence... Without Christ, even my neighbor is for me no more than a possibility of self-assertion through 'bearing the claim of the other.'"[47] It is through Christ, in other words, that I hear this claim as absolute and understand that I can bear the claim only in Christ: "The human being perceives the claim of the neighbor as the absolute only if God's absolute claim in Christ *has encountered* him and *given* him the answer to the question about himself."[48] In this way the encounter with Christ has ontological rather than temporal priority: "There is a boundary only for a concrete human being in its entirety, and this boundary is called *Christ*."[49] It is the church that the encounter with Christ takes place.

The Ontological Relation of Christ and the Church

Bonhoeffer unfolds the priority of Christ through his concept of the church as not simply a community of human beings, but fundamentally as "*Christ* existing as church-community."[50]

What is important in this formula of "Christ existing as church-community" is its ontological character. The church-community is not something which is somehow qualified by Christ, rather it is itself a form of Christ's existence: the church-community is "the present Christ himself."⁵¹ What consequences does this have for the question of where we experience a real encounter with the other?

Christ as the revelation of the absolute God is the only one who is able to claim me in an absolute way from the outside. Therefore it is *only through Christ* that human existence can be encountered. Moreover, because the church is the only form in which we now have access to Christ, this encounter with Christ must take place within the church: "[O]nly through the person of Christ can the existence of human beings be encountered, placed into truth, and transposed into a new manner of existence. But as the person of Christ has been revealed in the community of faith, the existence of human beings can be encountered *only* through the community of faith."⁵²

Why is this *present Christ*, who is *existing* in the church-community, so important for the idea of revelation? Finally, we come to the necessity of history. If God is a person then his revelation has to be such that the character of this personhood is preserved. In particular, personhood includes freedom and uniqueness, both of which are possible only in the context of history.⁵³ Human beings cannot themselves conceive of this contingency and cannot include it in their system of ideas. Here the freedom and uniqueness of the person in principle can be maintained. If God wants to reveal himself as person, history is therefore the only place where this can take place.⁵⁴ Whereas for Jesus' contemporaries this revelation of God in the historical person of Jesus of Nazareth really was contingent, however, we now hear the story of Jesus Christ as a story from the past. Yet the problem with past stories is that they are not really able to challenge us; we can too easily explain them by locating them in their context. For this reason the story of Jesus Christ can have relevance for us only where it encounters us today. This is why Jesus Christ has to encounter us as a present Christ. This is why he has to encounter us in the church as Christ's mode of being for us today. Specifically, this happens in the present proclamation of the church in word and sacrament. In this proclamation the past is incorporated into the present.⁵⁵

The concept of Christ existing as church-community, then, does *not* mean that Christ is existing *only* in the church-community and nowhere else (i.e., as some death of God theologians have maintained). As Bonhoeffer writes, "Christ has ascended into heaven and is now with God, and we still await Christ's coming." What this means is that a "complete identification between Christ and the church-community cannot be made."⁵⁶ Or as Bonhoeffer elsewhere puts it, "the tension between 'Christ existing as community' and the heavenly Christ, whom we await, persists."[57] In other words, the church-community is no more and no less than *one* mode of being of Christ: namely, that mode of being in which Christ is there for us today.

To be clear, "Christ existing as community" is not a metaphysical claim about the church. Rather, it describes what takes place concretely when one church member becomes *Christ to the other*. It is when we become Christ to the other in the church-community that then Christ is present. This occurs in the *structure* of being with-each-other and in the *action* of being for-each-other.[58]

On the one hand, the structure of *with-each-other* means that wherever one member of the church is, "the church-community is with this individual."[59] This sense is one in which we bear the burdens and sufferings of each other and become "Christ in relation to the neighbor."[60] At the same time, the action of *for-each-other* means that through "self-renouncing, active work for the neighbor; intercessory prayer; and ... the mutual forgiveness of sins"[61] we can again become "Christ to the other."[62] This fact that we exist *with each other* in the church is something that has to be believed.[63] Furthermore, faith is also necessary for being *for each other*; in order for this to occur one has to be able to hear the claim and need of the other as the claim of Christ, which is in turn only possible through faith.

Finally, the fact that the other is not only a You, who has a claim on me, but also an I, a person, who understands my claim as qualified absolutely through Christ, means that I can only fully experience this other when he or she *is revealed* to me *as love*.[64] This happens when the other is there *for me* in the church-community: "In the community of saints ... the You reveals itself to the I as another I, as heart, as love, as Christ."[65] My recognition of this revelation again depends on faith: "One person cannot know the other, but can only acknowledge and 'believe' in the other."[66]

In summary: the structure of the *with-each-other*, the action of the *for-each-other*, and the encounter with the other as a loving I are all only possible within the church and through faith.

There is one final aspect of the ontological relation of Christ and the church that requires our attention before we proceed to the final section: Bonhoeffer's concept of the collective person. This concept indicates how a community is more than only an accumulation of individuals standing in I-You-relations to each other; community is "a spiritual reality that is more than the sum of all the individuals."[67] As a collective person it has its own "center of activity."[68] With respect to the church, then, it is Christ who is both the center of activity of the church-community and its collective person.[69] At the same time, every single member of the church-community is able to represent the collective person; this is precisely why every member is able to become *Christ* to the other.

On this basis, then, it is apparent that Bonhoeffer's ontological account of the *church* has to be understood in personal categories: "The Protestant idea of the church is conceived in personal terms—that is, God reveals the divine self in the church as person."[70] It is in the church as the community qualified by Christ, then, that real encounter happens. Furthermore, it does so in a *historically* and *God established* way;[71] in the church we encounter revelation.

The Ontological Structure of the Church

It is finally possible, then, to directly examine the ontological structure of the church as the place where we encounter revelation. Bonhoeffer identifies three aspects of this ontological structure in particular. He insists, first, that in the church "the being of revelation can be conceptualized in continuity"; second, that "the existence of human beings is really affected"; and third, that "the being of revelation can be conceptualized neither as what exists, as something objective, nor as non-existing, as something nonobjective."[72] It is necessary to examine each of these aspects in further detail.

The significance of the first aspect, then, is that it again indicates how God has bound himself in revelation. The being of revelation is able to be conceptualized in continuity precisely because of its presence in the church. Further, it is the fact that God has bound himself to the proclamation of the church—specifically to its preaching and the sacraments—that allows for the reliable communication of this revelation.

In the church-community, then, people are not only able to talk about their personal experience of being forgiven, but "[t]he community of faith really does have the word of forgiveness at its disposal."[73] Bonhoeffer insists that "the congregation may declare in sermon and sacrament that 'you are forgiven.'"[74] In this sense Christ actually is the subject of this proclamation.[75] It is through this forgiveness which is at the church's disposal that the continuity of revelation takes place in the church.[76]

Second, the continuity of revelation requires that it *really* affects the individual; its continuity has meaning only because it addresses us. How does this affection of the individual become possible? Specifically, it becomes possible through the encounter with Christ which is in turn made possible by "Christ existing as church-community." It is because Christ makes the other's claim and love relevant to me in the church that revelation encounters me existentially.[77] It is also when this happens that I find myself within the collective person "Christ existing as church-community." For both the continuity and the existentiality of revelation, then, it is necessary that the church is a collective person.

This leads us to the third aspect: namely, the question of how the being of revelation in the church should be conceptualized. As Bonhoeffer writes, "the being of revelation can be conceptualized neither as what exists [*als Seiendes*], as something objective [*Gegenständliches*], nor as non-existing [*als Nichtseiendes*], as something nonobjective [*Nichtgegenständliches*]."[78] Although there has to be continuity and existentiality of the revelation, then, the ontological structure of the church cannot simply be understood as a synthesis of act and being. It is neither *Seiendes* (being) nor *Nichtseiendes* (act).

This is again necessary in order to preserve the existentiality and continuity of revelation. On the one hand, if revelation were to be "fixed in what exists" (i.e., *Seiendes*) it would be "existentially of no interest." Correlatively, were it evaporated into nonobjectivity (i.e., *Nichtseiendes*), then its continuity of revelation would be lost.[79] Consequently, the ontological character of revelation must, as Bonhoeffer writes, entail a "tension [*Schwebe*] between entity and nonentity."[80] In my own understanding, this indicates a third mode of being beyond *Seiendes* and *Nichtseiendes*. It is this third ontological mode that maintains revelation in its continuity and existentiality.

It is this third mode of being which can be found in Christ as "the revealed person of God and the personal community that is founded through God's person."[81] The person of Christ and the community of persons founded through Christ have "genuine objectivity" (which differs from the ordinary objectivity and of course from the non-objectivity).[82]

To be clear, this character of "genuine objectivity" in the strictest sense pertains solely to the person of Christ. Although Christ encounters us in objective things (*in Seiendem*), and specifically in the concretely visible[83] community of the church, Christ is not identical with them. He cannot be drawn into the circle of the I. Bonhoeffer is clear that the person of Christ "concretely stands-over-against" the I. It "does not let itself be drawn into the power of the I, because it itself puts limits on existence, since it is the 'outside' per se."[84] In other words, Christ encounters us in *Seiendem*, but is not himself *Seiendes*. However, because he encounters us in *Seiendem*, he is also not *Nichtseiendes*. Christ is neither act nor being, but, rather belongs to this third ontological category.

For this reason it is also only Christ who gives the other human being the same ontological character. Without Christ, the other human being remains "something that exists, a thing, a 'there is,' in relation to which a neutral behavior is possible which does not touch my existence."[85] It is only through Christ, and therefore in the church, that the other human being is qualified by a transcendent being who is beyond my disposal. It is *as* they are constituted by Christ, then, that those who are in the church have the ontological character of neither act nor being as well.

At the same time, there is another ontological structure present in the church—namely, the "dialectic of faith and church."[86] Human beings belong to the church only through faith: "In order to 'become' members of the church, human beings must believe."[87] The fact that human beings *are* in the church only through an act of faith again means that they understand the personhood of the others only through faith.[88] On the other hand, faith is in turn only possible for those who are within the church: "Faith has, as its presupposition, being in the church. Faith invariably discovers itself already in the church."[89] In other words, to believe means to discover that it is not we who constitute God's grace, but rather that God and his grace are already there. The fact that we now can encounter God only in the church means to discover that the church is already there,[90] or that we already *are* a member of this church. In this sense the act of faith itself becomes possible only through a preceding being.

If these claims initially appear contradictory—i.e., that the act of faith requires being in the church, and that being in the church requires the act of faith—they nevertheless belong together: "only in faith do humans beings know the being of revelation, their own being in the church of Christ, to be independent of faith."[91] Faith and being in the church mutually found or form a "synthesis of act and being."[92]

It is on this basis, then, that Bonhoeffer also speaks of the person as a synthesis of act and being.[93] Does this mean that I was mistaken in arguing that the person is neither an act nor a being? I do not think so;

it is possible to differentiate between what *constitutes* a person and what *characterizes* a person. On the one side, a person is constituted by the synthesis of the act of faith and the being in the church. As Bonhoeffer writes, persons "are what they are on account of membership in the new humanity ... All this they 'are' only in referential-act toward Christ," i.e., in faith.[94] He is also clear, however, that "their being-'in reference to'- Christ is rooted in their being in Christ, in the community of faith."[95] This describes how the synthesis of act and being in the church constitutes the person.

At the same time, the person is *characterized* as both existing historically (i.e., a person *does not* evaporate into nonbeing) and as constituted by something transcendent, namely Christ (i.e., a person is not a reified existing thing). The "being of human beings ... is *not* to be thought of as a reified existing thing *nor* as having evaporated into nonbeing [*weder als Seiendes erstarrt, noch ins Nichtsein verflüchtigt gedacht*]."[96] In this sense the person is and remains in "tension [*Schwebe*] between entity and nonentity."[97]

If it is true that faith is only possible in the church and that the church can only be understood by believing its claim to be the revelation of God, then it's absolutely clear why Bonhoeffer says that understanding the church is possible only "by stepping inside it,"[98] and that the essence of the church cannot be understood from *the outside*, but only from *within*.[99] What this ontological structure of the church means, then, is that only members of the church (i.e., believers) can properly understand. The essence of the church is available neither to sociology nor to philosophy. To quote Bonhoeffer one final time: "The church can in its essence be understood only *as a divine act, which means, through a statement of faith.*"[100]

This chapter has argued that for Bonhoeffer the character of the church can only be understood from a theological premise, because the church is established by God and even its historical shape has its reason in God's will and deed. It has explained Bonhoeffer's opinion that only in the church, through the encounter with the present Christ, human beings become persons. For only here they hear the absolute claim of the other which breaks open their self-centeredness and become aware of the other. Only in the church, which is the present Christ himself, am I able to understand the ethical claim of the other as absolute, and only in Christ am I able to bear and answer the claim of the other. The ontological structure of the church corresponds to these insights: the ontological continuity of the church allows for a reliable communication of the revelation of Christ and the ontological existentiality of the church makes revelation really touch human existence. Accordingly, Bonhoeffer conceives the personhood of Christ and—through Christ—of the members of the church as being a mode of being of its own which guarantees both.

4

Hegel, Bonhoeffer, and Objective *Geist*

An Architectonic Exegesis of Sanctorum Communio

JEFF NOWERS

THE PURPOSE OF THIS essay is to explore the relation of Georg Wilhelm Friedrich Hegel to Dietrich Bonhoeffer, a topic that remains a difficult and unsatisfactorily explored area of Bonhoeffer studies. One notable recent contribution comes from Adam Kotsko, who identifies Bonhoeffer's recrafted version of the Hegelian concept of objective *Geist*[1] as the central concern of Bonhoeffer's *Sanctorum Communio*. This central concern, Kotsko argues, though not explicitly named by Bonhoeffer in his subsequent writings, persisted throughout his life, even in the *Letters and Papers from Prison*.[2] My own thesis here stands in basic agreement with Kotsko. But whereas Kotsko finds objective *Geist* to be the basis of continuity in Bonhoeffer's overall thought, my aim is to focus squarely on *Sanctorum Communio*, Bonhoeffer's first dissertation. Assuming Hegel as a backdrop, I shall provide a logical accounting of the dissertation's structure that examines how objective *Geist* occupies a place of central concern within it.

To this end, I have approached *Sanctorum Communio* in a manner analogous to an architectural analysis. I thus identify four stages of construction, with Bonhoeffer's notion of objective *Geist* representing the most significant stage. The first stage pertains to Christology and ecclesiology, two dogmatic *loci* that Bonhoeffer weaves tightly together (he is a "Christo-ecclesiologist"). In the second stage, pneumatology comes to the fore, which accounts for the bond of Christology and ecclesiology. Yet these first two stages are linked to certain assumptions about community, which constitutes the third stage of construction. An examination of Bonhoeffer's understanding of community reveals, in turn, a fourth stage, namely, objective *Geist*.

It is important to note that these stages of construction are not presented as layers in Bonhoeffer's conceptual apparatus. That is to say, one stage of construction is not necessarily dependent on, or part of, another stage. The sequential order of the stages matters less than the logical relationship between them. It must also be noted that it is not at all clear whether Bonhoeffer himself would have envisioned such stages of construction in his work. The metaphor of architectural analysis is useful rather for *my own* exegetical accounting of the logical structure behind the final form of *Sanctorum Communio*. My overarching thesis is that Bonhoeffer's own theologically recrafted version of objective *Geist* undergirds his Christology, ecclesiology and latent pneumatology; objective *Geist* thus can be seen as the underlying central concern of the entire dissertation. Bonhoeffer's own stated purpose in *Sanctorum Communio* is to pursue a theological understanding of the church informed by social philosophy and sociology,[3] and my aim is to show that objective *Geist*, as a theologically-reworked social concept, lies at the heart of this project.

Hegel's *Geist*

Before I examine *Sanctorum Communio*, it is necessary that I first review the salient features of Hegel's *Geist* concept as a backdrop. *Geist*, for Hegel, is the historical unfolding of the dialectical process. If "the Idea"—reality *in toto*—is assumed as the most basic and pure singular category, it must also be assumed as logically indeterminate and devoid of feature; it is, therefore, nothingness. But in naming the Idea as nothingness, a crucial movement has already occurred: the Idea has passed from itself to that which qualifies it, namely, nothingness. The return of the Idea to itself is the goal of the dialectical process, but only insofar as this is a return to unity, such that the Idea is not merely as it began *in itself*, but is rather now *in* and *for* itself, which is its own actualization.[4]

This dialectical process, which for Hegel occurs at every level of reality, is reflected in the three-part structure of his *Encyclopaedia*, a work begun in 1817 and revised and expanded up to 1830, the year before his death. In the first part of the *Encyclopaedia*, Hegel deals with logic, followed by nature in the second part, and *Geist* in the third part. The overall movement begins from logic, understood as "pure" thought, which passes over to the concrete thought of nature (i.e., conceptions of differentiated objects of matter and life forms), and finally to *Geist*, which is the return of thought to itself, not as pure abstraction but as manifested historically in the world.

In its historical unfolding, *Geist* follows the same tripartite movement. Subjective *Geist*, or the mind of the individual subject—namely, consciousness, sense perception and memory—passes over to objective *Geist*, which is the collective product of the "I" and its thinking. Objective *Geist* thus has to do with institutions—law, morality, community and the state. The unity of subjective and objective *Geist* is found in absolute *Geist*. This is a movement into the domains of aesthetics, art, religion and, ultimately, philosophy, which for Hegel is the supreme manifestation of reason. Hegel finds in the Christian doctrine of the Trinity a resource for conceiving of *Geist* theologically. The Father signifies pure thought and consciousness, which passes over, in the begetting of the Son, into the world and its institutions; the Holy Spirit signifies the reconciliation of the world to God.[5] For Hegel, then, God is not metaphysically prior and other, but is rather the unfolding processes of mind that culminate in absolute *Geist*.

Stage 1: Christology and Ecclesiology

For the purposes of this essay, I am concerned with the middle movement of *Geist*—objective *Geist*. How does Bonhoeffer rework this notion? And how can objective *Geist* be identified as the central concern of his *Sanctorum Communio*? To answer these questions, I employ an architectural analysis of *Sanctorum Communio*, in which Christology and ecclesiology together constitute the initial stage of construction. In analyzing this stage, I show that the tightly woven bond of Christology and ecclesiology emerges from Bonhoeffer's understanding of Christ as

Stellvertreter (vicarious representative), which itself is predicated on a specific theology of sin.

In that theology of sin, Bonhoeffer posits a contrasting binary of Adam and Christ. All of humanity, according to Bonhoeffer, subsists in Adam, who is *der Mensch*, the "representative human being." Though Adam is representative, "everyone becomes guilty by their own strength and fault, because they themselves are Adam."[6] All of humanity, Bonhoeffer argues, "falls with each sin, and not one of us is in principle different from Adam; that is, every one is also the 'first' sinner."[7] It follows, then, that history is the history of Adam, and sin is the enslavement to that history. What breaks this historical juggernaut is *das Leben in der Liebe* (life that abides in love), a life revealed by Christ as *Stellvertreter*.

For Bonhoeffer, life-abiding-in-love is possible only by fulfilling the ultimate isolation engendered by the Jewish law.[8] This fulfillment takes Jesus to the cross—what Bonhoeffer describes as "the most profound solitude that the curse of the law brings upon human beings."[9] In assuming the totality of Adam's alienation in himself, Jesus' death becomes itself the finality of death and the transformation of history. Accordingly—and here is where Bonhoeffer makes a key move—in Jesus' resurrection "the humanity-of-Adam has become the church of Christ."[10] Adam has been superseded by *Christus als Gemeinde existierend* (Christ existing as church-community).[11] For Bonhoeffer, this church is not a mere historico-religious entity but rather *Gemeinde*, a reality of revelation. Yet in this distinction, a tension emerges in Bonhoeffer's reasoning. On the one hand, Christ does not "represent" the church, for "only what is *not* present can be represented."[12] Since Christ *is* present, he actually exists now as church-community. On the other hand, Bonhoeffer concedes that "[t]he reality of sin and the communio peccatorum remain even in God's church-community; Adam has really been replaced by Christ only eschatologically."[13] Can this tension between the now and the eschatological not-yet be overcome? Can Bonhoeffer show the church's existence to be "real"? Is the church actualized? The answer to these questions is illuminated by Bonhoeffer's view of the agency of the Holy Spirit, which constitutes the second stage in this essay's architectural analysis.

Stage 2: Pneumatology

The Holy Spirit in Bonhoeffer's theology is the nexus between Christ and the church. Bonhoeffer conceives of Christ as eternal Word, in whom the church has its eternal origin and finds its historical identity. But the Word does not enter history of its own determination and potency; it rather is joined to the Holy Spirit who actualizes it. That is to say, the actualization of Christ is the pneumatic rendering of the Word historically concrete. But this is also at once the actualization of the church, namely, the historical instantiation of what the church *is*—Christ existing as church-community. For Bonhoeffer, then, the identity of the Holy Spirit is the agent of actualization, of both Christ and the church. Indeed, apart from the Holy Spirit, Christ—both in his personal incarnation and resurrection—would be tantamount to an abstraction, divorced from time and space. Likewise, independent of the Holy Spirit, the very idea of church-community "would be individualistically dissolved from the outset."[14]

How does the Holy Spirit accomplish this parallel actualization? Bonhoeffer reasons that when the Holy Spirit imbues the human heart with divine love, Christ comes into the person, which means, he says, that "the church comes 'into' us."[15] The actualization of the church is thus the actualization of Christ. When Christ as church-community indwells the person, the "I" of the I-You relationship is consequently empowered to love the other as "You." By "love" Bonhoeffer means *agapé*, or "Christian love,"[16] a kind of love that St. Paul says is "poured into our hearts through the Holy Spirit" (Rom. 5:5). *Agapé* is therefore a pneumatic gift that translates into the self-surrendering will of the "I" for the "You."

This actualization does not mean that the church, in all its various particularities, is pneumatically transformed into a univocal oneness. For Bonhoeffer, the church always retains its distinctive elements. It is, he writes, "conscious community," "based on the separateness of persons," and thus "only real when constantly created anew by wills."[17] Yet in its actualization, these wills yield to a unity so intense that Bonhoeffer describes it as a "single life."[18] Members of the church, as "being-for-each-other," arrive at a place where their identities as "I" cannot be conceived apart from complete surrender to every "You" whom they encounter in the community. Such surrender, however, is not a one-time accomplishment. The church's actualization is an ongoing "movement" wherein the church finds itself, as Bonhoeffer says, breaking up "into the community-of-the-cross" and then being "built up" afresh "to become the Easter community."[19] In other words, in the recurring movement from cross to resurrection, Bonhoeffer is suggesting that the church is actualized through the Holy Spirit's conviction of sin and empowerment toward *metanoia*, whereby the "I" surrenders to the "You." The Holy Spirit therefore establishes the bridge from what the church, despite the persistence of sin, is eschatologically, to what it is *now*—Christ existing as church-community. Actualization occurs in the ongoing movement across that bridge.

It is important to note, however, that the Holy Spirit does not actualize individual members of the church but rather the church as a whole—again, neither as a univocal singularity nor as a totality of individual parts, but as *Kollektivperson*. This notion, which Bonhoeffer utilizes repeatedly, derives accordingly from a larger set of assumptions about community—and this constitutes the third stage of Bonhoeffer's construction of a theology of *Geist*.

Stage 3: Community

On close examination, Bonhoeffer's articulation of community finds its starting point in his understanding of the individual person. In attempting to distance himself from Hegelian Idealism, which he interprets as collapsing the personal and the social, Bonhoeffer contends that the person is distinctly real apart from community. Nevertheless, the person is also defined by ethical demands from outside the self, from the other. The moment of encounter with the other is therefore always an ethical moment, a crisis point, where the person must respond to the address of the other. The person's existence as "I" is thus contingent on standing before the other who is "You." In this sense, the "You" sets the limits of the "I."

Bonhoeffer recognizes that to speak of the "You" as giving shape to the "I" is already to speak of community on a most basic level. According to Bonhoeffer, community is insufficiently understood if it is merely equated with the empirical realities of social relations. A better approach, he says, is to ground such empirical social realities "in a phenomenology of sociality established in spirit [*Geist*]."[20] What does Bonhoeffer mean by *Geist*? For him, *Geist* occurs on two different levels—as individual and as objective. Individual *Geist*, which corresponds to Hegel's subjective *Geist*, "is the bond of self-consciousness and self-determination that documents [the human person's] structural unity"; it is, Bonhoeffer says, "the principle of receptivity and activity" that functions "in acts of thinking, self-conscious willing, and feeling."[21] Individual *Geist*, however, does not stand independently on its own, for it is necessarily open and expressive of itself while simultaneously cognizant of the boundary that delimits it in relation to what is other. Questions thus emerge about how the human person is both structurally[22] open to sociality and closed, for "the 'openness' of the person demands 'closedness' as a correlative, or one could not speak of openness at all."[23] Bonhoeffer seeks to hold such openness and closedness together in harmonious tension. He argues that human beings, on a basic emotional level, are innately open by virtue of the fact that they are able to understand and express themselves. And if this is so, then it follows that human beings can also be understood—which implies relation and sociality.

Bonhoeffer nevertheless is quick to assert the simultaneous closedness of the person. It makes little sense, for him, to speak of openness apart from the acknowledgment of closedness as its necessary correlate. Moreover, he recognizes that an over-affirmation of human openness runs the risk of reducing "person" to what he calls "apersonal spirit,"[24] a move made by Hegelian Idealism. Insofar as individual *Geist* arises in every "I," the "I" is carried along by the tide of sociality—or, more exactly, by the tide of objective *Geist*. This is not to suggest that the openness of individual *Geist* results in its subsumption into objective *Geist*, for human beings "really know their I only in the You-relation."[25] The I-You dialectic, then, remains in sociality and is not mitigated by it. Indeed, the I-You dialectic is constitutive of sociality, just as sociality is presupposed in any I-You relation. For this reason, Bonhoeffer understands individual *Geist* and objective *Geist* as correlative. Individual *Geist* cannot be conceived without objective *Geist* and sociality in view; likewise objective *Geist* presumes the reality of individual *Geist*.

Stage 4: Objective *Geist*

Objective *Geist* is what I argue in this essay to be the central concern of *Sanctorum Communio*. This notion, for Bonhoeffer, refers to the collision or union of personal wills wherein "a 'structure' is created—that is, a third entity, previously unknown, independent of being willed or not willed by the persons who are uniting."[26] It is the spirit of sociality objectified, and, as such, it brings human beings into an experience of community "as something real outside themselves, . . . rising above them."[27] In this "rising above," objective *Geist* remains "genetically dependent"[28] on the persons in a community while exerting itself as a singular will upon them. Just as individual *Geist* relates to the self-consciousness and will of the person, so objective *Geist* is the self-consciousness and will of the community as *Kollektivperson*.

In its dialectic with individual *Geist*, objective *Geist* constitutes the unified "center of activity"[29] animating community. For Bonhoeffer, then, objective *Geist* is what makes community possible in the first instance. Here it is instructive to note that Bonhoeffer distinguishes community from other forms of human collectivity. A "society," for instance, is nothing more than "an association of rational action"[30] that "bears no marks of personal vitality."[31] Similarly, in a "mass" the person belongs to the whole without any sense of his or her individuality.[32] Community, however, is a different reality. Whereas a mass is short-lived and cannot sustain itself indefinitely, and whereas a society is oriented beyond itself to a goal, a community exists *for itself*. A society is "timebound" within the unfolding of history, but a community is an eschatological phenomenon situated at the boundary of time and eternity.

Community, moreover, is characterized by will. On the one hand, the individual, by an act of his or her will, consciously participates in what the community is doing. On the other hand, community itself, as *Kollektivperson* endowed with objective *Geist*, possesses its own unified self-consciousness and will. This will of the *Kollektivperson* cannot be construed as simply the end toward which all personal wills run. For that construal suggests that individual wills run alongside each other toward a shared target, without direct reciprocity. In Bonhoeffer's schema, the will of *Kollektivperson* is marked by reciprocity, by individual wills directing themselves to one another. In their reciprocal relationship, individual wills unite in agreement, an event that forms the essence of "unity of will." The meaning of this agreement, however, must not be reduced to the moment of historico-empirical consensus or assent. Instead, "agreement" here is a complex notion that includes resistance and conflict. Such conflict is not intrinsically problematic, for "[o]nly in strife with other wills, in subjecting these to one's own will or being subjected, is strength and richness of will developed."[33]

Bonhoeffer's depiction of objective *Geist* and reciprocity of will is tantamount to his understanding of the actualization of the church.

According to Bonhoeffer, when the Holy Spirit imbues the human heart with divine love, Christ enters the person, which means that "the church comes 'into' us."[34] As a consequence, the individual person—the "I"—is empowered to love the other as "You." This self-surrendering of the will of the "I" for the "You" is itself the very reciprocity that Bonhoeffer finds at the heart of objective *Geist*. But since the "I" cannot surrender to the "You" without the Holy Spirit's empowerment, this human act of reciprocity must be simultaneously the work of the Holy Spirit. As it pertains to my core thesis in this essay, this coincidence signifies that the Holy Spirit's actualization of the church is co-terminus with the generation of objective *Geist* as the reciprocity of wills. In short, objective *Geist* emerges from the agency of the Holy Spirit in the actualization of Christ existing as church-community.

A recounting of the steps that I have taken in analyzing the architectural logic of *Sanctorum Communio* is now in order. The essay began with an analysis of the symbiotic relation of Bonhoeffer's Christology and ecclesiology, which revealed the Holy Spirit as the agent of Christo-ecclesial actualization. It was determined, however, that the Holy Spirit's actualization of the church is illuminated by Bonhoeffer's understanding of community, in which the category of "person" as the "I" is delimited by the "You." Bonhoeffer's insistence that community be understood as phenomenologically rooted in *Geist* brought the analysis of this essay, finally, to its central concern of objective *Geist*. For Bonhoeffer, objective *Geist* is the basis of genuine community, and this in turn is the work of the Holy Spirit in actualizing Christ ecclesially. The actualization of Christ existing as church-community is thus bound up with the pneumatic inspiration of objective *Geist*. Hence objective *Geist*, as that which lies at the heart of Bonhoeffer's theology of sociality, can be understood as his central concern in *Sanctorum Communio*.

Conclusion: Bonhoeffer the *Geist* Theologian?

In conclusion, I return full circle to the issue posed at the outset of this paper, that of the relation of Bonhoeffer to Hegel. In several respects, the two diverge sharply. For instance, Bonhoeffer's stress on the double nature of *Geist*, as both individual and objective, stands starkly at odds with Hegel's view that the "person" is ultimately accidental and absorbed into objective *Geist*.[35] Whereas Hegel sees subjective *Geist* as moving toward, and ultimately being sublated by, objective *Geist* in its movement toward absolute *Geist*, Bonhoeffer holds that individual *Geist* and objective *Geist* remain correlative. Moreover, whereas Bonhoeffer affirms an orthodox Christian ontology, which distinguishes divine and creaturely entities, Hegel dispenses with such ontology, thereby merging God's own being with the world. For him, the Holy Spirit thus merely symbolizes the final movement in the life of God, the historical reconciliation of thought to itself, which is absolute *Geist*. Bonhoeffer does hold that the Holy Spirit performs a mediatory agency between eternity and history, actualizing the eternal Word—Christ—in space and time. Yet he differs from Hegel precisely in holding that Christ and the Holy Spirit are actual persons, intervening in a concrete world they transcend, rather than mere symbols of the self-mediation of *Geist*.

These differences notwithstanding, Bonhoeffer appears to converge with Hegel at the end of *Sanctorum Communio*. There Bonhoeffer wonders about the eschatological significance of the church's objective *Geist*. What happens at that moment when the church, by virtue of the operations of the Holy Spirit, *is* Christ in a fully realized sense? Put differently, what happens when the church's eschatological reality becomes finally synonymous with its present reality? Bonhoeffer himself concedes a certain difficulty in imagining such a scenario, but he is convinced that it *will* happen. And when it does, he declares, the church's objective *Geist* "really has become the Holy Spirit."[36]

Does Bonhoeffer mean here that objective *Geist* is not merely the work of the Holy Spirit but is rather caught up into the Holy Spirit's own life, such that the respective identities of objective *Geist* and the Holy Spirit are virtually indistinguishable? If so, Bonhoeffer seems to be toying with his own unique version of *theosis*, in which it is the church's *Kollektivperson* that is subsumed into the Holy Spirit. If Bonhoeffer holds that humanity finds its ultimate end in the participation of the church's objective *Geist* in the life of the Holy Spirit, such that the church's objective *Geist is* the life of the Holy Spirit, then Peter Hodgson's description of Hegel as a "theologian of the spirit" might also be applied to Bonhoeffer.[37] Perhaps Bonhoeffer is a *Geist* theologian.

5

Dispossessed Science, Dispossessed Self

Dilthey and Bonhoeffer's Christology *Lectures of 1933*

Jacob Phillips

In May 1933, Dietrich Bonhoeffer began his *Christology* lectures at the University of Berlin. The lectures began on May 3rd and took place throughout the summer semester.[1] They were held on Wednesdays and Saturdays, between 8.00am and 9.00am.[2] One student who attended these lectures, Otto Dudzus, later recorded that the audience on those Wednesday and Saturday mornings was about two hundred. He also gave us his first impression, that when Bonhoeffer stepped forward to mount the platform, "he looked like a student himself." From this rather inauspicious-sounding beginning, however, Dudzus went on to say that "never had a lecture impressed [him] nearly so much."[3]

Twenty-eight years beforehand the philosopher Wilhelm Dilthey (1833–1911) retired with a series of lectures in Berlin, at the Prussian Academy of Sciences. The contrast with Bonhoeffer's lectures could not be more stark. Dilthey was at the end of a long and distinguished career— he held the Berlin Chair of Philosophy between 1882 and 1905. Bonhoeffer's academic career had begun only six years before his lectures, with *Act and Being*. In that work, Bonhoeffer acknowledges drawing on

Dilthey positively at key points.[4] Scholars point out that Bonhoeffer also drew on Dilthey in his latest writings. Ralph Wüstenberg's *Theology of Life*, for instance, highlights at length elements of Dilthey's philosophy in Bonhoeffer's *Letters and Papers from Prison* (DBWE 8).[5] In this chapter, however, I suggest that concern with Dilthey also appears in the 1933 Christology lectures (DBWE 12). In them, Bonhoeffer appropriates elements and concerns from Dilthey's philosophy while reconfiguring them significantly. Bonhoeffer thus promotes a particular counterproposal for scholarly inquiry into the self-conscious meaning of the "I." My claim is that this reconfiguration indicates a distinctive operation, which I am calling "the dispossession of the self." That is, Bonhoeffer's lectures function to "dispossess" his hearers of precisely the sort of scientific approach and the sort of subject inscribed by a certain form of early twentieth-century, hermeneutic philosophy executed by Dilthey, as well as others after him.

Making this claim requires some initial clarification. It is important to state that I am not asserting that Bonhoeffer's concern with Dilthey here displaces the key, foundational influences on these lectures (or indeed on Bonhoeffer's work more generally). I am not arguing that Dilthey is more important than, say, the well-acknowledged sources of orientation, such as Martin Luther or Karl Barth.[6] Substantively speaking then, I am not claiming that Bonhoeffer's use of Dilthey implies that the human sciences rather than revelation provided the key point of orientation for Bonhoeffer. To the contrary, as is well known, Bonhoeffer's appropriation of the work of diverse philosophers was conducted *from* the standpoint of the distinctly revelation-orientated position usually associated with Karl Barth.[7]

There is a further question here as to whether or not the concern with Dilthey's philosophy in these lectures is implicit or explicit. That is, whether or not it is indirect and coming via Dilthey's general influence on the philosophical milieu at the time (most notably Husserl and Heidegger), or that it is explicit, and an appropriation which occurred directly through Bonhoeffer's reading of Dilthey. This question requires a detailed reading of the literature of this milieu and so cannot be answered fully here.[8]

Nonetheless, I wish to suggest that the references in *Act and Being* mentioned above point to a high regard for certain aspects of Dilthey's thought, suggesting that Bonhoeffer saw him as a seminal resource, [9] Moreover, the *Christology* lectures utilize much of the language from

Dilthey's 1927 *Gesammelte Schriften VII*, particularly regarding the nature of the human sciences as involving a system of meaning (*Sinnzusammenhang/Sinnvoll Zusammenhang*), of structure (*Struktur*), of a mode of "being for me" (*für-mich-sein*) and the center (*Mitte/Mittelpunkt*) of human life.[10] As I will indicate, Dilthey uses the mode of knowing of the human sciences to criticize elements of the natural sciences. Bonhoeffer's lectures follow him closely in this criticism. However, I also wish to suggest that Bonhoeffer goes further, not only wielding Dilthey's criticisms of the natural sciences against Dilthey's explication of the human sciences, but also reintegrating Dilthey's terminology into his own articulation of a christological "science" and thus a christologically-formed "knowing self."

In the first section that follows I will describe Dilthey's own attempts to locate and describe a more vital mode of apprehension as an explication of the "given" that is "being-for-me," as well as his writings on "structure" and the "center of the individual." I will then turn to the parts of Bonhoeffer's lectures where he appears to reconfigure these aspects in light of Christology, thereby effectually dispossessing the theory of science and the self his hearers have come to know through Dilthey's influence.

Dilthey and the Philosophy of the Human Sciences

A key concern of Dilthey's philosophy is to delineate a theory of the sciences. He writes: "there are two great tendencies [that] come to play in all scientific (*wissenschaftlich*) endeavors." The first is that of natural science, which seeks to establish "uniformities" in the physical world. The second involves the analysis, not of just the physical world, but of our "lived experience" of it. Dilthey considers the intelligibility of each tendency to occur by way of the "categories" of "cause" and "meaning" respectively.[11] Dilthey's use of the term "category" bears certain similarities to the Kantian usage in that it refers to necessary conditions of understanding. However Dilthey would part company with Kant in seeking to ground these categories as an *a priori* which cannot be derived from looking at the world.[12] Dilthey adheres strictly to *describing* our experience of the world, and consciously seeks to avoid *explaining* ultimate grounds for its character.[13]

What Dilthey calls "real categories" refer to the necessary conditions by which conclusions are drawn in each of the two types of discipline. These conditions play an important role in allowing Dilthey to delineate between the natural and human sciences. To elucidate this, we can look at Dilthey's primary "real categories" for each group of sciences respectively. The primary 'real category' of natural science is "causality."[14] This means that the underlying pattern of thought by which an object is understood in the disciplines of natural science is the explanation of how a phenomenon occurs.

For the human sciences, the fundamental category is "meaning" (*Bedeutung*).[15] An object is intelligible according to these disciplines, says Dilthey, through the underlying condition of a cognitive tendency to locate its meaning. This conclusion arises from his view that meaning "provides the relation that ... articulates the apprehension of the course of a life." In studying human life, Dilthey sees the category of meaning arising from the description of memory. As someone looks back over their life, certain events are considered meaningful to the whole of that life, and the sense of the whole in turn imparts meaning to the parts. To render an object intelligible in this way, involves imparting to it "significance." This distinctive part-whole relation, which Dilthey detects in human "recollection" of a "life course," constitutes the most basic example of the category of meaning. The category also extends beyond a single life, to providing the conditions by which we can "grasp and explicate simultaneous and successive life-courses in history."[16] Dilthey sees the basic work of the human sciences to be gathering together the parts of certain phenomena, relating them to some whole, and allowing this relation to feed back into the understanding of the parts. Dilthey describes the human sciences as thus referring its object to a "system" of "meaning" (*sinnvollen Zusammenhang*).[17]

Dilthey then specifies why the mode of intelligibility of the natural sciences cannot be extended into the human sciences. According to him, the natural sciences operate by abstracting from lived experience. He sees the scientist conceiving of a natural object by way of an abstract construct of thinking, such as the formula H_2O for water. He describes the concepts by which this process of abstraction happens as being created by thought, i.e., the chemical symbol H_2O is a product of human cognition, rather than necessarily authentic to the given character of water itself. Dilthey describes this process as the "subordination" of nature to thought, which allows us to 'gain control' over the natural world.[18]

By using these constructions, we are enabled to "explicate conditions for the given into a framework."[19] This explication occurs by way of hypotheses, that is, through *inferring* likely causes and outcomes from the interrelation of these constructions. Not only do the natural sciences "supplant phenomena by adding thought" but they seek "hypothetical causal grounds" for the interrelation of those phenomena.[20] The kind of hypothesis which Dilthey has in mind would involve mostly inductive inference, inference to probability. For example, in the nineteenth century the germ theory of disease became widespread, based on an inductive inference that if people consuming water from a certain source all suffer the same disease, the probability is that there is something in the source that communicates the disease.

Such abstract constructions, being created by cognition, behave according to cognitive expectation, i.e., according to the logical demands of rational inference. Dilthey speaks of an "immanent antinomy" between the phenomena themselves and the way in which they are grasped in science. This antinomy, Dilthey claims, is responsible for the systems of science which are "surreptitiously assured" by the very theories that seek to explain it, so that the explanations they provide are "circular."[21] For Dilthey, the manner of representing cognitively the objects of knowledge in natural science, and of organising their interactions, ultimately rests on the internal authority of human cognition. It thus *prevents* the more vital encounter with something extrinsic to cognition; the human sciences, he claims, are then more faithful to the extrinsicality of this encounter. So Dilthey's criticism of natural science is that the fundamental condition of its possibility is grounded in the knower.

Hermeneutics and the Descriptive Method

Dilthey goes on to describe this more vital encounter with objects of knowledge. His philosophical *raison d'être* was to locate and describe an epistemological foundation for the human sciences. He sought to achieve this foundation through a descriptive method, which seeks to explicate what is given.[22] Dilthey sees the human sciences as being founded on lived experience as precisely this given; it is "an articulation . . . [of] the general structures of historical life." These sciences strive to "attain objectively engaged and objectively valid conceptual cognition of the interconnectedness of lived experiences in the human-historical-social world."[23]

For example, sociology is one such articulation of human experience: the society, which subsists in the lived experience of human beings in the historical world. The disciplines of law or economics likewise rest on descriptions of lived, historical social processes, from which they derive their character and content. Dilthey saw the "task of the human sciences" as an analysis of the "human-historical-social world" which sought to proceed "without losing sight" of the "original togetherness" of the "concrete concerns of ordinary life."[24] This articulation of the task of the human sciences is a deliberate attempt to avoid those elements of natural scientific thought of which he was suspicious.

There is also a more specific manner in which Dilthey seeks to question the presuppositions of natural science. His description of our knowledge of the "human-historical-social world" considers it to be ultimately rooted on unreflective moments of apprehension, which are not grounded conceptually but simply "are." He calls this level of primary reflexive awareness "objective apprehension" (*Gegenständliche Auffassen*).[25] This allows Dilthey to make a clear delineation between the natural and human sciences. The natural sciences are spoken of as seeking to "construe" physical objects, whereas the human sciences are concerned with "what is given to us in lived experience and in reflection upon it."[26] He says of the descriptive method, "there are no hypothetical assumptions that impute (*unterlegen*) something to what is given."[27]

Dilthey describes moments at this primary reflexive level as "being-there-for-me" (*da-für-mich-sein*). They are "there-for-me" in the sense that they are not accounted for by any explanatory theory, or hypothesis. They are "there-for-me" in the sense that they are simply given, they *are*, and accordingly they should only be described. To explain them is to become locked in thought, on one side of the "immanent antinomy." "Being-there-for-me" can be designated as a facet of "lived experience" because if something is simply "there," it has not been posited noetically. An object which is "there-for-me" exists, for Dilthey, in a real objective sense, in that it is not grounded conceptually as something inferred to exist in a certain way with or without me.[28]

The Structure of Experience

Another key aspect to Dilthey's attempts to describe an epistemological foundation for the human sciences is his understanding of the "structure"

(*Struktur*) of human encounter with the world as a precondition for understanding the world. For Dilthey the pattern by which I experience various occurrences exhibits a structure that ties my experience of the world together into a unity. That this structure rests on the grounding of apprehension as "being-for-me" means in turn that the fundamental condition for the possibility of knowledge in the human sciences is not grounded in the knower, but in the givenness of that which simply "is."

For Dilthey, this structure arises because its constitutive moments of objective apprehension exhibit "inner relations" that have a certain constancy.[29] Dilthey considers this structure to extend also into more developed and complex forms of apprehension. This structure provides a pattern according to which a human being develops over time, through on-going lived experiences of varying complexity.[30] As something which fundamentally undergirds the development of human experience, it could be said that Dilthey considers this structure as something like that which other philosophers refer to as a "self."

The word "self" is often used to refers to a stable unit, which can be delineated separately to the experiences it undergoes. To locate the term "structure" as referring to something like the term "self" could present "structure" as referring to such a stable unit. However, Dilthey scholar Fritjof Rodi points out that a more stable notion of the term "structure" is commonplace today, as consequence of the philosophical school of "structuralism." But, Rodi tells us, in the early nineteenth and twentieth centuries (before the growth of "structuralism"), the word "structure did not always refer primarily to [such] static relationships."[31]

Rodi describes the Dilthey's concept of 'structure,' as it developed throughout the progression of his corpus. Dilthey's early work uses the term "articulation" (*Gliederung*) in order to "make visible" what he called "the actual relation of the psychophysical unity [i.e., the individual] to the external world."[32] In a work from the middle period of Dilthey's life, he develops the term "structure" to further define this idea in terms of an "interaction of a living body and an external world which constitutes its milieu."[33] For Rodi, "structure" names Dilthey's uncovering of the "interplay between self and milieu in its various modifications and differentiations."[34]

So when the mature Dilthey speaks of structure, he refers to patterns with a distinct constancy, but these patterns are not separable from those experiences themselves. In Dilthey's descriptive method, he specifically resists grounding or explaining this constancy by locating a "self" apart from experience. Instead, he describes constancy as it arises in the succession of experiences.[35] Structure, the perceived unity of a life unit (human being), thus exists at the point at which the entity undergoes lived experiences, and not something on one side of this meeting-point. To use an alternative term, we could think of Dilthey's structure as an "interface" which arises in the description of experience. So structure is the characteristic pattern of the *meeting* of self and world. Thus, Dilthey's use of the term "structure" is distinct from the notion of discrete "self," as it is often understood in light of the development of "structuralism."

Because Dilthey's use of structure, as the interface between self and milieu, allows us to describe the patterns by which apprehension occurs, it is the basis of understanding the expressions of the experiences of others. Dilthey says that a "hermeneutics of all existing human intercourse is based precisely on the permanent structural relations that emerge regularly in all spiritual (*geistigen*) manifestations of life." The "structural relations" are seen as making "our interpretation of all spiritual processes possible."[36] Taking spiritual (*geistig*) as that which pertains to self-conscious mind, we can paraphrase Dilthey here as claiming that we understand the encounters of other self-conscious minds with the world on the basis of the patterns by which our minds encounter the world.

The Center of the Individual

As mentioned above, Dilthey's primary category for the apprehension of objects in the human sciences is "meaning." For him, meaning arises in relation to each individual being "centered in itself." Meaning becomes perceptible precisely by gaining an awareness of the common strata of an individual "life-course."[37] Dilthey thus speaks of each "personal life-nexus" as having "an individual nucleus," which is its point of unity. Every experience of individuals has in common this nuclear center, the point where the moments of a "life course" converge. Yet the individual's specific "form of unity" is unique to each, since it is "centered in itself."

This relationship between centeredness and meaning acquires further detail in Dilthey's consideration of meaning and the relationship between the "parts of life to the whole."[38] He writes: "[T]he connectedness implicit in life obtains its explication only in the relation of the meaning of events of life to the understanding and the sense (*Sinn*) of the whole of life."[39] What particular events *mean*, then, is something made intelligible in relation to the point at which they converge, the common strata, or sense of the whole, which is unique to that individual life-course. Our understanding of the meaning of the parts of life involves locating them in relation to the point in the center of an individual's life.[40]

Bonhoeffer's Christology Lectures

I will now show how Bonhoeffer's *Christology* lectures display a concern with these aspects of Dilthey's philosophy. In what follows, I will indicate how Bonhoeffer both applies Dilthey's criticisms against the natural sciences to the human sciences, thus subverting Dilthey's approach, and yet reconfigures important elements of Dilthey's philosophy for his own theological purposes.

Bonhoeffer's concern with Dilthey appears near the outset of his lectures, when Bonhoeffer lays out the same basic view of the natural and social sciences as Dilthey: "[A]ll scholarly [*wissenschaftlich*] questions can be reduced to two." The first is "what is the cause of X?" and the second is "what is the meaning [*Sinn*] of X?" The first question "covers the realm of the natural sciences [*Naturwissenschaften*]" and the second, "that of the arts and humanities [*Geisteswissenschaften*]." With regard to the natural sciences, says Bonhoeffer, "the object X is grasped ... by being understood in its causal relationship to other objects." For the arts and humanities, he states, "the object X is grasped ... by its being understood in its relationship of meaning [*Sinnzusammenhang*] with other known objects." In both cases, then, the grasping occurs by way of "classification." This classification provides an interrelated network of associations, which form the ground for comprehending the object X. These classification systems are therefore "immanent" to the knower; they are at the disposal of the human being, as human "logos classification system[s]" (DBWE 12, 301).

Bonhoeffer points out that our comprehension requires the foundation of such classification systems. Yet, in doing so, he also implicitly performs a critique of Dilthey. For the latter, to ground the behavior of natural phenomena in the interplay of cognitive constructions through hypothesis leading to "cause" is circular, and leaves the knower locked-in-thought.[41] Bonhoeffer agrees: asking "how" a phenomenon occurs causes us to remain in our own frame of reference, "mirroring" ourselves to ourselves.[42] Yet Bonhoeffer also shows that, on Dilthey's own terms, the question "what" asked by the arts and humanities can be reduced to the question "how," insofar as it can be reduced to ultimately self-referential components, as exhibited by Dilthey's understanding of "meaning." Thus Bonhoeffer sees the task of comprehending *either* cause or meaning as asking the question: "how does the object X fit into the classification that I already have at hand?"[43] Thus, Bonhoeffer would extend Dilthey's criticisms of the problems of self-enclosed natural science to *both* forms of scholarly inquiry. According to Bonhoeffer then, Dilthey's attempts to find a more objective basis for knowledge are not robustly objective enough.

Christological Science

Bonhoeffer, however, sees one science as distinctively different: the theological discipline that is rooted in Christology. In Christ, we are confronted with an object that cannot be known according to the cognitive tendencies of the human *logos*. Christ is the "counter Logos," which "appears, somewhere and at some time in history, as a human being, and as a human being . . . says 'I am the truth.'" At this point, from which the discipline of Christology begins, "it is no longer possible" to fit the object into either of the classification systems. This "object" of study, the "Word made flesh," signals the moment at which "every possibility of classification must fall short."[44]

Regarding Christ, Bonhoeffer claims the appropriate mode of questioning is to ask, "who?" Asking "who" is a question "about transcendence." This means it is a question asked in acknowledgement that the answer cannot be provided according to the means at the disposal of the questioner. So the question "who" is a question that humans cannot really ask, insofar as we have no grounds upon which to comprehend the answer. Moreover, the knower continues to ask "how," seeking to bring the counter Logos into an "immanent classification system." Yet, "the immanent question of 'how' can never comprehend [Christ]" because "the One who is questioned is the Son himself." That we persist in asking "how," Bonhoeffer says, indicates the fact that we "are chained to our own authority,"[45] that we wish to ground the claim to truth which confronts us in our own means of comprehending truth and to make of it our own possession. Therefore, we are in a situation where we "*must* ask *who*" but we "*can* not."

At the heart of Bonhoeffer's *Christology* lectures, there is this uneasy tension: we "*must* ask *who*" but we "*can* not." That the question "who" actually *is* asked provides the foundation of his endeavor. For Bonhoeffer, the human logos asks the question, "Who are you, Jesus Christ?" Nevertheless, "it is up to the human logos" to "understand the given question," and "to reflect upon and analyse it as it exists."[46] The issue here, then, is to delineate how the question exists. Asking "who" occurs only because the questioner is confronted by the object of christological study, "the Word of God."[47] Accordingly, to "understand the given question" suggests seeking to make intelligible the question "who" in a manner which is mindful of the key point: that it can only be asked after the human logos is confronted by the counter-Logos. This seeking to make intelligible the givenness of the question itself ensures that it always remains the question "who" and is not brought under the authority of the questioner. Likewise, to "reflect upon and analyse the question as it exists" demands that we do not seek to render the question more intelligible, or more meaningful, according to the demands of the human logos. This means we cannot supplement the question, by tidying-up its difficult and awkward parts, and seeking to make more palatable for the human logos the fleshly assertion, "I am the truth." This approach, Bonhoeffer says, *brings out* the "ontological structure of the *who*." It reflects the "is-ness" of the object, the reality of its existence as it *is* and not as it might be rendered more intelligible for the human logos. The purpose of the question "who" is to maintain a particular noetic posture in the apprehension of the object.[48]

The confrontation with the Counter Logos, and the givenness of the question "who" which results from it, can be seen to exhibit more than one tension. Bonhoeffer is clear that that the key element which prevents a self-referential classificatory move on the part of the human logos is Christ's being incarnate in *empirical history*.[49] That the claim to truth is spoken by a flesh and blood human being circumvents human rationality, which must, by its very nature, seek to understand truth in disembodied universal principles outside of time and space. However to this could also be added the point that there is a further tension in that it is the *fallenness* of the human logos which is affronted by its own inability to comprehend the claim to truth on its own terms, and seeks to bring the Counter Logos into its classification system. In somewhat typical Bonhoefferian fashion, then, issues of philosophical epistemology are blended with certain points of Christian doctrine. The givenness of the question "who" thrusts the questioner into a posture which circumvents both certain aspects of human rationality itself, and its fallen grasping at self-mastery, in which it is "chained to its own authority."

The foundational tension at the heart of these lectures is given from the encounter with the genuinely exterior: the "counter Logos." Bonhoeffer presents the fact of the encounter with genuine exteriority, not only as the presupposition for scholarly inquiry into Christ, but also as the presupposition of scholarly inquiry itself. He describes Christology as "logology," suggesting that it is the scholarly discipline of reflecting on the center of scholarly disciplines, which are often recognisable by a distinctive "-logos." Christology is "knowledge par excellence" (*Wissenschaft katexochen*), the knowledge that "makes all knowledge possible."[50] These expressions aim to show that by resisting immanent classification, the Word of God provides the "ultimate question for critical thinking." The counter-Logos offers a starting point that promises an outward orientation for human knowing through the exterior givenness by which it confronts the questioner.

Structure Dispossessed

Bonhoeffer's "dispossession" of the human sciences by Christology clearly indicates a strong critique of Dilthey's overall program. Yet, as this and the next section will show, Bonhoeffer nevertheless seeks to incorporate elements of Dilthey's philosophy of the human sciences into his own Christology, whilst re-configuring these elements so as to dispossess Dilthey's knowing "I."

Bonhoeffer goes on to elucidate the being of the Counter-Logos in more detail. He states, "the being of Christ's person is his being-for-me" (*Sein Christus-Sein ist sein Pro-me-Sein*).[51] Bonhoeffer's describes his understanding of Christ as "there-for-me" in terms of a threefold form (*Gestalt*) as "Word, sacrament and church-community" (*Gemeinde*). This description in terms of the givenness of Christ in "Word, sacrament, and church-community" offers an objective ground that supports the noetic posture described above. Here Bonhoeffer gives the knower a determinate orientation from which to formulate knowledge, on the basis of the being of Christ "as it exists."[52]

This framework can be seen to take up two specific aspects of Dilthey's philosophy. First, Dilthey's grounding the orientation to knowledge in lived experience is similar to Bonhoeffer's grounding of knowledge in the experience of Christ's presence in "Word, sacrament and church-community." Second, both aim similarly for a mode of apprehension not grounded on the "subordination" to, or "authority" of, the human mind. Dilthey attempts to describe a primary level of "objective apprehension" without any noetic grounding, which he calls the mode of things "being-there-for-me" (*da-für-mich-sein*). For Bonhoeffer Dilthey's philosophy could not be expected to adequately describe the genuinely exterior; yet he proposes his own method for an genuinely *objective* grounding to the sciences under the modality of Christ as "being-for-me" (*Für-mich-sein*).[53]

With this, I claim, Bonhoeffer thus appropriates precisely Dilthey's idea of "structure" while simultaneously reconfiguring it. For Dilthey, the structure of the life unit is the necessary precondition of the human sciences, for it makes the understanding of others possible. For Dilthey, structure is something like an interface, the pattern according to which a self encounters a milieu. Bonhoeffer's use of the term structure can also be seen in similar terms, as an interface, the pattern of relations in an encounter. But the key point is that the structure is the interface where *Christ* encounters the world of space and time. The "pro-me" structure, for Bonhoeffer, is the point where Christ is present in space and time, and it is precisely *Christ's* presence in space and time that becomes the foundation of the sciences, as the moment of encounter with genuine exteriority.

The Center of Human Existence

In this way, Bonhoeffer "dispossesses" the human life-unit at the center of Dilthey's schema. At the same time, consistent with his claims that christological science can actually be seen as grounding the other sciences, Bonhoeffer also reconfigures certain elements of Dilthey's philosophy of the human sciences into his own christological "structure."

Toward the end of the Christology lectures, Bonhoeffer claims that the question "who" can also be translated into spatial language as the question "where is Christ?" Bonhoeffer gives a threefold answer to the question "where is Christ?" that provides the means for his reconfiguration of certain aspects of Dilthey's philosophy: Christ is "the center of human existence, of history and of nature."[54]

When Bonhoeffer describes Christ as "the center of human existence" he means that Christ is the fulfilment (*Erfüllung*)[55] of human existence. Christ as the fulfilment of human existence is related to Christ being considered as the perfectly fulfilled human being. Bonhoeffer considers Jesus as the perfect fulfilment of human life, the only one in whom the law could be fulfilled. So Bonhoeffer's assertion that "Christ is at the center," means that he stands in the place where all the parts of human life are brought to perfect fulfilment, as a center refers to a nucleus, a place where all the parts of something converge. However, Bonhoeffer also considers Christ as the boundary (*Grenze*) of human existence. Human life, made for perfect obedience and fellowship with God, is unable to reach its fulfilment. This fulfilment, then, comes from outside. In Christ, says Bonhoeffer, we meet the boundary we cannot cross. In this way, he states, "Christ is seen as the boundary and center of history's being."[56]

As we have seen, Bonhoeffer seeks throughout his lectures to avoid to making the "Counter-logos" intelligible on the basis of a human classification system, such as that of the human sciences (*Geisteswissenschaften*) in which an object is grasped "by being understood in its relationship of meaning [*Sinnzusammenhang*] with other known objects."[57] Nonetheless, at precisely this point in the lectures, in his discussion of Christ as the "center of history," he speaks of Christ as the "meaning of history" (*Sinn der Geschichte*).[58] But this is meaning arrived at as an explication of the "who," a question which cannot be answered by the means at the disposal at the questioner. So Bonhoeffer's meaning of history is not some locatable center which can be reached by history itself. It is then, both boundary and center: he says the meaning of history is "swallowed up" in the cross.[59]

To locate meaning as "swallowed up" in this event where promise meets fulfilment constitutes a particular appropriation of the category of meaning. Unlike in the human sciences, however, this meaning proceeds not by locating the objects under discussion *in relation to* other objects, but, instead, in accepting their being related to a "hidden center."[60] This constitutes a powerful challenge for the academic discipline of history, which was seen as the emblematic human science in the German academy. Bonhoeffer here reconfigures the understanding of history according to the "ultimate question for critical thinking," the "who," and so points toward a radically open approach to interpreting events of the past, according to a "hidden center" of meaning given in the encounter with the counter Logos. We find the same approach in Bonhoeffer's discussion of understanding the "I." Christ is spoken of as the "center of human existence," but this is "not the center that we can see here." So we cannot posit

Christ at the very nucleus of our perceptible being, at the point where all converges. As with history, we live "in a fallen world" so "the center is at the same time a boundary." Referring to this center is an "ontological-theological statement,"[61] referring to things as they *are* in a way which can only be seen by God. That is, Bonhoeffer would say God sees the "I" in perfect fulfilment; in perfect obedience and fellowship with him.

For Bonhoeffer, this "I" is *made possible* by Christ; it is the "I" which one cannot reach alone. Christ is then the boundary, the point beyond which the "I" cannot go. Again, Christ is also the "center," the "I" which only God can see, in perfect fulfilment. In sum, "as the limit, Christ is at the same time the center that I have regained."[62] This mirrors the dynamic we saw in Christ as the "center of history," where we see a way of understanding both the "I," and history, which is "swallowed-up" in the cross. In other words, Bonhoeffer considers that we can understand what things mean, but only in a way which ensures "meaning" is based on the "who": based on the question that can only be asked on the basis of an encounter with that which cannot be made intelligible by the means at the disposal of the questioner.

From here we can see Bonhoeffer's distinctive counter-proposal. For Dilthey, the individual human life-course is understood on the basis of its structure. This occurs through locating each part of a life in relation to a central point from which we gain the sense (*Sinn*), which feeds back into the parts. Bonhoeffer dislodges the place held by the structure of Dilthey's individual, and places there the "ontological structure" of Christ. But we cannot posit Christ at the very nucleus of our perceptible being, as he is a "*hidden* center." Therefore, understanding what the parts of a life mean requires our locating of them in relation to a point which is given from outside. The sense of our life, the point of unity where the significance of our life events can be perceived, is on the other side of the boundary we meet in Christ. This understanding of the human being is an explication of the "who." It is an abdication of the right to award significance to the events of our life from our being centered in ourselves, and proceeding instead from a dispossessed noetic posture whereby the point in relation to which meaning can be attributed is given from outside.

6

Shame and the Other

Bonhoeffer and Levinas on Human Dignity and Ethical Responsibility

---

BRIAN GREGOR

DESPITE SOME IMPORTANT DIFFERENCES in presuppositions, the works of Dietrich Bonhoeffer and Emmanuel Levinas reveal a striking convergence on a number of themes. One such theme is that of ethical responsibility for the other person. There are interesting reasons for this convergence in attending to the theme of "the other"—most significantly, its prominence in European thought during the 1920s and 1930s, due to such thinkers as Karl Barth and Franz Rosenzweig.[1] My purpose in this chapter is not, however, a conceptual genealogy. Instead, I will consider what we can learn from Bonhoeffer and Levinas on the theme of ethical responsibility, along with another shared theme: shame. For both thinkers, shame testifies to a fundamental nakedness—not as the literal absence of clothing, but as the exposure of one's being. Shame testifies to the burden of being, as well as the inner divisions of the self. Levinas discusses this theme in two early essays (*On Escape* and *Existence and Existents*), while Bonhoeffer's discussion is rooted in his theological interpretation of the creation and fall narratives in the book of Genesis.

Bonhoeffer's argument is particularly intriguing since he argues that after the fall, a certain sense of shame is *necessary* in order to preserve the dignity of the human being. On its own, however, shame is not *sufficient* to ground that dignity. Levinas joins Bonhoeffer on this last point; both argue that human dignity is rooted in the concrete encounter with transcendence. For Levinas, we encounter this transcendence in the face of the other, and it is only in ethical responsibility for the other that genuine humanity occurs. Similarly, Bonhoeffer argues that human personhood is constituted in the ethical response to the other, but he goes further by grounding his conception of humanity in a robustly christological ontology. In this grounding we encounter a crucial difference between the two thinkers, since Levinas is a Jewish philosopher attempting to offer an ethics without ontology. Given such different commitments, there might seem to be no point in trying to bring these two thinkers into dialogue. Nevertheless, I will argue that both thinkers provide important insights regarding the burden of being, while Bonhoeffer's christological ontology offers significant advantages for thinking about human dignity and ethically responsible relations with others, since it differentiates between creation, fallenness, and the orders by which God graciously preserves the world for the sake of Christ.

Levinas: Shame and Subjectivity

In the introduction to his 1935 essay *On Escape*, Emmanuel Levinas examines the philosophical conception of the human subject in conflict with being, "the discord between human freedom and the brutal fact of being that assaults this freedom," and the struggle that "sets the 'I' [*moi*] against the 'non-I' [*non-moi*]." This conception leads to an ideal of heroic self-sufficiency in which the "I" flourishes, not by overcoming internal conflicts, but by overcoming external threats.[2] In modernity we find this ideal in the romantic and idealist pictures of the "I," as well as the bourgeois conception of the "I," whose capitalist enterprises of "initiative and discovery" aim "less at reconciling man with himself than at securing for him the unknowns of time and things." The peace of the bourgeois "I" is threatened by the vicissitudes of material existence and the unknown variables of the future, which the "I" seeks to master, preferring "the certainty of tomorrow to today's enjoyments."[3] Peace resides in the security of the self-sufficient, self-identical "I" as the master of all that is foreign to itself.

In Levinas's view, these modern conceptions of the "I" are in keeping with the understanding of being that pervades the history of Western philosophy. Starting with Parmenides, being is self-contained, self-sufficient, and self-identical. To the extent that something truly *is*, these attributes belong to it as perfections. Moreover, being is governed by the logic of the *conatus essendi*—the effort to persist in one's own being. The logic of being is a logic of self-preservation. Such is the order of things.[4]

From the perspective of being, then, particular beings are imperfect to the extent that they lack these attributes of self-sufficient identity and unity. Imperfection thus arises in finitude as a limitation of one's being.[5] Philosophy sets out to transcend the limitations of finite being in favour of infinite being, in whatever form it might take: the realm of the Platonic Ideas, the God of onto-theology, or Hegel's Absolute *Geist*. Yet Levinas suggests that this preoccupation with transcendence does not hold the same priority in the mood of modern society—something expressed profoundly by modern literature. This contemporary mood is a malaise, a "world-weariness" marked by a sense that all is not well with being; it is an overwhelming awareness that "*there is being*—a being that has value and weight," which "is revealed at a depth that measures its brutality and seriousness." This awareness emerges as "the discovery not of a new characteristic of our existence, but of its very fact, of the permanent quality [*l'inamovibilité*] itself of our presence."[6] The permanent presence, the ineluctable weight of being—certainly not its "unbearable lightness"—arouses the desire for escape. This is not a desire to escape merely *finite* being, as is the case with the poet's flight from "'lower realities,'" the romantic refusal of "social conventions," and "the philosophical and religious evasion of the material world." These projects touch on the "horror" of finite *experiences* of being, but they do not touch the more fundamental horror of being *qua* being.[7] Like Heidegger, Levinas locates the question of being *qua* being at the heart of philosophy. But for Levinas, this question arises out of the desire for escape.

Escape to where? We do not desire to go somewhere in particular, "only to get out [*sortir*]" of being. It is not a desire for death, since "death is not an exit, just as it is not a solution." Rather, it is a need for transcendence, for that which exceeds one's own being, or to use Levinas's neologism: *excendence*.[8] And so within the self-sufficient, self-contained, and self-identical realm of existence, a duality emerges. The identity of the "I" is no longer a tautology, a pure I = I; self-consciousness is marked by the desire to escape from oneself, from "*the fact that the I [moi] is oneself [soi-même]*."[9] Again, the problem is not finitude, i.e., that one's own being is limited; rather, it is the very *being* of one's self that one desires so desperately to escape. Thus the hope for eternity does not necessarily offer consolation, since eternity only intensifies the burden of being.[10]

Levinas proceeds to describe different manifestations of this need in the phenomena of malaise, pleasure, shame and nausea. *Malaise* is a dynamic state that "appears as a refusal to remain in place, as an effort to get out of an unbearable situation." This effort has no determinate goal or object but is rather "an attempt to get out without knowing where one is going, and this ignorance qualifies the very essence of this attempt."[11] Malaise might seek an escape in *pleasure*, but in the end pleasure "is a deceptive escape."[12] Pleasure never delivers the ecstasy it promises—namely, to deliver the "I" from itself. The ensuing disappointment pronounces the failure of pleasure, a failure that "is underscored by *shame*."[13] The transition from pleasure to shame might suggest that shame arises out of remorse over this or that illicit pleasure. For Levinas, however, shame is more fundamental than particular actions or passions: "It is the representation we form of ourselves as diminished beings with which we are pained to identify. Yet shame's whole intensity, everything it contains that stings us, consists precisely in our inability not to identify with this being who is already foreign to us and whose motives for acting we can no longer comprehend."[14] Shame regards our internal division: the conflict between the obligation "to claim responsibility for ourselves,"[15] the simultaneous desire to distance ourselves from ourselves, and the impossibility of doing so. Shame is a manifestation of the inescapable fact that one is "riveted to oneself."[16]

Levinas follows this with a provocative claim: "Shame arises each time we are unable to make others forget [*faire oublier*] our basic nudity. It is related to everything we would like to hide and that we cannot bury or cover up." Nakedness is not strictly a lack of clothing—it "is not only the body's nakedness," but rather the exposure of that which "one seeks to hide from others, but also from oneself."[17] The shame that accompanies nakedness "means that we cannot hide what we should like to hide,"[18] namely, "the nakedness of our total being in all its fullness and solidity, of its most brutal expression of which we could not fail to take note." The intimate self-awareness of shame thus "reveals not our nothingness but rather the totality of our existence."[19] Again, shame is not a consequence of finitude or lack, but rather the fullness and presence of our being. The self is riveted to itself, unable to escape. Here the self is not pitted against external threats; shame exposes the more fundamental threat of division within the self.

Bonhoeffer: Shame and Subjectivity

Like Levinas, Bonhoeffer recognizes shame as a more fundamental phenomenon than remorse over a particular wrong. If "we lower our eyes whenever we meet the eyes of another," this shame is not due to remorse over a fault, but to the reminder of "our own nakedness" and "the lost wholeness of life."[20] Shame is that "irrepressible memory" of our estrangement from God and the other human. Bonhoeffer accounts for this estrangement through the theological doctrine of the fall, which he examines in his lectures from the Winter Semester of 1932–33 at the University of Berlin. In these lectures Bonhoeffer shares Levinas' sensitivity to the burden of being (in Bonhoeffer's view, *post-lapsarian* being), which results from the internal division within the self.

Bonhoeffer's interpretation of the Genesis narrative offers powerful insight into how the primordial event of the fall altered the ontological structure of the human being. Prior to the fall, human existence was characterized by the recognition of limits: Adam recognized the limits of creaturely being, as distinguished from the Creator,[21] and he knew these limits as signs of grace. Similarly, he recognized the other human as limit. Adam experienced the woman as a limit, yet he loved her as a limit.[22] After the fall however, Adam no longer knows these limits as grace but as frustration. He hates them. He "no longer regards the other person with love," and thus "the limit is now the mark of dividedness."[23] Prior to the fall, Adam lived in free relation with the other, but after the fall this freedom is lost and the self curves in on itself in sin.

Several consequences follow from this incurvature. First, the human refuses "to recognize any limit at all" in the relation to the other, giving rise to obsessive desire and the lustful ambition "to possess the other."[24] Second, there emerges a need to clothe oneself out of shame. This shame over nakedness is a new phenomenon. In the prelapsarian state, "Nakedness is the essence of unity, of not being torn apart, of being for the other, of respect for what is given, of acknowledging the rights of the other as my limit and as a creature. Nakedness is the essence of being oblivious of the possibility of robbing others of their rights. Nakedness is revelation; nakedness believes in grace. Nakedness does not know it is naked, just as the eye does not see itself or know about itself. Nakedness is innocence."[25] After the fall, however, the human being sees only itself.[26] Shame testifies to the rupture that now divides human existence: "Shame expresses the fact that we no longer accept the other as God's gift but instead are consumed with an obsessive desire for the other . . . Shame arises only in a split-apart world [*in der Welt des Zweispalts*]."[27] Ironically, shame testifies to those creaturely limits that human beings refuse to acknowledge: "In their shame human beings acknowledge their limit . . . The shame of human beings is an unwilling pointer to revelation, to the limit, to the other, to God."[28]

A third consequence of the fall is the transition from being created in the image of God (*imago dei*) to becoming "like God" (*sicut deus*). As the serpent promised, human beings became "like God" by transgressing the Tree of the Knowledge of Good and Evil. Bonhoeffer contrasts the two conditions: "Imago dei—humankind in the image of God in being for God and the neighbour, in its original creatureliness and limitedness; sicut deus—humankind like God in knowing out of its own self about good and evil, in having no limit and acting out of its own resources, in its aseity, in its being alone."[29] In coming to be *sicut deus*, human beings also come to know about death. They die. Now humankind "lives in a circle";[30] humankind "lives out of its own resources, yet it cannot live. It is compelled to live, yet it cannot live."[31] Death means "no longer being able to live before God, and yet having to live before God."[32] Death "means to have life not as a gift but as a *commandment*. But from this commandment no one can escape, not even by choosing oneself to die, for to be dead is itself to be subject to the commandment to life. *To be dead means to-have-to-live.*" There is no escape from this commandment to *be*. It "demands from me something that I am not in a position to fulfill. It obliges me to live out of myself, out of my own resources" and this is precisely what the self cannot do.[33]

Adam's existence is marked by an internal division, torn between death and life: He yearns for death, hoping to "rescue his life from the bondservice and drudgery [*Frohn*] of having to live without life."[34] This is not a nihilistic hatred of existence. It is a desire for life, but a desire that cannot escape the inability to live. This inner division entails "a continuing, renewed rebellion against this existence [*Dasein*]; it is a quarrel with life, a grasping at the life that would put an end to *this* life, that would be the new life. What Adam wants under any circumstance is *to live*."[35] Yet it would seem there is no escape.

Social Life and Shame(lessness)

As we noted earlier, Levinas contends that the modern conception of subjectivity fails to recognize the burden of being and the internal division that threatens the self. In an essay entitled "Reflections on the Philosophy of Hitlerism," published a year prior to *On Escape*, Levinas levels this objection against the subject as conceived by liberalism. Levinas sees a link between the Christian doctrines of liberating grace and the philosophical notion of rational autonomy. However disputable this connection might be, Levinas suggests that Christian conceptions of salvation as liberation from being give rise to a vision of the rational subject that stands free from being (most notably the body and the rest of the material world), dispassionately reasoning and choosing between logical possibilities.[36] Since the liberal view maintains that "consciousness or reason determines being," one can escape being merely by *thinking otherwise*.

This sort of disengaged, idealistic thinking not only fails to recognize the burden of being and shame; it is also unable to deal with these burdens. In his 1947 essay *Existence and Existents* Levinas raises the issue of nakedness once again. Keeping in mind the point that nakedness is not simply a lack of clothing, he suggests that it "is the true experience of the otherness of the other." This experience stands in contrast to everyday social life, in which the nakedness of the other human being "is taken to be unhealthy" and is concealed by forms—roles, responsibilities, activities, conversations—that mediate the naked other, tempering the shame that would otherwise make such exposure unbearable.[37] Levinas insists that "[t]hose we encounter are clothed beings." We put on clothes, and we attend to our appearance. The human in this state "is clean and abstract. Life in society is decent. The most delicate social relationships are carried on in the forms of propriety; they safeguard the appearances, cover over all ambiguities with a cloak of sincerity and make them mundane." Those unmentionables that do not fit into such forms are relegated to the privacy of home, under the cover of night.[38]

A certain romanticism might lead one to conclude that these modes of concealment are hypocritical, and to insist on a more honest, "authentic" level of interaction. Yet Levinas never makes this argument, and neither does Bonhoeffer. In fact, Bonhoeffer argues that we *need* this sort of covering to preserve shame and the awareness of our disunity. To this end Bonhoeffer suggests the positive social role of the mask, which is not a disguise to deceive others, "but the necessary sign of the estrangement and disunion that exists. As such it must be respected. Beneath the mask lives the desire for the restoration of the lost unity."[39] The mask is not bourgeois hypocrisy but a means of preserving modesty, and therefore a condition for maintaining a sense of dignity regarding oneself and others.

Why preserve shame, then? Precisely because it cannot be overcome. Whether one's motives are romantic or cynical, the proud honesty that purports to be totally devoted to truth ultimately overlooks "the decisive truth, namely that after the fall there is a need for covering [*Verhüllung*] and secrecy [*Geheimnis*]." Honesty and truthfulness "does not at all mean that whatever exists must be uncovered. God himself made clothing for human beings, that is, *in statu corruptionis* many aspects of the human being are to remain concealed, and when one cannot root it out, evil is likewise to remain hidden."[40] Bonhoeffer's point is not that the body is evil, nor is he calling for the cultivation of prudery or hypocrisy. His point, rather, is to oppose any vision that seeks to overcome shame and reclaim humanity's prelapsarian nakedness on its own terms. We cannot repair the rupture in our being; we live in a "split-apart world," and yet human beings still presume to be able to "escape from themselves."[41]

Prior to an eschatological reconciliation of that which is split apart, clothing thus allows us to inhabit a "dialectic of covering and uncovering,"[42] and must be honoured for two reasons. First, clothing testifies to our brokenness, and our inability to escape this division on our own. Second, clothing acts as what Bonhoeffer calls an "order of preservation" (*Erhaltungsordnungen*), by which God upholds and preserves fallen humanity (DBWE 3, 139). Clothing is a means by which God affirms the fallen world, yet also reveals its limits. Clothing preserves those limits that fallen humanity longs to transgress, restraining the obsessive desire that seeks to overcome the otherness of the other.[43]

It is important to recognize that these orders of preservation do not possess any ultimate worth in themselves. They are established by God, but they are provisional insofar as they are directed eschatologically toward Christ, through whom the fallen creation will be resurrected in the new creation.[44] They are penultimate, and only exist in reference to the ultimate—i.e., the eschatological revelation of Christ and his ultimate reconciliation of all things. In using the language of "orders *of preservation*"

Ontology and Ethics

Bonhoeffer offers a critique of the Lutheran tradition of "orders of creation" (*Schöpfungsordnungen*), according to which the established orders of nation, race, family, culture, etc., are grounded in creation and thus the self-evident outworking of God's will. Bonhoeffer insists that this doctrine is dangerous because it allows these orders to remain autonomous and impervious to critique. One could then claim divine legitimation for the *status quo*, even when it involves economic exploitation and injustice, nationalism, violence, and war.[45] In a further effort to distance himself from this doctrine, Bonhoeffer eventually abandons the terminology of "orders" altogether, writing in *Ethics* of "divine mandates" instead.

Bonhoeffer had good reason to oppose the notion of autonomous created orders, since he saw the dangers of that theology manifested in the way German Christendom accommodated the ideology of National Socialism. The same circumstances also gave Levinas reason to be wary of any sort of ontological fatalism. In the closing passages of *On Escape* he writes: "Every civilization that accepts being—with the tragic despair it contains and the crimes it justifies—merits the name 'barbarian.'" The advantage of European civilization "consists incontestably in the aspirations of idealism," since the fundamental impulse of idealism is the desire "to surpass being." However, not all ways of surpassing being are equal. Despite its aspirations, Levinas argues that idealism—much like liberalism—cannot escape being because it "undervalues" it. Imagining "it has surpassed being, it is invaded by being from all sides." For idealism, being remains "always the same, having relinquished none of its characteristics."[46]

In the Germany of the 1930s, the inability of liberalism and idealism to surpass being acquired new gravity with the rise of a philosophy that merits the name "barbarian" to the fullest extent. In his analysis of "Hitlerism" Levinas articulates its conception of the human being, in which being claims to be insurmountable: "The mysterious urgings of the blood, the appeals of heredity and the past for which the body serves as an enigmatic vehicle, lose the character of being problems that are subject to a solution put forward by a sovereignly free Self." Being is destiny. In this context being means nation (*Volk*), blood (*Blut*), and soil (*Boden*): "[T]he self is constituted by these elements. Man's essence no longer lies in freedom, but in a kind of bondage [*enchaînement*]."[47] Consciousness no longer determines being, but vice versa: "Man no longer finds himself confronted by a world of ideas in which he can choose his own truth on the basis of a sovereign decision made by his free reason. He is already linked to a certain number of these ideas, just as he is linked by birth to all those who are of his blood. He can no longer play with the idea [*jouer avec l'idée*], for coming from his concrete being, anchored in his flesh and blood, the idea remains serious."[48] Relating this to the Nazi ideology of racism and war, Levinas contends that the very dignity of the human is at stake.[49] History shows how correct Levinas was on this count.

But how does shame figure into all of this? Here we must look to Bonhoeffer, who argues that shame is crucial to preserving human dignity, since shame recognizes the fundamental dividedness of the self. In contrast, *shamelessness* names the refusal to acknowledge or respect this dividedness. Shameless social gestures and social structures insist that every aspect of one's being be fully manifest, on public display. Even the gaze that refuses to turn aside when one makes eye contact with a stranger, the refusal to allow the other that privacy, already seeks to overcome all that is other. Bonhoeffer recognized this kind of shamelessness in the National Socialist regime. Jean Bethke Elshtain offers an insightful remark to this effect:

> One of the reasons Dietrich Bonhoeffer was so repulsed by Nazism was precisely because of its aberrant shamelessness. Nazi ideology dictated erasing any barrier between public and private, between that which should be open to public scrutiny and definition and that which should not. The horrific denouement of an ideology that required breaching the boundaries of shame was the shamelessness of death camps where human beings were robbed of dignity, stripped of privacy, deprived, therefore, of an elemental freedom of the body in life and of the respect we accord the bodies of the dead after life is no more. Scenes of starved, naked bodies, piles and piles being shoved by bulldozers into lime pits is a nigh inexpressible instance of shamelessness, with the dead reduced to anonymous carcasses.[50]

In Nazism the world saw the refusal of shame and the violation of the other taken to tragic depths of depravity.

Transcendence, Eschatology, and Human Dignity

Is it possible to resist this sort of shamelessness and thereby preserve the dignity of the human being? Where could we find the resources to do so? This is a question Levinas and Bonhoeffer both confront. Levinas poses this question in a 1990 prefatory note to his essay on Hitlerism: "Does the subject arrive at the human condition prior to assuming responsibility for the other man in the act of election that raises him up to this height?" Levinas then makes his trademark point, which he had not yet developed in the 1930s: "This election comes from a god—or God—who beholds him in the *face* of the other man, his neighbor, the original 'site' of Revelation."[51] For Levinas the ethical summons of the other provides an escape from the burden of being.

In *Existence and Existents*, Levinas describes the burden of being in terms of the *il y a*, the sheer *there is* of being, which is prior to all significance and meaning. Levinas describes such phenomena as indolence and fatigue as indicative of the inability to take up one's being and begin. The "I" is not self-positing, because it is unable to bear the burden of beginning to *be*. The future poses a threat, and thus "[b]eginning does not solicit [the future] as an occasion for rebirth, a fresh and joyful instant, a new moment; indolence has already brought it about beforehand as a weary present." Could it be that "the future, a virginal instant, is impossible in a solitary subject"?[52] Levinas concludes that time—the future, the new instant—is something with which the "I" "cannot endow itself." The I falters under overwhelming abundance of being, but in itself the "I" lacks the resources to constitute itself as a particular, personal being amidst impersonal being. It is a matter of moving, as the French title suggests, *de l'existence a l'existant*—but the I cannot hope for salvation by itself because this move can only come through the other.[53] And this alterity is *radically* other. The other is not simply *another me*: "He is what I am not: he is the weak one whereas I am the strong one; he is the poor one, 'the widow and the orphan.'"[54] Only in response to this vulnerable other can the solitary subject escape from the oppressive burden of being. Only in this instant is the "I" constituted as such.[55]

In subsequent works Levinas will develop this theme of the turn to the other more explicitly as ethical responsibility.[56] Levinas describes this ethics as an eschatology, since it originates from beyond being, beyond history, beyond any sort of self-contained, systematic totality.[57] The moment of ethical responsibility for the other is an eschatological disruption of being, and it is only in this moment that true humanity emerges. Levinas thereby presents us with a "humanism of the other": whereas classical liberal humanism locates the basis for human dignity in freedom and rationality, Levinas argues that the true vocation and dignity of the human consists in ethical responsibility, which initiates with the summons of the other.[58]

Bonhoeffer's description of ethically responsible subjectivity is quite similar to Levinas—albeit with some crucial differences. In his earliest works Bonhoeffer describes responsibility as arising in the moment (*Augenblick*) of being addressed by the other. In the moment of decision, of movement into the concrete situation of responsibility, the human being is "created" as a real person. Ethically speaking, human beings "do not exist 'unmediated' qua spirit in and of themselves, but only in responsibility vis-à-vis the 'other.'"[59] As he writes in *Sanctorum Communio*: "The I comes into being only in relation to the You; only in response to a demand does *responsibility* arise."[60] Moreover, the other does not present itself within the ontological horizon of the "I"; instead, in words that seem to anticipate Levinas, Bonhoeffer writes: "'You' says nothing about its own being, only about its demand."[61] And this is an unconditional, absolute demand, which means that the "I" has no claim of its own, but rather "is claimed by this absolute demand."[62] Also like Levinas, Bonhoeffer sees ethical intersubjectivity as fundamentally asymmetrical. The other person is "the concrete ethical barrier"[63] who "sets the limit for the subject." [64] The other "places me before an ethical decision,"[65] and only in the moment of ethical decision do I enter the condition of true personhood and humanity.

For Bonhoeffer the encounter with the transcendent other is also the condition for the escape from the burden of being—from the impossible situation of having to live, yet being unable to live. But whereas Levinas sees this escape as taking place through the ethical encounter with the other human, in Bonhoeffer's view it is the Creator who upholds his creation and redeems it in Christ who makes escape possible. In Christ, God reconciles the fallen creation to himself, and only this reconciliation overcomes shame: "Shame can be overcome only by being put to shame through the forgiveness of sin, which means through the restoration of community with God and human beings. This takes place in confession before God and before another human being. Human beings are clothed with God's forgiveness, with the 'new human being' that they put on."[66] That said, the ultimate overcoming of shame is an eschatological word, and does not obviate the penultimate conditions of existence here and now. Shame remains with us in the "twilight" in which we presently reside, and therefore clothing remains as a means of preservation.[67] This preservation is God's work, and not ours. We cannot repair the wounds in our being, nor can we overcome shame through sheer voluntary fiat. We must instead accept God's preservation—not as something eternal or ultimate, but as pointing to the coming of Christ, who reconciles that which is torn apart.

This is a vital insight, as Bonhoeffer insists that our eschatological hope must not lead to impatience or contempt for the world. Christ's resurrection makes possible our resurrection and the new creation, but God also upholds and preserves this fallen world in affirmation for the sake of Christ, in whom God and the world are reconciled.[68] Even in the face of the German Christian appeal to orders of creation and the accompanying idolatry of *Volk*, blood, and soil, Bonhoeffer insists that we should not seek to surpass creation, the world, or being altogether. Christ brings about the reconciliation of God with the world. Bonhoeffer sympathizes with Nietzsche's critique of that Christian religiosity that merely wants to escape the difficulties of life on the earth. All too often the desire to "surpass being" arises from an unwillingness to engage with the world; if life becomes difficult, this otherworldly religiosity allows one, with a quick and bold leap, to soar "relieved and worry-free, in the so-called eternal realm."[69] Of course, the possibility of such an escape is dubious in the first place. To recall Levinas, eternity does not necessarily offer consolation, since it can intensify and radicalize the weight of the burden of being. It is therefore significant that Christ does not overcome our finitude, but brings reconciliation to the rifts in our finite being, here and now, relieving us of the burden of having to live out of our own resources.

Bonhoeffer argues that God's activity in the world does not aim at an otherworldly eternity, but the establishment of His Kingdom. This is something Christian radicalism cannot accept; whether it attempts to flee the world or to change it through revolutionary means, radicalism is rooted in a "hatred of creation. The radical cannot forgive God for having created what is." Instead of reconciliation one finds "bitterness, suspicion, and contempt for human beings and the world."[70] Yet contrary to the pious 'No!' to the world, with his "unfathomable 'Yes!'" God binds himself to the earth. And "where God is, there is God's kingdom."[71] For Bonhoeffer, then, there can be no question of utterly surpassing or escaping being altogether, but only of God's reconciliation. Therein lies the genuine escape from the burden of being—not as a pious departure from the reality of this life, but in reconciliation.[72] The human being is reconciled with existence, in a christologically-transformed being-in-the-world.

This christological reconciliation not only undermines the otherworldly interpretation of Christian faith; it also poses a significant challenge to Levinas. Although Levinasian eschatology has a decidedly this-worldly focus, it is nevertheless directed entirely beyond being. Levinas wants an ethics without ontology. By contrast, Bonhoeffer's Christology—characterized by incarnation, crucifixion, and resurrection—allows for a robust affirmation of being in a way that Levinas cannot countenance. We could sympathize with Levinas *if* he is correct in claiming that the logic of being is reducible to the drive to persist in one's own being as self-contained, self-sufficient, and self-identical. But is this the best way to understand being? The strength of Bonhoeffer's ontology is to show that being must be understood in terms of the drama of creation, fall, and reconciliation—a narrative dynamic that is clearly not part of the Levinasian description of being. Levinas provides a striking hermeneutic of postlapsarian being, but it is not clear how he can see being as having been created good,[73] nor how being might be healed and reconciled. Instead, for Levinas eschatology indicates a transcendence entirely otherwise than being. By contrast, Bonhoeffer's ontology interprets being through the story of its original created goodness and its severe wounding and self-division through sin, but also according to its healing and reconciliation through Christ's incarnation, crucifixion, and resurrection. This christological ontology allows us to understand the burden of divided being and the role of shame in preserving us, but also our ultimate source of hope for the healing of being in Christ.

7

Bonhoeffer, Kierkegaard, and the Teleological Suspension of the Ethical

The Beginning or End of Ethics?

MATTHEW D. KIRKPATRICK

SIMILARITIES BETWEEN THE THOUGHT of Søren Kierkegaard and Dietrich Bonhoeffer have often been suggested by scholars on both sides. However, until recently, little or no comprehensive study has been conducted of this relationship.[1] Analysis has been limited to footnotes, digressions, and the occasional article. One may easily surmise at least part of the reason for this state of affairs. Despite certain similarities of motifs and phrases, the overall emphases of the thinkers seem, to many scholars, finally and fundamentally incompatible. Bonhoeffer's theology finds its center in his profound ecclesiology and sense of community. Individualism, by contrast, characterizes Kierkegaard's work. For some, however, the difference between these writers is more pronounced. Kierkegaard's individualism, they suggest, rests on an even more fundamental "acosmic" perspective.[2] That is, Kierkegaard jettisons not only community but even the reality of world per se. In more theological terms, many cite this "dismissal" of the world as a form of Gnosticism, which affirms individual spirituality at the expense of the physical realm. In his influential *Theology of Dietrich Bonhoeffer*, Ernst Feil argues that in contrast, Bonhoeffer takes aim precisely at the "latent acosmic perspective" that had defined Protestant theology since the middle of the nineteenth century through the influence of Kierkegaard and others.[3] Furthermore, according to Feil and David Hopper, Kierkegaard's greatest influence on Bonhoeffer was briefly *seducing* him from his critical path toward the somewhat anti-worldly message of *Discipleship*.[4] Even Kierkegaard scholar David Law comes out strongly in favor of Bonhoeffer's attack on Christendom over against Kierkegaard's "Gnostic" version.[5]

Acosmism and Gnosticism are serious charges, for when they characterize epistemology and spirituality, the concrete bases for an ethic of earthly flourishing also appear endangered. Yet among the many intriguing, challenging, and even mystifying stories found in Christian scriptures, some in fact seem to tilt toward an ethically-problematic disavowal of the "goods" of the cosmos. Kant is hardly theologically orthodox, yet most would offer a certain sympathy for his description of Abraham, in his near-sacrifice of Isaac (the Akedah), as a butcher who shunned the ethical precepts of reason for the subjectively discerned voice of God.[6] Moreover, one might wonder how Christian theology could possibly reconcile Abraham's action with the scriptural call to love every human person. Not so for Kierkegaard in *Fear and Trembling*. Far from skipping over these aspects of the story, Kierkegaard emphasizes them and appears to grant this "teleological suspension of the ethical" the utmost validity for theological ethics. To acosmism and Gnosticism, one can therefore add two further charges: not only is Kierkegaard a moral nihilist for having discarded ethical rules, but he has also thrown out the neighbor. As Kierkegaard scholar Brand Blanshard writes, Kierkegaard's Abraham "is a man whose leading concern is not the welfare of others, but his own 'eternal happiness.'" Furthermore, he writes, "What we have in this strange version of Christianity is thus an insistence on the selfish character of the religious motive, combined with an insistence that the values of the Christian life, so far as these can be understood, are provisional only, and may at any time be overridden."[7]

Stephen Plant, in his excellent introduction to Bonhoeffer's thought, reaches a similar conclusion. Although Plant hesitantly draws attention to Kierkegaard's influence, he argues:

> Kierkegaard's *Fear and Trembling* proposes . . . that in the duty to love one's neighbor it is not God we meet, but merely the neighbor, since our duty to God can cause us to 'suspend' our ethical obligation to our neighbor. For Bonhoeffer, the choice between God and neighbor was false because God meets us in our neighbor. It was true, for Bonhoeffer, that Kierkegaard has correctly turned away from Kant in presenting a critique of philosophical ethics from the biblical point of view: but Kierkegaard had wrongly followed Kant in making the individual central to ethics. For Bonhoeffer . . . individuals meet God in community, not in isolated individualism.[8]

Space does not allow an in-depth analysis of Kierkegaard and Bonhoeffer together. This I have done elsewhere.[9] In this paper, rather, I hope to use *Fear and Trembling* to highlight the intensity of this relationship that spans the breadth of Bonhoeffer's corpus, and thus to point out the importance of Kierkegaard for Bonhoeffer scholarship. However, I also will show how Bonhoeffer is of significance to Kierkegaardians as an interpreter of Kierkegaard. For not only does Bonhoeffer use the "teleological suspension of the ethical" as the necessary basis for his "communitarian" ethics, but in so doing he offers a profound contradiction to the stereotypes that this suspension necessarily implies acosmism and Gnosticism. Although it is beyond the scope of this essay entirely to address whether Kierkegaard has in some ways lost the world, by showing that the teleological suspension need not lose ethical rules and the neighbor, I will suggest that the charges of acosmism and Gnosticism are fatally flawed. In conclusion, I will argue further that in Bonhoeffer we find someone who salvages *Fear and Trembling* for ethical theory by affirming that the teleological suspension is not the nihilistic end of ethics but rather its beginning.

Before addressing these aims, I must first offer an overview of *Fear and Trembling* from which we can discern Kierkegaard's influence and apply Bonhoeffer's interpretation.

Kierkegaard: An Overview

In order properly to grasp Kierkegaard's understanding of "ethics" and its "teleological suspension," some background is required. For Kierkegaard, there are two spheres of reality: the "outward and visible world," and the "world of the spirit." The latter is the reality perceived and defined by

God where "there prevails an eternal divine order."[11] In contrast, a human reason and understanding that has rejected its identity as 'creature' and set itself in the place of God defines the former. For Kierkegaard, systematic, idealist thought, which has sought to conquer everything and place it under its control, in fact *creates*, or projects, this outward world. Such thought shuns any limits to rationality, denies the divide between thought and reality, and awards itself a "spectator knowledge" of existence.[12] Thus, Kierkegaard's two realities are not simply dissimilar due to the limitations of the human mind but contradictory due to its sinfulness in projecting a false reality.

As Kierkegaard defines it in *Fear and Trembling*, "the ethical" is the product of such systematic thought, as typified in the work of Hegel and Kant. It is a universal, moral requirement to which all must submit. The ethical so defined is no longer a means to some higher end but rather holds its telos within itself. It becomes itself "the good" and therefore acts not simply as the absolute judge of human action but also the key to its salvation.[13] Effectively, it thus becomes the divine and so replaces the individual's relationship to God.[14]

Against this backdrop, Kierkegaard describes the knight of infinite resignation and the knight of faith in light of the Abrahamic story. The knight of infinite resignation is one who would be obedient to God's command in the present. He remembers that Isaac is the object of God's promise, yet believes that God, in asking him to kill Isaac, must simply have changed his mind. However, the knight can enact such a heinous deed only if he separates himself from his earthly life, by resigning his love for Isaac and the world, and placing his hopes and desires for happiness in eternal life. The knight of faith is likewise obedient and makes a movement of resignation. For Kierkegaard, both thus deserve praise because they relate to God directly, rather than through the universal requirement. Both thus to some degree effect a suspension of the ethical in favor of a higher telos—absolute obedience to God. However, the knight of faith makes a pivotal, second movement. Although it is entirely absurd, the knight of faith believes God's word in its entirety: he believes that he will kill Isaac and yet have him back again in order to fulfil God's earlier promise through him.

Correlatively, Kierkegaard can then define the actions of both knights according to the two spheres of reality. The knight of infinite resignation remains in the outward and visible world, seeing the command of God through the logic of human reason.[15] Isaac will die, and both he and the promise will remain dead. The knight of faith, likewise, recognises the impossibility of the situation and resigns Isaac to death. However, through the leap of faith, he jumps into the world of the spirit where "for God all things are possible" and believes he will receive Isaac back again.[16] Only the knight of faith then *fully* gives up the whole of temporality—both his understanding of and relationship to ethics, community, spirituality, and the cosmos as a whole. And yet, in so doing, he—and only he—also then receives it back again through the eternal. The question of course, which Kierkegaard does not perhaps make clear in this work, is exactly what world the knight thus receives and how the purification works.

What is clear is that Kierkegaard believes that the teleological suspension, which occurs through the individual's direct relationship with God, is essential for the sake of morality itself. Without this corrective, ethics subtly usurps God by standing in his place: "The ethical is the universal and as such, in turn, the divine. It is therefore correct to say that all duty is ultimately duty to God; but if one cannot say more one says in effect that really I have no duty to God. The duty becomes duty to God by being referred to God, but I do not enter into relation with God in the duty itself."[17] Kierkegaard's individualism, then, arises from his effort to secure what is most central to morality. Thus does Kierkegaard attest in *Fear and Trembling*, "the wonderful glory achieved by that knight [of faith] in becoming God's confidant, the Lord's friend, and . . . in addressing God in heaven as 'Thou.'"[18] Vice versa, as he later confirms in *Concluding Unscientific Postscript*, anyone who gives up his individuality to be obedient to the universal in itself is simply "selling his relationship with God," the very basis for morality.[19]

With this overview in place, this essay now may turn to a consideration of Kierkegaard's influence on Bonhoeffer through *Fear and Trembling* and of how Bonhoeffer's interpretation specifies the teleological suspension so as to salvage it from the abovementioned stereotypes.

Kierkegaard's Influence

Throughout especially his first period of authorship we find Bonhoeffer strongly echoing Kierkegaard's attack on systematic philosophy.[20] Evidence shows that Bonhoeffer was familiar with much of Kierkegaard's corpus, including the strong attacks evidenced in works such as

Matthew D. Kirkpatrick   *The Teleological Suspension of the Ethical*

Concluding Unscientific Postscript and *The Concept of Anxiety*.[21] However, I want to argue, Bonhoeffer particularly follows the configuration of the attack found in *Fear and Trembling*. Like that text, Bonhoeffer both diagnoses the problems of modern philosophy as rooted in an epistemology and frames his own response in terms of the absolute difference between two planes from which one may perceive reality. Like that text, I also want to argue, Bonhoeffer supplies a cure through prioritizing a certain kind of "individualism."

These parallels become most clear and explicit at what is perhaps the midpoint of Bonhoeffer's corpus, *Discipleship* (1935-37). The description of the Akedah in the chapter, "Discipleship and the Individual," particularly shows Bonhoeffer using both broad concepts and specific language resonant with Kierkegaard's portrayal of that event: "[Abraham] receives the call as it is given. He does not try to interpret it, nor does he spiritualize it. He takes God at God's word and is prepared to obey. Against every natural immediacy, against every ethical immediacy, against every religious immediacy, he obeys God's word."[22] Like Kierkegaard, Bonhoeffer attacks any system that purports to render an ethic immediately, i.e., in itself. Vice versa, as Kierkegaard describes Abraham as giving Isaac up, only to receive him back again through the eternal, so Bonhoeffer paraphrases: "Abraham received Isaac back, but he has him in a different way than before. He has him through the mediator and for the sake of the mediator. As the one who was prepared to hear and obey God's command literally, he is permitted to have Isaac as though he did not have him; he is permitted to have him through Jesus Christ."[23]

Alongside these textual parallels, a further piece of evidence makes Bonhoeffer's direct use of *Fear and Trembling* unequivocal—his selection of central scriptural texts. In *Fear and Trembling*, alongside Genesis 22, the only other biblical passage that Kierkegaard directly cites and expounds is Luke 14:26.[24] Perhaps unsurprisingly, Bonhoeffer likewise begins his chapter with the verses of Luke 14:26: "If anyone comes to me and does not hate his father and mother, his wife and children, his brothers and sisters—yes, even his own life—he cannot be my disciple." To this passage, which clearly sets out the "suspension" of all moral valuation arising in the knower, we will return.

Though *Discipleship* is the pre-eminent work in which to see Bonhoeffer directly adopting Kierkegaard's framework, his corpus both before and after also clearly uses it, often with specific allusions to Kierkegaard. By way of example, *Act and Being* (1929-31), Bonhoeffer's *habilitationschrift*, is essentially a sustained attack on systematic philosophy that largely parallels Kierkegaard's own. Like Kierkegaard, Bonhoeffer finds that despite the deification philosophy has awarded itself, human thought ultimately remains trapped within itself. It is an enclosed circle, bound to the limited and sinful ego.[25] It has failed to recognise that its only pronouncements are those of *possibility* and never *actuality*.[26] By creating a system, philosophy universalizes existence and fails to recognise its contingent and uncertain nature. As Bonhoeffer then summarizes, "Kierkegaard said, not without justification, that such philosophizing obviously forgets that we ourselves exist."[27]

Likewise, the dichotomy between two ways of knowing appears already, perhaps in its starkest form, in Bonhoeffer's early Barcelona lecture, "Basic Questions of a Christian Ethic" (1932). There Bonhoeffer declares, "one absolutely cannot speak about specific ethical problems from the Christian perspective. There is absolutely no possibility for establishing universally valid principles, since each individual moment lived before God can confront us with completely unexpected decisions."[28] Bonhoeffer here mirrors Kierkegaard's belief that, for the knight of faith, so specific and temporal are the commands of God—spoken *hic et nunc*—that they defy the communicability that universal ethics embodies and demands. Likewise, he thus closely parallels Kierkegaard in claiming that when ethics arises as the product of idealist thought, as "a child of the earth," it has absolutely nothing to do with Christianity.[29]

In *Creation and Fall* (1932–33) and *Ethics* (1940–43), Bonhoeffer continues to press the attack, claiming that human knowledge is then not just materially incorrect at points; rather it fundamentally sets itself up as an alternative to God's knowledge. In *Creation and Fall*, he thus argues that Adam and Eve's corruption did not simply involve gaining knowledge of good and evil. Rather, the cunning of the serpent's question was not to directly contradict God's word but, by sowing the seeds of doubt, to set Adam and Eve up as judges of that word. That "first religious conversation," in the way it speaks about God, encourages human beings "to sit in judgment on God's word instead of simply listening to it and doing it."[30] As Bonhoeffer then describes in the later *Ethics*, the serpent's question is thus the "prelude" to the problem of ethics, which is itself the child of systematic thought.[31] Through this question, the knowledge of good and evil created the "complete inversion of their knowledge," i.e., the knowledge now formulated by human philosophy.[32]

Ethics also shows Bonhoeffer framing the possible approaches to knowledge according to two levels, particularly in his use of "Jesus" and "the Pharisee" as types for moral epistemologies. For Bonhoeffer, the judgment of the Pharisees against Christ for deliberately flouting the law most clearly displays the problem of current approaches to ethics. The point here is not that Jesus and the Pharisee simply disagree about the content of ethics. Rather, as Bonhoeffer writes, "The Pharisee and Jesus speak on completely different planes."[33] Here Bonhoeffer once more echoes Kierkegaard's contrast between those who, like Abraham, view the world from the other side of the "leap" into God's promise and command and those who operate through the epistemological lens of their own immediate apprehensions of what is, supposedly, ethical.

Furthermore, there is evidence that Bonhoeffer also follows Kierkegaard in his turn to the "individual," standing before God, as the beginning of genuine ethics. Student notes from Bonhoeffer's lectures on "Creation and Sin," for instance, show Bonhoeffer applauding Kierkegaard for essentially discovering the Christian concept of the individual.[34] This Kierkegaardian individual is also very much in evidence in Bonhoeffer's subsequent framing of the task of ethics. In *Discipleship*, Bonhoeffer declares that "followers of Jesus are always completely alone, single individuals who can act and make decisions finally only by themselves."[35] And, as the *Ethics* essay "Ethics as Formation" makes clear, it is only "the person who clings to the commandments, the judgment, and the mercy of God that proceed anew each day from the mouth of God" who is able to stand fast.[36] Again and again in his mature work, Bonhoeffer repeats this claim that God himself directly gives both knowledge and the moral obligation of command.[37] Christianity and morality, then, are a matter of direct relationship with God.

What then of the strong emphasis on community, for which Bonhoeffer is so deservedly well known? And what, in particular, of Bonhoeffer's opinion of Kierkegaard in his first dissertation *Sanctorum Communio*, which most systematically develops Bonhoeffer's conception of community? At this point in his authorship Bonhoeffer did believe that Kierkegaard had rejected the church—a stereotype I believe Bonhoeffer corrected by the time of writing *Discipleship*.[38] However, this does not mean that Kierkegaard's positive influence is absent from the dissertation. To see this influence, we must first remember that Bonhoeffer's ecclesiological understanding of community is complex. Indeed, a close reading of *Sanctorum Communio* shows that this understanding has its basis in a form of individualism. There Bonhoeffer argues that although the individual is created by the community, the individual, drawn out into total solitude, is also the building block of the community, which thus recognizes and preserves that constitutive influence. As Bonhoeffer explains: "Everyone believes and experiences their justification and sanctification in solitude, everyone prays in solitude, everyone breaks through to the certainty of their own eternal election in solitude, everyone 'possesses' the Holy Spirit and Christ completely 'for themselves' . . . It is the solitude of the individual that is a structure of the created order, and it continues to exist everywhere."[39]

More strongly, Bonhoeffer appears to have drawn this understanding of the individual from Kierkegaard and, in particular, *Fear and Trembling*. For appended to the above quotation is a footnote directly citing *Fear and Trembling* and suggesting that Kierkegaard knew how to speak about solitude like few others. Thus, although the notion of community in Kierkegaard's thought is famously illusive, Bonhoeffer makes explicit that it is Kierkegaard who provides the foundation for his own communitarianism.

Through an analysis of these textual and conceptual parallels in Bonhoeffer's thought, and *Discipleship* in particular, it should now be clear that *Fear and Trembling* was a significant influence on Bonhoeffer. Like Kierkegaard, Bonhoeffer sets up the dichotomy between the ethical principles of systematic thought, and the obedience of the individual to God's direct and momentary commands. With this affirmation of the individual, the overcoming of ethical principles, and the absolute obedience to God, it can further be argued that the teleological suspension of the ethical rests at the foundation of his ethics—even his "communitarian" ethic.

Bonhoeffer's Interpretation

So far this essay has addressed the first of its aims: establishing Kierkegaard's influence on Bonhoeffer's ethics. We are now in a position to consider Bonhoeffer's further interpretation of the resources in *Fear and Trembling*, and how this overcomes the stereotypes that Kierkegaard and the teleological suspension must discard both the neighbor and ethical rules. It is to the neighbor that we turn first.

Mediation and the Neighbor

As we have seen, Bonhoeffer's presentation of the Akedah in "Discipleship and the Individual" is a close, if perhaps more christological, reading of the teleological suspension prescribed by *Fear and Trembling*. What is particularly significant is that in Kierkegaard's interpretation Bonhoeffer discerns the concept of mediation—a term that lies at the foundation of Bonhoeffer's understanding of community.[40] As Bonhoeffer makes clear in *Life Together* and *Discipleship*, direct relationships inevitably lead to the sinful claim of one person upon another. Morally good relationships in contrast come about as individuals meet each other through the mediation of Christ. For Bonhoeffer, the story of the Akedah, as seen through Kierkegaard's eyes, does not then represent the destruction of concern for the neighbor but rather its establishment. Here the significance of Luke 14:26 returns in force. For both Kierkegaard and Bonhoeffer, this verse establishes that one only enters into true relationship with the human other when one has first actively given them up—that is, when from the sphere of human reason and immediacy the individual is acting as if they hated the human other. Where Kierkegaard explains that "the ethical expression for what [Abraham] does is this: he hates Isaac,"[41] Bonhoeffer declares in parallel that true discipleship is to "accept the reproach of hatred for humans."[42]

Edward Mooney is one of the few Kierkegaardian commentators to suggest that *Fear and Trembling* has this relational side. Indeed, his reading is so close to that of Bonhoeffer that one wonders whether there may be some influence in that relationship. What Mooney underscores is that Kierkegaard's Abraham did not simply have a human claim upon Isaac as his father, but also a divine claim upon him as the object of God's promise. Consequently, God's command is not an arbitrary test simply to confirm Abraham's faith, but a specific act of God's love, one that re-established Abraham's relationship with Isaac by divorcing it from Abraham's attempt to execute the project of his *own* immortality *through* Isaac. This is precisely Bonhoeffer's point. God's command forced Abraham to place his hope back onto God himself rather than Isaac—to release the direct and sinful claim that Abraham had over Isaac. Furthermore, Mooney's suggestion that *Fear and Trembling* affirms the notions of "independence-in-relationship"[43] and "separateness-in-love"[44] could also identify the key themes of *Sanctorum Communio*.

It should be admitted at this point that *Fear and Trembling* is by no means explicit in offering this interpretation. Furthermore, Kierkegaard scholars are not in agreement that Mooney's is necessarily a correct representation of *Fear and Trembling*. However, whatever the objective merits of Mooney's interpretation—which I would suggest are substantial—what is important for this discussion is how Bonhoeffer understood Kierkegaard over against other possible interpretations. And to this we can argue two important points. First, despite the stereotypes of Kierkegaard as individualistic and perhaps even acosmic, common at the time of Bonhoeffer's writing, Bonhoeffer did not so interpret Kierkegaard, especially by the time he wrote *Discipleship*. Secondly, Bonhoeffer's understanding of the Akedah as relationally-restorative mediation is not simply an idea he added on top of *Fear and Trembling* but something that he saw naturally within it. To justify these bold claims we must return to Bonhoeffer's own library.

By the time of writing *Discipleship*, Bonhoeffer had become heavily influenced by a collection of Kierkegaard's journals, edited by Wilhelm Kütemeyer, entitled, *Kierkegaard—Der Einzelne und die Kirche*. The significant textual parallels between *Discipleship* and this collected volume were first suggested in the short appendix to the doctoral dissertation of Heinrich Traugott Vogel in 1968.[45] Vogel's analysis was picked up again a few years later in Geffrey B. Kelly's dissertation. Here Kelly interviewed Eberhard Bethge who confirmed not only that Bonhoeffer had been reading *Der Einzelne und die Kirche* at the time of writing *Discipleship*, but believed that it was from this source that Bonhoeffer gained inspiration for his descriptions of cheap and costly grace.[46] This thesis is further substantiated by Bonhoeffer's own copy, which is filled with underlinings and annotations, some of which we will explore momentarily.

It is not surprising that this collection should have stuck out for Bonhoeffer. Kütemeyer's 1934 publication of the collection puts Kierkegaard forward as a social and ecclesial commentator who was deeply relevant for Germany under Nazi rule. As the publisher's sleeve declares, "Is this book a current contribution to the religious crisis? That it most assuredly is. It concerns more than just Kierkegaard's lifetime." Although Kütemeyer's selection prefers Kierkegaard's later entries concerning his "attack on Christendom" he also emphasizes sections that offer constructive criticism for both the nature of community and church.

Consequently, it is not surprising that Bonhoeffer should vigorously mark his copy when Kierkegaard writes:

> The definition of "Church" found in the Augsburg Confession, that it is the communion of saints where the word is rightly taught and the sacraments rightly administered, this quite correctly (that is, not correctly) grasped only the two points about doctrine and sacraments and has overlooked the first, the communion of saints (in which there is the qualification in the direction of the existential). Thus the Church is made into a communion of indifferent existences (or where the existential is a matter of indifference)—but the "doctrine" is correct and the sacraments are rightly administered. This is really paganism.[47]

Kierkegaard's understanding of true community and the nature of "indifferent existences" is clarified a few entries earlier where he writes, "In the 'public' and the like the single individual is nothing; there is no individual . . . In community the single individual is; the single individual is dialectically decisive as the presupposition for forming community, and in community the single individual is qualitatively something essential and can at any moment become higher than 'community' . . . The cohesiveness of community comes from each one's being a single individual . . . Every single individual in community guarantees the community; the public is a chimera."[48]

In returning to our two claims, if Bonhoeffer had at one point accepted the stereotype of Kierkegaard as an individualist who rejected the church and world, this interpretation was no longer possible. In these passages, Kierkegaard reveals himself as standing in profound agreement with Bonhoeffer's own understanding of the *sanctorum communio*, bound to the isolation and mediated union of individuals. Here we find further explication of what Mooney describes as "independence-in-relationship" and "separateness-in-love." If Bonhoeffer was reading these journal articles alongside *Fear and Trembling* at the time of writing *Discipleship*, as Bethge affirmed, it is no leap to suggest that he would have interpreted *Fear and Trembling* in the light of them. For Bonhoeffer, therefore, Kierkegaard's reading of the Akedah, defined around the teleological suspension of the ethical, offers the foundation for true, Christian community by establishing the right relationship between individual and neighbor. Far from undermining relationships, therefore, Bonhoeffer considered *Fear and Trembling* as offering the foundation for their existence.

Moral Nihilism?

With the neighbor-relation not only affirmed by secured on a firmer basis, what about our second question: Is the teleological suspension of the ethical still a form of acosmic "moral nihilism" that rejects ethical structures for the subjectively discerned voice of God? Although this is relevant for Kierkegaard, as we have shown Bonhoeffer's ethics to be founded on the Akedah and the Kierkegaardian individual, it is equally pertinent for Bonhoeffer.

For Bonhoeffer, Abraham exemplifies the necessity for the individual to discern God's command for each situation in each moment. This is given its clearest definition in the essay, "Ethics as Formation." Here Bonhoeffer writes, "Only the person who combines simplicity with wisdom can endure. But what is simplicity? What is wisdom? How do the two become one? A person is simple who in the confusion, the distortion, and the inversion of all concepts keeps in sight only the single truth of God . . . Because of knowing and having God, this person clings to the commandments, the judgment, and the mercy of God that proceed anew each day from the mouth of God. Not fettered by principles but bound by love for God, this person is liberated from the problems and conflicts of ethical decision, and is no longer beset by them."[49] Given this foundation, many have criticized Bonhoeffer's ethics as a form of "situation ethics," i.e., a fully subjective form of ethics. And certainly one can see how a superficial reading could lead one in this direction. Indeed, where Kelly and Nelson criticize the aforementioned Barcelona lecture, "Basic Questions of a Christian Ethic," for not adequately distinguishing itself from a situational position,[50] so the situationalist Joseph Fletcher went so far as to make Bonhoeffer's statement in *Ethics* that "[moral] principles are [but] tools in the hands of God"[51] his battle cry.[52] However, it can only be a superficial reading that justifies this situational interpretation since, for Bonhoeffer, a God of order richly qualifies the individual's discernment.

To begin with, Bonhoeffer fundamentally rejects the idea that individuals are to discern God's will through either emotional enthusiasm or some revelatory bolt from the blue. Rather, one must draw together all one's faculties—of "heart, intellect, observation, and experience"—in the discernment process.[53] Furthermore, existence contains within itself God-ordained structures, such as the divine mandates and more generally the "intrinsic laws" that provide basic, stable forms of social life.[54] God is not a God of anarchy, but one who creates order that preserves human life. Bonhoeffer's discernment process is thus deeply earthly and embodied, demanding the individual to draw all his faculties together in the search for God's revelation through the structures God has put in place. In addition to engaging the mandates and the intrinsic laws of life, ethics thence will involve concrete elements including the preaching of the church, personal study of Scripture, the influence of conscience transformed into Christ, the voice of the human other who has become Christ to me, and the inspiration of the Holy Spirit. In prioritizing the individual's discernment of God's command, Bonhoeffer thus does not consign his ethics to the kind of Fletcherian antinomianism that such thinkers as Paul Ramsey charge with being a form of "moral nihilism."[55]

Rather, Bonhoeffer's teleological suspension provides the authentic framework within which the individual "receives back" the ethical in purified form. Indeed, there are even indications that Bonhoeffer anticipates the direct relationship with God that can recast and sharpen the supposedly "rusty swords" of ethical principles. The first English volume of Bonhoeffer's collected lectures, letters, and notes, published by Collins under the title *No Rusty Swords*, made famous this characterization of principles. Yet perhaps this metaphor does not imply that Bonhoeffer simply looked to discard such implements. Perhaps instead the metaphor proves extremely apt for illustrating Bonhoeffer's understanding of the restorative power of teleological suspension. Just as with any other metal tool, the reason why swords go rusty is not because they have stopped working but because they are no longer being used and properly looked after. The same is the case for ethical principles which have been converted into absolute universals. By being misused in this way they have become brittle, blunt and are no longer of any use. However, they shine once again when they are restored to their intended state as tools *in the hands of God*. For Bonhoeffer, the rules that clarify the cosmos and attune one to it are not undermined but truly affirmed by being received from God, but only from God. We must not relate to God through ethical principles, but relate to ethical principles through God. Just as the individual must give up the neighbor to receive them back again through the mediation of Christ, so it is with ethical principles. Nothing in human experience can be received directly, outside of this mediation.

In some contrast to Bonhoeffer, Kierkegaard is by no means explicit in describing a God of order. Although Lutheran, he offers very little affirmation of that tradition's "orders of creation," or similar divinely ordained social structures. However, although he is not explicit, Kierkegaard hints at the redemption of ethical principles. In *Fear and Trembling*, for instance, Kierkegaard declares that the knight of faith "determines his relation to the universal through his relation to the absolute, not his relation to the absolute through his relation to the universal."[56] This quotation suggests that there *is* an actual determination of the ethical universal through the relation to the absolute. My suggestion is that what we find in Bonhoeffer is one who accepts Kierkegaard's central premises of individual discernment and the teleological suspension of the ethical while also showing these to be not only compatible with, but necessary for, the presence of profound ethical order.

Whereas some may consider the teleological suspension to be the end of ethics because it allows the individual to prefer the contradictory demand of God, Bonhoeffer's interpretation redeems the concept by suggesting this criticism misunderstands the nature of "suspension." In faith, suspension does not mean momentarily putting the ethical aside like a naughty child temporarily excluded from school. Rather, as a perpetual leap, faith suspends the ethical by permanently holding and encasing it in the direct relationship and command of God. In Bonhoefferian language, one might then better speak of the "teleological *mediation* of ethics." It is only through the mediation of Christ that one can approach ethical principles. One must go first to God, who will then direct one to the structures and principles that God has created and continues to affirm. The teleological suspension of the ethical is then, for Bonhoeffer, not the end of ethics but rather its beginning. It is the very first movement from which all ethical structures and principles will find their affirmation and fulfilment.

In describing this teleological suspension, it may be surprising that we have not yet made reference to Bonhoeffer's involvement in the assassination attempt. On first glance, this may appear to be the most substantial evidence of a Kierkegaardian-inspired Abraham moment—Bonhoeffer's personal teleological suspension of the ethical. This it certainly was. However, it is only now, at the very end, that we can properly understand how this event *fits* into Bonhoeffer's more holistic framework. For in Bonhoeffer's mind, it is not simply this decision that was an Abraham moment. Rather, for him, every decision needs to be an Abraham moment—giving up the ethical, and then receiving it back again through the eternal.

Concluding Postscript

Kierkegaard's influence is of course important for understanding Bonhoeffer's thought. However, the burden of this essay is to argue that in Bonhoeffer, we find a significant interpreter of Kierkegaard for the present day. Far from condemning Kierkegaard to the rubbish heap of overly individualistic theologies, Bonhoeffer saw in Kierkegaard's work an important affirmation of proper social life in the world. While Kierkegaard scholarship has moved on from the outdated understanding of Kierkegaard as an irrationalist, it has yet to embrace Kierkegaard the cosmic communitarian. In Bonhoeffer, we find someone who might point the way.

8

Bonhoeffer on Law Breaking
A Reassessment of the Ethical Exception to the Divine Command

Jeremy K. Kessler

As a theologian and a participant in the conspiracy to assassinate Adolf Hitler, Dietrich Bonhoeffer felt compelled to explain human actions that he believed were ethically necessary yet contrary to divine commandments. Specifically, he sought to square his own autonomous decision to break the law with his belief in the persistent presence and sovereignty of God. This chapter argues that Bonhoeffer's response to the problem of breaking the law of this God led to a subtle but crucial shift within the *Ethics* manuscripts and paved the way for his prison theology.

In the 1942 *Ethics* manuscript "History and Good [2],"[1] Bonhoeffer argued that in the exceptional, borderline case (*Grenzfall*), ethics could require the human to break a divine commandment. Such an ethical violation could never be justified beforehand, and required both recognition that God's law was being broken and the consequent taking on of guilt for such a violation (*Schuldübernahme*). Yet because all human action ultimately derives its ethical pedigree from its responsiveness to a single, divine reality mediated through Christ, Bonhoeffer worried that the very idea of an ethical violation of divine law might imply a contradiction in God—a contradiction between divine will in the borderline case and divine law as it operates in the rest of life.

In the subsequent *Ethics* manuscript, "The 'Ethical' and the 'Christian' as a Topic," Bonhoeffer moved away from his divisive analysis of ethical action, which emphasized the exceptional, law-breaking case, and emphasized instead the expansiveness, coherence, and vitality of divine command. The command of God "encompasses all of life."[2] This holism of command—marked by a diminished focus on the commandment's exception—secures both the unity of divine reality and a relatively stable ground for human action.

My thesis is that Bonhoeffer continued to develop this vision of the accessibility and unity of divine reality in his prison writings, but in language not based in "command." This paper thus reads the seemingly novel interests of Bonhoeffer's 1944 theology—particularly its reception of Wilhelm Dilthey's history of human autonomy and maturity—as a continuing response to the problem of divine law-breaking that Bonhoeffer encountered in 1941. Bonhoeffer's vision of a "world-come-of-age" depicted an exceedingly close fit between what Larry Ramussen has called "divine presence and human power."[3] This close fit minimized any potential antagonism between ethical human action and divine normativity.

From Formation to Commandment

In his classic study, *Von der Kirche zur Welt*, Hanfried Müller identified two, overlapping methodological motifs in Bonhoeffer's ethical thought: "Ethik als Gestalt" and "Ethik als Gebot."[4] Following Müller, Larry Rasmussen has traced this relationship between ethics as formation and ethics as commandment within Bonhoeffer's *Ethics* manuscripts, particularly by comparing and contrasting the early "Ethics as Formation" with the late "The 'Ethical' and the 'Christian' as a Topic."[5] Pointing toward the *Letters and Papers from Prison*, where discussion of commandment drops out almost entirely, Rasmusssen argues that "ethics as formation is not only the more original methodological motif in Bonhoeffer; in the end it is also the reigning one."[6] Rasmussen's conclusion appears sound. From the beginning to the end of Bonhoeffer's corpus, the close correspondence between human reality and christological reality is perhaps the central presupposition. Yet, in *Ethics*, Bonhoeffer employed the language of command as a supplement to the language of formation at a crucial moment in his life, when the ethics of his own actions were most fraught. To understand why Bonhoeffer might have turned to the language of command in the *Ethics* manuscripts, it is first important to note the contemporaneous development that occurred in his christology.

Bonhoeffer's earliest theological work already emphasized the relationship between the form of Christ and human reality. In Bonhoeffer's dissertation, *Sanctorum Communio*, he introduced "Christ existing as church-community," community formed in Christ, as the knowable form of God.[7] As Clifford Green has noted, even God's transcendence is realized as a kind of intimacy: "Transcendence is not God's otherness beyond humanity and above the world; the holy, creating, sustaining, and reconciling love of God which is revealed in Christ is God's lordship *in* the world *among human beings*."[8] Likewise, in *Act and Being*, Bonhoeffer insisted that "God is not free from human beings but for them. Christ is the word of God's freedom. God *is* present . . . not in eternal nonobjectivity but . . . 'haveable,' graspable in the Word within the church."[9] In his christology lectures, Bonhoeffer made clear the ontological priority of Christ, in ethics as in other matters, when he explained that Christ can be "seen as the center of human existence, of history, and of nature."[10] And all the more so in *Discipleship*, where Bonhoeffer wrote, "Our goal is to be shaped into the entire form of the incarnate, the crucified and the risen one."[11]

Even as it reaffirms the importance of christological formation, *Ethics* introduces a crucial christological development—what Rasmussen calls "the expanded area of conformation."[12] Dating back to *Sanctorum Communio*, Bonhoeffer witnessed the work of conformation primarily in the church community. In *Nachfolge*, where Bonhoeffer explicitly discussed the ethics of discipleship in conformational terms, this "ethics as formation [was] predominantly a churchly ethic."[13] In *Ethics*, however, *all* of reality is conformed to Christ: "in the body of Christ all humanity is accepted, included, and borne."[14]

The signal symptom of the extension of conformation to the whole world is the system of mandates which Bonhoeffer unveiled in a 1941 insert to the first *Ethics* manuscript, "Christ, Reality, and Good."[15] In living within the mandates, humans participate in the reality of Christ, irrespective of their particular relationship to church community: "The world stands in relationship to Christ whether the world knows it or not. This relation of the world to Christ becomes concrete in certain *mandates of God*."[16] The mandates of "work, marriage, government, and church" all subsist "through Christ, toward Christ, and in Christ."[17] Strikingly, this formative christological labor is accomplished only through the command of God: "Not because there *is* work, marriage, government, or church is it *commanded* by God, but because it is *commanded* by God, therefore it *is*."[18] Thus, it is at the moment when Bonhoeffer's conformational Christology expands to encompass the whole of life that the language of commandment is introduced in earnest.

Of course, Bonhoeffer had spoken about commandment before this late date. Rasmussen notes in particular Bonhoeffer's 1932 address "On the Theological Basis of the Work of the World Alliance" in which Bonhoeffer called upon the church to preach "only commandments," not "timeless principles," and explained that a "commandment must be definite, otherwise it is not a commandment."[19] Later the same year, Bonhoeffer wrote to a friend that, "At bottom everything hangs on the problem of ethics, that is, actually in the question of the possibility of the proclamation of the concrete command by the church."[20] Yet, as Rasmussen notes, Bonhoeffer did not develop an "explicit hermeneutic of ethics as command" until the *Ethics* manuscripts.[21] There, such an ethic would be founded in the innovation of the mandates—a system of concrete commandments.

The mandates, then, mark the *convergence* of an ethics of conformation and an ethics of command. The moment when Bonhoeffer expands the ethics of formation to embrace the whole world is *also* the moment when Bonhoeffer first elaborates an ethics of command. As Rasmussen writes, the mandates are *both* "the media of conformation" by which the world is formed in Christ *and* "definite historical forms of the command of God."[22] Similarly, Ralf Wüstenberg suggests that we understand the mandates as the explicit normative elaboration of Bonhoeffer's longstanding thesis of Christ's centrality in the world.[23] In essence, the mandates are "a Christocentric alternative to natural law";[24] the mandates are what happens when reality gains normative structure thanks to the commanding, conforming presence of Christ.

Yet as much as ethics as conformation and ethics as command appear to converge and affirm one another in the mandates, the two ethics do retain different emphases. Specifically, it is within the language of command that Bonhoeffer makes a crucial distinction between moral life, generally speaking, and the exceptional nature of ethical decision-making. "Commandment" is an essential term in this distinction, because "commandment" is that which the ethical decision at times must violate.

Breaking the Commandment

In the *Ethics* manuscript, "History and Good [2]," Bonhoeffer emphasizes the concrete context of ethical thought and action: "We ask about the good not in abstraction from life, but precisely by immersing ourselves in it. . . . The question about the good can no longer be separated from the question of life, of history."[25] But in subtle distinction to Bonhoeffer's treatment of concrete life and worldliness in later *Ethics* manuscripts and the prison writings which follow upon them, concrete life in "History and Good [2]" is typified by a radical tension. Bonhoeffer writes: "There are occasions when, in the course of historical life, the strict observance of the explicit law of a state, corporation, a family, but also of a scientific discovery, entails a clash with the basic necessities of human life. In such cases, appropriate responsible action departs from the domain governed by laws and principles . . . and is instead confronted with the extraordinary situation of ultimate necessities that are beyond any possible regulation by law."[26]

Bonhoeffer calls such a situation, where "strict observance" contradicts "basic necessities," the "borderline case."[27] In the borderline case, the responsible actor "must completely let go of any law, knowing that here one must decide as a free venture." A necessary adjunct of this free venture is "the open acknowledgement that here the law is being broken, violated; that the commandment is broken out of dire necessity, thereby affirming the legitimacy of the law in the very act of violating it." Although Bonhoeffer insists that the law is affirmed even in its violation, this "acknowledgment" alone cannot secure the rectitude of the free venture. Whether in a given instance it is better to submit to the commandment or to violate it is the "ultimate question" that "must be kept open." "[I]n either case," however, "one becomes guilty, and is able to live only by divine grace and forgiveness."[28] Consequently, the response to the borderline case must always involve the taking on of guilt (*Schuldübernahme*).

At the unfinished end of "History and Good [2]," Bonhoeffer considers a worrisome entailment of his analysis of responsible action in the borderline case. He asks whether "the law of God as revealed in the Decalogue, and the divine mandates of marriage, work, and government" do not establish an "an inviolable boundary," one whose transgression would "amount to an insubordination against the revealed will of God?"[29] The import of this question is that the borderline case seems "to introduce a contradiction into the will of God itself."[30] Given Bonhoeffer's over-riding christological perspective, what could it possibly mean for the law of God to be in conflict with the "basic necessities of human life," which themselves can only arise in conformity with Christ? The very conditions of the borderline case seem to establish an instance when divine reality is split along a seam that separates divine law from divine exception. The language of commandment and exception risks disrupting the holism—the embrace of the whole of life—that the language of conformation and the mandates promised.

Unsurprisingly, Bonhoeffer suggests a christological resolution to this potential contradiction. The truly responsible actor "does not separate the law from its giver," whom he recognizes as Jesus Christ, "the ultimate reality to whom [the actor] is responsible."[31] Both the divine law and the divine will rest in Jesus Christ. As a result, any apparent contradiction between commandment and necessity, between law and freedom, will be reconciled through Christ himself; it is "through Christ" that the responsible actor "will be freed from the law for the responsible deed." This sentence almost suggests that Christ suspends the law so that no actual contradiction in divine reality occurs. Yet Bonhoeffer insists that law is *both* broken and sanctified in the "deed that arises out of freedom."

If "History and Good [2]" leaves us with an unresolved worry about the possibility of a divine contradiction—an interruption or disagreement within divine person—it also leaves us with the possibility of a contradiction within the human person. On the one hand, Bonhoeffer's responsible actor must operate in "the sphere of relativity, completely shrouded in the midst of the countless perspectives from which every phenomenon is seen."[32] He must renounce "ultimately dependable knowledge of good and evil."[33] And he must always bear in mind that he is breaking a law, committing a transgression against God's command, and is thus guilty. On the other hand, he "is not torn apart by destructive conflict, but instead can with confidence and inner integrity do the unspeakable."[34] While surely anything is possible through faith, Bonhoeffer's demands upon the responsible actor are experientially daunting, requiring both a constant awareness of willful commission of the "unspeakable" and a constant equanimity about this commission.

Reconciling the Commandment and the Ethical

In the late *Ethics* manuscript, "The 'Ethical' and the 'Christian' as a Topic," Bonhoeffer returned to the question of the relationship between law and freedom, commandment and exception.[35] Although "Topic," in keeping with "History and Good [2]," maintains a distinction between an ethical "boundary event" (*Grenzereignis*)[36] and quotidian moral life under the mandates, it views the boundary event with a certain suspicion. Bonhoeffer warns against "the unhealthy takeover of life by the ethical, that abnormal fanaticizing, that total moralizing of life, which leads to a constantly *interrupting* stream of judging or exhorting comments."[37] The very event of ethical decision-making, the kind of responsible action limned in "History," here is acknowledged as a threat to the "totality of life."

Alluding to the ontological and experiential aspects of the potential contradiction introduced by the borderline case, Bonhoeffer remarks that the "ethical phenomenon is a boundary event ... both in its content and as an experience."[38] Within community as structured by the mandates, "the ethical phenomenon, the ought, is dormant and not apparent in its objective and subjective sides." As Clifford Green notes, this means that there is neither the objective, divine imperative, "You ought," interrupting reality within the mandates, nor the subjective experience of the "I ought."[39] It is notable that Bonhoeffer calls the ethical phenomenon—the "ought"—"dormant" *in* rather than absent *from* or external *to* "community" and "order."[40] While in "History and Good [2]" the ethical venture operates outside of and *against* pre-existent law, Bonhoeffer describes the venture here as internal to the mandated structures of formed life, even if it is best understood as a boundary event.

To be sure, Bonhoeffer does not reject the ethical outright. Quite the contrary, he continues to insist that the ethical serves as a boundary to mark the fact that "any community is in a real sense always disintegrating."[41] Because of the imperfection of communal reality, there will "undoubtedly [be] situations and times in which what is moral is not self-evident ... During such periods the ethical becomes a topic for discussion."[42] It is thus incontrovertible that "the ethical" remains a topic in "Topic."

Yet the conceptual and rhetorical burden of "Topic" is on the limitation of the ethical, not its emancipation. This emphasis is in distinction to the argument and rhetoric of the "History" manuscript, which aimed to set the ethical free from fear of violating the law. The language of the

"Topic" manuscript identifies the ethical closely with the extant human order, setting the human free from fear of the ethical's dramatic excesses. Bonhoeffer explains: "The ethical is . . . not a principle that levels, invalidates, and shatters all human order. Instead, it inherently involves a certain order of human community and entails certain sociological relationships of authority. Only in their context does the ethical manifest itself and receive the concrete authorization that is essential to it."[43]

This idea of *authorization* for ethical action already marks an emphasis different from that found in "History." There, the responsible ethical actor was called, at least in certain situations, to "completely let go of any law."[44] Here responsible ethical action derives from pre-existent authority. At the end of "History," of course, Bonhoeffer *did* seek to ground the venture of free responsibility in an authoritative foundation—Jesus Christ himself. There, Bonhoeffer said that when acting responsibly, one is responding to Jesus Christ, in whom both God's law and God's will are located. The ground of responsible action is Jesus Christ, full stop. Putting it in this simple way, Bonhoeffer was able to elide—or defer—the worry about divine contradiction. Christ would somehow reconcile the divine law and the divine will which seems to will against the divine law.

In "Topic," the ultimate ground will remain Christ. But now, Bonhoeffer gets to this ultimate ground by a different path: the "sole authorization for ethical discourse" is the "commandment of God."[45] Bonhoeffer defines the commandment of God as "the total and concrete claim of human beings by the merciful and holy God in Jesus Christ."[46] Unlike the ethical, which now seems more partial and peripheral, the commandment "encompasses all of life." As Rasmussen explains, "the ethical is *part* of the command of God. It is far from the whole."[47] This emphasis reverses Bonhoeffer's rhetoric at the end of "History." There, Bonhoeffer treated the commands of God—such as "keeping the Sabbath holy" or "honoring one's parents"—as only one aspect of the "ultimate reality" of Jesus Christ, attaching equal prestige to the "responsible deed," for which such commands could be abrogated.[48] Here, the "command of the God" itself stands in for the ultimate divine reality, and the ethical, the space of the responsible deed, is identified as "far from the whole."

If Bonhoeffer's rhetoric now downplays the importance of the ethical, its explication of the commandment-as-"whole," is equally striking. Bonhoeffer explains that the "historical form" that the commandment takes is the system of the mandates itself: *"the commandment of God revealed in Jesus Christ is addressed to us in the church, in the family, in work, and in government.*"⁴⁹ In a sense, the *Ethics* manuscripts have come full circle, from the mandates-as-media-of-formation, to their status as laws which the ethical act may violate, to their re-appearance as the foundation of the ethical. Now, within the ambit of the mandates, rather than through their violation, Bonhoeffer sees the ethical arising.

The emphasis hereafter is on what Bonhoeffer calls the "pre-ethical," the "*flow* of life." ⁵⁰ Bonhoeffer deploys the language of "life" where he wishes to emphasize the dependence of the ethical upon the mandated structure of reality. Where the ethical was prized in "History" for the way in which it interrupts the daily strictures of life, enabling freedom, in "Topic" this interruption is minimized: life and its total structure is always present to cast a cooling shadow on the hot irruptions of ethical action. Bonhoeffer writes: "The commandment of God revealed in Jesus Christ embraces life as a whole. It does not merely guard, like the ethical, the boundaries of life that must not be crossed, but it is at the same time the center and fullness of life. It is not only ought, but also allowed. It not only prohibits but also liberates us for authentic life and for unreflective doing. It not only interrupts the life process whenever it goes astray, but it accompanies and guides it without our needing to be consciously aware of it."⁵¹ Bonhoeffer's chief concern is not to privilege one mode of normative activity (whether moral or ethical) over another but to highlight the ontological—christological—unity of normativity, "the comprehensive unity of God's command," the absence of "fragmentation."

This new emphasis on unity, totality, and wholeness responds to the possibility of divine contradiction raised at the fragmentary end of "History and Good [2]." There, the possibility of contradiction arose because of the way in which the ethical was formulated—as an absolute exception to commandment. How could it be that both the exceptional action and the mandates were in conformity with the divine presence, the form of Christ? Here, Bonhoeffer suggests that the mandates are not so much violated by as accommodating of the ethical, the ethical now becoming part of a larger, normative whole encapsulated as "the commandment of God."

As the manuscript continues, Bonhoeffer increasingly focuses on what he calls the "positive" content of the commandment, with his examples stemming from activity recognizably within the mandates.⁵² Bonhoeffer writes: "The commandment's goal is not avoiding transgression, not the agony of ethical conflict and decision, but rather the freely affirmed, self-evident life in church, marriage, family, work, and state."⁵³

What is so striking about the near-disappearance of the ethical from this discussion of commandment is that Bonhoeffer *introduced* the commandment of God in this manuscript as the *foundation* of the ethical, the "sole authorization of ethical discourse." Over the course of the manuscript, Bonhoeffer has become increasingly distanced from his major preoccupations in "History and Good [2]." There, his language treated the ethical deed, the guilt-ridden decision between wrong and wrong, as exceptional but vital. In "Topic," the ethical is not "vital" in the most basic sense, not the business of life. Indeed, in one striking passage, Bonhoeffer views "the ethical" as neurotic: "The 'ethical' can always only seek to interrupt this life, to confront it anew at any given moment with the conflict between its duties . . . It can only dissolve [life] into countless individual decisions."[54]

In general, the human experience of conflicting or contradictory duties seems to be actively minimized by the commandment: "Vis-à-vis God's commandment, a human being is not Hercules standing in perpetuity at a crossroads . . . worn out by conflicting duties."[55] It is as if the arena of self-evidence, which even at the beginning of the "Topic" manuscript is restricted to the space of the mandates, is now extended over the whole of reality. Through the commandment, humans "are allowed to know the proper decision as something that is truly behind them." By the end of the manuscript, the ethical is no longer even an event, but a heuristic. It "merely identifies the limits formally and negatively."[56]

From the human perspective, what the mandates offer is the experience of self-evidence. As Bonhoeffer puts it at the end of "Topic," humans operating within the mandates "are allowed, entirely without any inner conflict, to do one thing and not the other."[57] As further evidence that a subtle movement away from the conflictual reality of "History and Good [2]" has taken place, note the absence of any discussion of "guilt" in the post-"History" manuscripts.[58] If there is no longer anxiety about a contradiction between commandment and ethical action, then the need for active consciousness of guilt is diminished. Of course, this shift in emphasis does not mean that Bonhoeffer has rejected the reality of guilt, only that he does not think it should be a central preoccupation of the human moral agent in the world.[59]

The transition in "Topic" toward a holistic vision of human life, utterly conformed to Christ, and uninterrupted by ethical or ontological anxieties about the breaking of divine law casts helpful light on the striking—and seemingly novel—preoccupations of Bonhoeffer's prison theology. Particularly, Bonhoeffer's adoption of the Diltheyan motifs of human autonomy and the world come of age can be understood as a continuing expansion throughout human reality of the self-evident, empowering normativity that Bonhoeffer formulated in the mandates as the historical form of the encompassing commandment of God. In other words, just as the mandates represented an expansion of the scope of conformation beyond the church community, Bonhoeffer's emphasis on life, holism, and worldliness in the prison writings marks the expansion of the mandates even into the space that had once been occupied by the *Grenzfall*, the space where the mandates were earlier said to give out.

While in "Topic," the experience of life having a "unified direction" is enabled "by the commandment as by a good angel," in the prison writings, Bonhoeffer will attribute this experience of self-evident decision-making, of confidence and strength in life, to human autonomy, as made possible by Jesus Christ, "the human being."[60] The language of commandment has been displaced by a christological naturalism and humanism. This naturalism and humanism are not new to Bonhoeffer's thought, of course; we see them at work in *Sanctorum Communion* on forward. But in the 1944 theology they truly take center stage, after several attempts in *Ethics* to develop a commandment-based ethic. What Rasmussen reads as a privileging of an ethic of formation over an ethic of command in the prison writings, tracks this shift. The language of the mandates as structures of *command* disappears, but their essential role remains, now expressed in the language of human autonomy and worldliness.

Why might Bonhoeffer have moved away from the language of commandment altogether? Perhaps the very semantics of commandment could not but imply a division inimical to the full coherence of christological and human reality. For instance, in the last *Ethics* manuscript, "The Concrete Commandment and the Divine Mandates," we find Bonhoeffer moving closer to the formulations he would achieve in the prison writing, but still negotiating the divisiveness introduced by the language of commandment. In "Concrete Commandment," he explains that a "life of *genuine* worldliness is possible through the *proclamation* of the crucified Christ."[61] Here, it is the commanding word of Christ in the church that secures an authentic worldliness, to be distinguished from the "pseudo-worldliness" of the world "in opposition to the proclamation of the cross of Christ."[62] The language of commandment implies that something always must be added *to* the world: "Left to its own devices, the worldly is neither willing nor able to be only worldly."[63] But if something must be added to the world, then this suggests that the world is not always already "accepted, included, and borne" in the body of Christ. The language of commandment ultimately underrates the efficacy of Christ's formative relationship to the whole of reality. Only if the world "left to its own devices" was already Christ's world could it be said that Christ "embraces all of life."

From Commanded Life to Life Itself

As Rasmussen notes, "[o]nly once is the command of God even mentioned" in the prison letters, and then in a "passing remark" about a commentary on the first three of the Ten Commandments upon which Bonhoeffer was working.[64] The language of this *"Exposition on the First Table* of the Ten Words of God" is more formal and didactic than his letters, and the general tone is of an earlier Barthian register. Rasmussen notes that Bonhoeffer did not feel "sufficient excitement to share with Bethge" any of his specific arguments in the "Exposition."[65] There is, however, at least one noteworthy aspect of Bonhoeffer's presentation. He notes the "exceedingly remarkable fact" that: "Throughout history people have reflected on the fundamental orders of their life . . . and the results of nearly all such reflections overwhelmingly correspond with one another and with the Ten Commandments. Whenever the conditions of human life descend into disorder through powerful external or internal crises and upheavals, those persons who are able to hold on to clarity and discretion in their thoughts and judgments recognize that without fear of God, without reverence for parents, without protection of life, marriage, property, and dignity . . . no human life in community possible."[66]

This passage seems to be influenced both by Bonhoeffer's experience with his secular co-conspirators[67] and by his recent reading in the intellectual history of natural law.[68] Beyond the natural morality it endorses, what is so striking about this passage is its claim that reliance on such natural regularities is proper in times of *crisis.* Here, as opposed to in "History and Good [2]," times of disorder *do not* elicit the boundary, the exceptional case, the necessarily-broken commandment, but rather the self-evident and naturally-occurring norms of natural law.

Indeed, the two most distinctive aspects of Bonhoeffer's 1944 theology—the critique of religion and the coordinate embrace of the language of maturity, autonomy, and worldliness—mark a continuation of the trend away from a guilt-ridden ethic of law and exception and toward a more self-confident ethic that relies upon a unified moral reality accessible to the human actor.

In Bonhoeffer's April 30, 1944 letter to Eberhard Bethge, generally considered to be the beginning of the "new" theological reflections,[69] Bonhoeffer announces that the "age of religion" is "past."[70] He associates several different though related phenomena with religion, but I will focus on what Ernst Feil calls religion's "partiality." [71] One of Bonhoeffer's continual objections to religion in the prison letters is the way it cordons off different aspects of reality. Thus, in a climactic passage, after Bonhoeffer has surveyed several biblical events to discern the true meaning of conversion and faith, he writes: "There is nothing about a religious method [here]; the 'religious act' is always something *partial*, whereas 'faith' is something whole and involves one's *whole* life. Jesus calls us not to religion but to life."[72]

Indeed, it is religion's tendency to divide that makes worldliness the true antonym of religion.[73] To be worldly is to embrace the whole of reality, without exception or reliance on something or somewhere beyond life. Thus, Bonhoeffer calls on Christians to understand themselves no longer "religiously as privileged, but instead . . . as belonging wholly to the world."[74] Bonhoeffer's analogy of religion to circumcision is deeply resonant with this understanding of religion-as-partiality: "Freedom from *peritomé* [circumcision] is also freedom from religion."[75] Circumcision literally separates flesh from flesh, one form of life from another.

Bonhoeffer's choice of circumcision as the paradigmatic case of religious partiality suggests that he associates such partiality with law more generally. The law of circumcision, like every law, introduces divisions into life—between those who know the law and those who do not; those who obey or disobey; those who are exempt. As Wüstenberg notes, Bonhoeffer's "comparison of religion with circumcision or with the law occurs in various guises in Bonhoeffer's writing."[76] Thus, when Bonhoeffer criticizes Christian apologetics for attacking the "world's coming of age" he calls such apologetics "unchristian" because they "confuse Christ with a particular stage of religiousness, namely, with a human law."[77] The apologists seek to impose religious laws, creeds, and practices on those who are already mature, autonomous, independent.[78] They seek to constrain and harry what has already been made whole and calm.[79]

But if Bonhoeffer's critique of religion is a critique of the tendency of religious law to sow division and disquiet, is his late theology then a truly antinomian one, granting all legitimacy to the whims of human actors? Not at all. Rather, continuing the trend of his *Ethics*, Bonhoeffer's prison letters describe what Larry Rasmussen has called a "Christocentric alternative to natural law,"[80] a kind of normativity that applies to the whole of reality and is evident to human actors, regardless of their particular religious practices. In "Topic," Bonhoeffer announced that the commandment of God embraced the whole of life, freeing the human to live within the self-evident moral structures of reality as formed in Christ. In the prison writings, Bonhoeffer has moved away from the language of commandment—perhaps because of its connotations of religious partiality and division—but still embraces much of the moral vision endorsed by the *Ethics*. It was Bonhoeffer's discovery of Dilthey's *Weltanschauung und Analyse des Menschen seit Renaissance und Reformation* that provided him with a new narrative language with which to re-describe and extend the ethical vision of the later *Ethics* manuscripts.[81]

This narrative, which described a centuries-long "movement toward human autonomy,"[82] involved a transition from an age of commandments, imposed from above, to an age of naturally-emergent laws, which Dilthey described as "universally valid concepts" that "inhere in the entirety of life and draw from life their persuasive power."[83] As Bonhoeffer explained to Eberhard Bethge, by these natural laws, "the world lives and manages its affairs in science, in society and government, in art, ethics, and religion."[84] Bonhoeffer specifically referred to Montaigne and Bodin, who had "substitute[d] rules for life for the commandments," and Hugo Grotius, who had "set up his natural law as an international law, which is valid *etsi deus non daretur*, 'as if there was no God.'"[85] Dilthey's story offered Bonhoeffer a wider context in which to place his own movement away from the language of commandment and the kind of partiality it tended to introduce.

These naturally-emergent laws about which Bonhoeffer read could subsist "as if there was no God" because they emerged from the world itself and its host of physical and personal relationships. Such a world, Bonhoeffer recognized, need not be the world of an atheist who denies the reality of God, but rather a world that is uninterrupted by exceptions, miracles, lightning strikes of personal inspiration. It is a world that cannot be escaped through a journey into the self or above to some higher power. It is world that requires humans to stand on their own feet, and it provides the ground on which to do so. Bonhoeffer did not doubt for a moment that the ground of such stability was Christ. Rather, he connected his embrace of the "world come of age," a world of human maturity, to the theology of the cross: "God consents to be pushed out of the world and onto the cross; God is weak and powerless in the world and in precisely this way, and only so, is at our side and helps us."[86]

In what does the help of the weak God consist? Precisely in throwing us back upon our autonomy: "God would have us know that we must live as those who manage their lives without God."[87] Christ as God does not distinguish himself by separating himself from reality, but by choosing the world. Human autonomy obtains because of Christ, *the* autonomous human being who himself was forsaken by God. Christ, however, does not promise some *additional* intervention or command or support; the ground we are given through Christ is our autonomy.

Bonhoeffer did not believe that autonomy was a good as such. Rather, it was through his new emphasis on autonomy that Bonhoeffer was able to return to the basic ethical issue that had driven him for so long—the question of responsibility. In their autonomy, humans correspond to Jesus Christ, who is not just autonomous but uses his autonomy to choose to be-for-others. As Bonhoeffer writes in his "Outline for a Book," "Jesus's 'being-for-others' is the experience of transcendence!"[88] The ethical imperative of "being-for-others" *is* christological reality: "The transcendent is not the infinite, unattainable tasks, but the neighbor within reach in any given situation. God in human form!" There is little reason to think that the specific content of "being-for-others"—if Bonhoeffer had elaborated it further—would have differed greatly from much of what he wrote in the *Ethics* manuscripts about the mandates and natural, formed life.[89]

In sum, since the initial stages of his theological career, Bonhoeffer had defined responsibility as response to the reality of Jesus Christ. But the way in which Bonhoeffer analyzed this reality developed over time. In "History and Good [2]," as we have seen, Bonhoeffer flirted with a reality divided between enduring divine laws and their exceptions, a reality in which law must be broken in order to sanctify it. This analysis introduced both experiential and ontological problems, as humans seemed torn between confident law-breaking and guilt-bearing, and God himself seemed torn between his law and his will. The later *Ethics* manuscripts, particularly "Topic," sought to move beyond these problems, emphasizing the unity of divine reality and the general self-evidence of moral action, humans being conformed to divine reality through the commandment of God.

Then, in Bonhoeffer's prison writings, the language of autonomy, maturity, and worldliness replaced the language of command, achieving an astonishing degree of coherence between ethical human action and divine reality. As Feil has noted, Bonhoeffer came to embrace modernity—which even in the last *Ethics* manuscript attracted his suspicion—for ethical reasons: "He affirmed modernity as a command [for humans] to have positive dominion over the world."[90] Modernity and autonomy act as a world-historical call to responsibility; like the commandment of God in "Topic," they turn humans out into the world, but now the commandment is experienced from below, emergent and inextricable from the "natural life" of the world. As always for Bonhoeffer, this "natural life" is "formed life," life conformed to Christ, and thus structured in a particular way.[91] But now even the command to dwell in this life has come from life, discovered through the exercise of human autonomy, the paradigm case of which is the life of Christ. Such a command may not be violated without denying the presence of Christ himself, and thus does not admit any ethical exception.

9

Liturgy, Kenosis, and Creation

Bonhoeffer and Lacoste on Being before God without God in the World

KENDALL WALSER COX

IN THE WAKE OF Martin Heidegger's break with theology and turn toward methodological atheism, we are faced with the phenomenological and theological question of whether—and *how*—one can live before God as a radically finite being in an intranscendable world. Constricting the meaning and bounds of being locally and temporally seems to frustrate talk about God and "the beyond" and raises doubts about the intelligibility of standing face-to-face with God. This is the problem Jean-Yves Lacoste assumes in *Experience and the Absolute: Disputed Questions on the Humanity of Man*, where he proposes a "liturgical reduction"[1] that makes thinkable turning toward God in a "natively" Godless world. Resonating throughout Lacoste's leading back of the human to "liturgy"[2] is Dietrich Bonhoeffer's unfinished inquiry into what it means that "before God and with God we live without God."[3] But while Bonhoeffer suggests that living in the world "*etsi deus non daretur*"[4] situates the human at the center of existence, Lacoste, in striking contrast, describes being-toward-God-in-the-world as a transgressive dwelling at the frontier. It seems this divergence is rooted in the ways they understand and relate the terms "world" and "creation." Where Bonhoeffer's treatment of world and creation indicates significant conceptual overlap, the coherence of Lacoste's analysis depends upon not only an opposition between world and creation but also an elliptical sidelining of creation itself. In light of this, even if we take up Lacoste's impressive phenomenological rendering of human identity in excess of worldly existence, we might not wish to leave behind Bonhoeffer's reckoning of the human situation.

In what follows, I first offer Lacoste's project as a particularly rigorous attempt to think methodological and experiential atheism *theologically*. As such, it is a compelling response to a number of the questions and challenges bequeathed to theology in Bonhoeffer's late letters and papers. While the trajectory of Bonhoeffer's thought has branched out in various directions—with catch phrases such as the "worldliness" of faith, "religionless Christianity," and "a world come of age" now pervading contemporary theology—it is fitting that this cluster of concepts find its way back to its phenomenological root through Lacoste's work. Bonhoeffer too wrestled with and was informed by the strictly immanent philosophy of Edmund Husserl and Heidegger—as is explicit in earlier works such as *Sanctorum Communio*,[5] *Act and Being*,[6] and *Creation and Fall* and evident in his later writings as well. Second, however, while Lacoste grafts himself into Bonhoeffer's legacy[7] and they share certain common ground, it is clear that Lacoste's account of the humanity of the human tends away from some of Bonhoeffer's deeper impulses—namely, concerning the original and eschatological unity of world and creation. While this is by no means the only or most obvious point of contrast between them, it is the fulcrum for my engagement here. Third and finally, a number of Bonhoeffer's well-known concepts are flagged as resources for rethinking world *as* creation and being-in-the-world *as* being-before-God. Rather than culminating in a counter-argument, this initial juxtaposition is an invitation for further engagement between phenomenology and theology, particularly around the question of the human vocation of creatureliness.

Lacoste's Liturgical Reduction to Kenotic Existence

Lacoste's liturgical reduction culminates in "a kenotic treatment" of humanity. He claims we "say" what is most essential about ourselves when we "accept a *kenotic* existence."[8] The "ontological poverty" of humanity manifest in birth and death should be affirmed in "concrete gestures" of voluntary dispossession, for "whoever desires poverty . . . wants nothing other than to accede to the truth of [human] being." Thus abnegation becomes "a path we can follow that is faithful to what we are."[9] According to Lacoste, it is the human's "eschatological destiny" to attain itself by "being rid of what is most *natively* proper" to itself.[10] To be (truly) human, then, is to accept a certain "beneficial violence."[11]

Setting aside immediate objections (humanist, feminist, or otherwise) that such an ascetic anthropology betrays an underlying disdain for physical existence, as well as longstanding precedents for such kenoticism (e.g., John of the Cross, who lurks in the background of this work), it is worth observing how Lacoste arrives at his conclusion. While his meticulous and expansive train of thought cannot be summarized here, several conceptual moves are particularly integral to the cogency of "kenotic existence": (1) the Heideggerian typology and eschatology of Dasein; (2) the description of liturgy as "encounter" and "inexperience" rather than conscious experience; (3) a critical engagement with Hegel's eschatology through a Bonhoefferean "splitting in two of the end"; and (4) a focused theology of the cross that grounds an *anthropologia crucis*.[12]

First, Lacoste carves out a space for liturgy, or being-before-God, within a Heideggerian topology. In uncovering the structure of being as *Dasein* and *Insein*, Heidegger has taught us that the question "who am I?" is preceded by the question "where am I?"[13] Topology is part of ontology.[14] But, on all fronts, "location, as a transcendental feature" of Dasein means it is destined to understand itself in "an essentially intranscendable world."[15] Being-there means being-in, *not* as a thing inside another thing—e.g., a fish in an aquarium—but according to the logic of *inherence*: the world as *horizon* recedes as it enfolds.[16] Because of this, the originary relationship of Dasein to the world is that of not-being-at-home (*Unzuhause*) and foreignness (*étrangéité*).[17] Yet there is no other place for Dasein, no beyond-the-world from which it comes or toward which it is oriented.

This being-there-in-the-world is governed by temporality and thus yields a certain eschatology.[18] Heidegger says in his 1923 lectures, *Ontology—The Hermeneutics of Facticity*, "the character . . . of 'our' 'own' Dasein [is] its being-there for a while at a particular time."[19] Thus Dasein "finds itself *face to face* with the 'nothing' of the possible impossibility of its existence."[20] Standing "*coram morte*," to use John D. Caputo's phrase,[21] has structurally supplanted the Augustinian *coram Deo*.[22] This is so, for Heidegger, not just ontically, but *ontologically*: the shape of Dasein's being is determined by its "not-yet" as its "way to be."²³ Its telos, its "ownmost potentiality," is "the possibility of impossibility," the impossibility of existing.²⁴ Thus Dasein is fundamentally *Sein zum Tode*: being toward death.²⁵

However, the "world" of *Being and Time* is not the only *topos* of humanity for Heidegger. In his later commentaries on Friedrich Hölderlin, "earth" figures in the "the Fourfold" (*Geviert*) as the familiar homeland of the "mortal."²⁶ It complements the sky, as the mortal the deities—all under the sovereignty of "the sacred" (*das Heilige*) and oriented toward, in the poet's words, "the infinite relation."²⁷ Although theology might be tempted to insert itself here, God can neither be identified with deities relegated to a finite locale nor with a purely immanent or pagan sacred. The fourfold, then, does not annul the topology of *Being and Time*. Yet Lacoste exploits the dialectic that surfaces between the atheism of the world and the sacred of the earth.²⁸ If "the native conditions of experience" already go "hand-in-hand with a logic of ambiguity,"²⁹ place might be determined otherwise for liturgy.

Second, siding with Hegel against (a certain reading of) Schleiermacher, Lacoste maintains the priority of knowledge over immediacy.³⁰ By "liturgy" Lacoste does *not* mean immediate or affective experience of God or any human act of worship, but "the logic that presides over the encounter between [the human] and God."³¹ Now, given the topological determination of ontology, whatever the human does cannot be thought *atopically*. Therefore, liturgy must "subvert topology from within" by negating and transgressing its boundaries.³² In contrast to "religious experience" (which Lacoste rejects), the encounter with God must be thought in terms of *nonplace, nonexperience, nonevent*, and *nonaccomplishment*.

Briefly, the liturgical non-place is a matter of bracketing "being-there" for the sake of "being-*toward*"³³—or, symbolically subordinating being-in-the-world to being-before-God.³⁴ This act is generally marked by nonexperience, not because God is "absent" or "nonexistent," but simply because the "immediate" naturally "keeps the Absolute veiled over." God is not given according to the logic of "historical and worldly regimes of presence."³⁵ It follows that the liturgical encounter accepts itself as a non-event, or the non-advent of God.³⁶ The one who prays knows that (for the most part) nothing happens—or more precisely, nothing happens for consciousness. This is not to say God is not *there*—for God is omnipresent—or that God *cannot* be there—for God is omnipotent. What is in question is not two regions of being—"this side" and "the other side"—but rather, two orders of experience. So to be before God is simply "to expose [oneself] to God"—to *expect*, to wait. Liturgical time is consequently reconstituted as an "*entr'acte*"—an intermission between the factical and the eschatological; it is the nighttime of existence defined by inoperativity.[37]

This brings Lacoste to a more precise definition of liturgy as "the *expectation or desire for Parousia in the certitude of the nonparousical presence of God*."[38] The sleepless vigil—the pre-eminent figure of liturgy for Lacoste—is a matter of doing nothing necessary, not even the diurnal work of ethics.[39] But this non-necessity is, in Eberhard Jüngel's sense, a *beyond*-necessity; it proves "the surplus of meaning we give our humanity."[40] Liturgy thus fundamentally contests Heidegger's assertion that "one is what one does."[41] It appears as "time wasted" but it is "existence gained." So Lacoste has identified another important gap—between facticity and vocation, necessity and freedom, situation and identity, location and orientation.[42]

A third related thread in Lacoste's work is his critical engagement with Hegel's eschatology through a Bonhoefferean "splitting in two of the end." In his *Phenomenology of Spirit*, as in his lectures on the philosophy of religion, Hegel claims the Christian faith is the *Revealed* Religion[43] that contains the entire content of the truth of Spirit—the complete manifestation of the Infinite in the finite, the absolute knowledge of the reconciliation of God and the human. The truth of Spirit is achieved on Good Friday, when the Infinite fully enters into the finite experience *par excellence*: death. Importantly, for Hegel, as for Bultmann after him, Christ's death *is* itself the resurrection of Spirit into the community of faith.[44] That is to say, Easter Sunday is folded into the negative moment of the cross: the resurrection is simply the *meaning* of the crucifixion—the transmission of Christ's knowledge of reconciliation.[45] The paradox of Hegelian eschatology, then, is only the "paradox of a delayed interpretation."[46] For Hegel, it is the ignorant human who lives as if God is not there.

While Lacoste agrees with Hegel (against Kant) on the possibility of the knowledge of God, he contests Hegel's interpretation of the resurrection because it renders the eschaton immanent in the world.[47] The manifestation of God in Christ is indeed "insuperable, the last word proffered in history." However, Hegel has forgotten that this last fact is also a *promise*—yet to be fulfilled.[48] In Bonhoeffer's language, reconciled existence is not "the ultimate" but the "penultimate."[49] The interval between the end (the cross) and the end (the eschaton) must be maintained. God is not available in the mode of parousia and so, against Hegel, knowledge is not absolute. Rather, knowledge "consecrates itself to the distance that separates [humanity] from the definitive fruition of" God.[50] Further, since the eschaton will "render conceptual mediations obsolete,"[51] knowledge *only* has its privilege *preeschatologically*. In other words, knowledge and inexperience are inextricable: "We know and do not 'see.'"[52] For Lacoste, against Hegel, it is precisely the one who *does* know God who still lives *as if* God is not there.[53]

A final theme fundamental to the integrity of Lacoste's liturgical reduction is his theology of the cross. What we have said so far is that the *identity* of the human is already eschatological (oriented toward God) while the *situation* of the human is still preeschatological (or factical); Bonhoeffer and Lacoste generally agree here. The question is *how* to live an eschatological identity out of an intranscendable empirical situation. For Lacoste this is a matter of what he calls "pure *exposition* to God."[54] Turning toward God entails a "disorientation of consciousness," a decentering of the subject, in which human intentionality is subordinated to "God's intentions" for humanity.[55] In relation to God, the "I" is never "spectator." Experience is reversed and "the order of aims" inverted. The human becomes "nothing but the object of an aim,"[56] "nothing but its opening to God."[57] According to this reduction, the essence of the human is not the will-to-power, as for Nietzsche, but the will-to-powerlessness.[58] Likewise, contrary to Heidegger's concept of authenticity, disappropriation demonstrates that to be oneself is not to possess oneself.[59] It appears as foolishness or madness, but Lacoste says the ascetic life is motivated by "an extravagant rationality."[60]

Finally we can clarify Lacoste's concluding *anthropologia crucis*.[61] He says, human destiny "becomes intelligible only in light of another destiny, that of the Crucified." This is Lacoste's *a posteriori* justification for denying the privilege of experience: the silence of the cross.[62] The cross indicates that God can be nearest when only known by the senses as an absence[63]—and this is what validates his description of liturgy in terms of *nonvision* and *nonfeeling*.[64] The one who turns toward God in the world "symbolically dwells in Good Friday."[65]

What is faintly intimated here is the extent to which this reduction depends upon a certain kind of paschal trinitarianism and a certain description of the *imago Dei*. In his concluding sentence, Lacoste claims we say who we are "most precisely" when we "accept an existence in the image of a God who has taken [on] humiliation."[66] The *imago dei* tends to evoke the first chapters of Genesis; we might ask why in this case it does not.

The Question of Creation

What is curiously faint in Lacoste's otherwise rigorous inquiry into the humanity of the human is his conception of creation.[67] It is not there "in the beginning," or at the "origin;"[68] it is not mentioned alongside the incarnation, the cross, the resurrection, the image of God, the Kingdom, or even "the eschaton." It seems the world has nothing to do with creation and only concerns the meaning of humanity inasmuch as it obscures it. But what does not get asked here is whether the worldly or factual conditions of finitude might actually be *creational*.

Included in his profound concession to Heidegger is Lacoste's definition of the world.[69] He says, "there is *no equivocation between the phenomenological concept of the world and the theological concept of the world* that differs from creation . . . and that a denial of creation governs."[70] In the language of Ephesians 2:12: the world is *atheios*.[71] On Lacoste's understanding, this means "the world, *as world*, draws a veil between Dasein and God."[72] But this elision of definitions perhaps stems from a problem in Heidegger's own thought. As Hannah Arendt points out, Heidegger is aware of Augustine's dual use of *mundus*—which means, on the one hand, the divine creation of heaven and earth (*ens creatum*) and, on the other, "worldliness" or love of the world (*dilectio mundi*). But, Arendt says, Heidegger is ultimately "confined" in his understanding because he "interprets only the latter" despite the fact that it is derivative of the former.[73] He attempts to divest *mundus* of any metaphysical or theological sense as created,[74] reducing it to a neutral, immanent structure of being—which is what Lacoste assumes in coordinating the phenomenological (Heideggerian) and the theological (Pauline) senses of "world."[75] In doing this, what Lacoste gains is the right to describe the atheism of the world as humanity's originary fallenness, divertissement, and in-authenticity.[76]

World, then, is not identified with "fallen creation," nor is it destined for redemption; it is that which must "pass away" (1 Cor 7:31).[77] For Lacoste, the true human dwelling place is the relation sealed between God and humanity—a "location" which is notably abstract—and this relation is essentially determined by a "noninterpositioning of 'world' and 'earth' between God and me."[78] So we are left with the question: *Where* is creation?

With recourse to the logic of the gift, Lacoste describes creation as "the gift of Being." The world, in contrast, is "the denial that Being is a gift"; it is a "reality *entirely different* from creation" because it is governed by forgetfulness.[79] This helps us make sense of Lacoste's enigmatic question—can I be present at my own creation?[80] It seems that "world" and "creation" must be conceived as two conflicting comportments toward being—much like Heidegger's own description of authenticity and fallenness as "intentional how[s]" rather than "objective event[s]."[81] When we, in our worldliness, forget the gift, we forget that "the border between Being and non-being *actually passes through our present*, and that we cannot face God *without admitting that [God] continues [this] benevolent giving*."[82] Liturgy, as Lacoste conceives it, maintains the fragile link between gift and giving through the practice of disappropriation or dispossession. Facing God involves a "perpetuation" of "creation," which Lacoste calls our "first passivity."[83]

We might ask here whether the work of dispossession is merely another permutation of the self-realization that Lacoste reproaches in the Nietzschean will-to-power and the Heideggerian logic of appropriation. But more to our point, what if—and this is something Paul Tillich, for example, readily concedes—God's intention for humanity precisely ordains the making of life one's own?[84] Is disappropriation really a response in kind? The *reception* of *the* gift itself is perhaps as crucial as the *acknowledgement* that it is *a* gift. As gifted, humans are—in fact—no longer poor.

This compels us to ask what creation as "the gift of *Being*" could mean if it is pitted against the so-called theological definition of "world" and, concomitantly, the phenomenological "being-in-the-world." If, theologically speaking, being is what God gives and, phenomenologically defined, being is Dasein and Insein, then how could being-before-God demand a violation of these conditions and how could "world" be "completely different" from "creation"? To challenge the enclosure of the worldly horizon is one thing, but to do violence to the reality of being-in-fact seems like another form of forgetfulness: it does not forget that Being is *a* gift, as the "world" does, but it appears to forget what *the* gift is: creaturely existence—local, temporal, finite.[85]

Interestingly, the only objections Lacoste seems to imagine to his reduction are Nietzschean (that it is nihilistic) and Hegelian (that it is slavish and unhappy).[86] However, we might take exception to the "minimal" human on other grounds as well.[87] May we expect more from being human and from the encounter with God than existential attenuation, negation, and cruciformity?

Bonhoeffer and Being before God in the World as Creation

In speaking of the "world come of age," Bonhoeffer refers, like Lacoste after him, to the fact that the encounter with God is not necessary or basic to worldly experience. God has been discarded as a "working hypothesis."[88] But for Bonhoeffer, reconciled existence in the time of the penultimate is not a matter of dispossession and ascesis only, but of worldliness, ethics, strength, and joy. Their dissimilarity here is bound up with the fact that, for Bonhoeffer, creation and world *overlap* rather than, to use Lacoste's word, "collide."[89]

This is signaled throughout Bonhoeffer's theology, not least by the fact that he frequently uses the terms "world," "earth," "creation," and "reality" interchangeably or to qualify one another. In *Creation and Fall*, for example, Bonhoeffer identifies the world (*Welt*) with "what has been created," "the earth," "God's kingdom," "creatureliness," "*we ourselves*," etc.[90] Of course, Bonhoeffer also recognizes the full range of meanings of "world," including those with negative associations. In his early Barcelona sermons, he sometimes refers to the "transitoriness," "wickedness," and vanity of a "world" governed by time and death.[91] However, even in those texts and especially as his thought develops, Bonhoeffer opposes the kind of Christianity that attempts to desert or negate the world or relegate it to a discrete sphere. Endorsing Nietzsche's critique of "otherworldly" or "afterworldly people" (*den Hinterweltlern*),[92] Bonhoeffer emphasizes the closeness of the human (*ha-'adam*: the earthling) to the earth (*ha-'adama*), saying, "What is to be taken seriously about human existence is its bond with mother earth, its being as body. Human beings have their existence as existence on earth. They do not come from above; they have not by some cruel fate been driven into the earthly world and been enslaved to it."[93]

Against the gnostic inclinations alluded to here, Bonhoeffer describes life before God in a baptismal address as "wholly in the world, deeply rooted in the earth."[94] While a comprehensive analysis of his treatment of creation would show this more clearly, it is worthwhile to recall several of Bonhoeffer's concepts that are funded by a nonopposition between world and creation and thus stand out as resources for recasting "liturgy."

First, Bonhoeffer's appeal in *Ethics* to "natural life" introduces an important third term that helps mediate between creation *per se* and the order that opposes it.[95] Expressing concern that "the Protestant church" of his day was delivering "a static proclamation of divine grace" in which "everything human naturally sank into the night of sin" and the "antithesis to the natural was no longer the unnatural but the word of God," Bonhoeffer sought to recover the category of "the natural" for Protestant thought from Catholic ethics. He writes, "We speak of the natural as distinct from the *created*, in order to include the fact of *the fall into sin*. We speak of the natural as distinct from the *sinful* in order to include *the created*." In contrast, "the unnatural is that which ... closes itself off from the coming of Jesus Christ."[96] Bonhoeffer thus aligns the natural with "fallen creation" and differentiates it from the unnatural, or evil, which attempts to destroy it. Here he echoes *Creation and Fall*, where he speaks of "the reality of the fallen world, which is *the creation upheld*,"[97] and "Christ, Reality, and Good," where he describes the world during the "penultimate" as "preserved," "loved and reconciled by God."[98]

Second, inasmuch as Bonhoeffer has an *anthropologia crucis*, it compels humans to activity rather than passivity. While Lacoste grounds liturgical nonaccomplishment in the kenosis of the cross, for Bonhoeffer, the cross leads to "vicarious representation or action (*Stellvertretung*) in concrete situations *for the sake of others*."[99] It is significant that Bonhoeffer does not refer to the revelation of God in the humiliation of Christ apart from its soteriological purpose. He writes, "God consents to be pushed out of the world and onto the cross; God is weak and powerless in the world"—*but*: "in precisely this way, and only so, is at our side and helps us."[100] On Good Friday, we know God as the one for whom we are "you;" we know Christ, as the icon of God, "is there for others."[101] As a result, when Bonhoeffer speaks of something like the imitation of Christ through voluntary dispossession, it is not in existential or individually[102] "liturgical" terms but in relational and ethical terms. Life ordered to the cross is not a matter of self-denial and renunciation for its own sake but of "service and self-giving"[103] on behalf of "the neighbor within reach in any given situation."[104] Thus, although ethics might not be inscribed in the structure of Dasein or even Mitdasein—as Lacoste interprets Heidegger against Emmanuel Levinas[105]—it is inscribed in the being of Christ and therefore in humanity's vocational identity.[106] That is to say, for Bonhoeffer, actively being-with-and-for-others-in-the-world is itself a mode of being-toward-God.[107] This association is thorough and reciprocal: it is not only the case that, as "the Crucified One," Christ's "'being-for-others' unto death" mediates our own humanity to us, but also that our "being there for others" mediates "our relationship to God."[108]

Third, alongside Luther's theology of the cross, Bonhoeffer's Christology is also informed by Irenaeus's sense of "recapitulation"[109] (*anakephalaiosis*)—Christ's "summing up" of all things in heaven and on earth (Eph 1:10).[110] Dasein finds itself "thrown" into the middle (*Mitte*) of existence, at a distance from its origin and telos. But the human meets the beginning and end together in Christ the Mediator (*Mittler*) who redeems by recapitulating all of creation in himself. For Bonhoeffer, eschatology and creation are tightly intertwined—the beginning is determined by the end; salvation is (re)creation. He introduces his lectures on Genesis 1–3 saying, "The church of Christ witnesses to the end of all things. It lives from the end, it thinks from the end, it acts from the end ... The new is the real end of the old; the new, however, is Christ ... The church speaks within the old world about the new world ... it sees the old world only in the light of the new world."[111] Bonhoeffer, like Lacoste, "sees the beginning only in dying, from the viewpoint of the end." But while for Lacoste, Good Friday is the first and last word of human existence in the world, when Bonhoeffer says "beginning," he has Genesis in mind and when he says "end," he means the cosmic renewal inaugurated in the incarnation. Thus Lacoste's revised Heideggerian sense of living from one's own future onward would still constitute, for Bonhoeffer, a return to worldliness. The incarnation, then, is not a justification for living "in the most tenuous way possible"[112] the experiences and categories of human existence but, quite obversely, that which calls humans into the "polyphony of life," to live "many dimensions at once."[113]

This helps us clarify Bonhoeffer's later analysis of the gap between the penultimate and the ultimate.[114] The penultimate is not simply a "worldly" time that leads to death and is utterly discontinuous with true life; it already includes human existence revived, redefined, and reoriented as creaturely. Bonhoeffer says, "in the fallen, old world [we] believe in the world of the new creation."[115] This eschatological re-visioning of the present is made possible by the one "Christ-reality,"[116] in which "the whole reality of the world is already drawn into Christ and bound together in Him"[117] (2 Cor 5:19). Reconciled existence is not just a matter of the union between God and the human but also between *God and the world*—and therefore between the human and the world as well. "Nothing is excluded" from God's love for the world in Christ (John 3:16).[118] It is consequently both possible and proper to "encounter the reality of the world [as] always already sustained, accepted and reconciled in the reality of God."[119] Of course, this reconciliation is not yet ultimate or absolute; it lives on a promise—but precisely a promise to "bring again" what is *earthly*. Commenting on Ecclesiastes 3:15, "God seeks out what has gone by," Bonhoeffer writes Bethge, this "apparently means that nothing of the past is lost, that God seeks out with us the past that belongs to us to reclaim it." In the end, as Paul Gerhardt's hymn reads, Christ "will restore it all."[120]

Finally, the preceding concepts serve as interpretive clues to Bonhoeffer's enigmatic recommendations of "this-worldliness" and of a "worldly" or "religionless" Christianity.[121] As he says earlier in *Ethics*, "It is a denial of God's revelation in Jesus Christ to wish to be 'Christian' without being 'worldly.'"[122] Bonhoeffer sometimes uses "worldly" quite differently to mean "godless" or "without God." For example, worldliness, non-religiousness, and godlessness can refer variously to the fact that God is not a perceivable and demonstrable entity, that there is no *deus ex machina* to solve the insoluble, that the world has come of age and is autonomous, or that a "false" (ontotheological) notion of God has been abolished.[123] But "worldly" also—and perhaps primarily—concerns God's mode of being-with-us in Christ. When considering how to reinterpret Christian doctrines "in a 'worldly' way," Bonhoeffer says he means "worldly" "in the Old Testament sense and in the sense of John 1:14"[124]—which is to say: creational and incarnational. Here Bonhoeffer specifically sets "worldly" over against "religious," "mythological," and "metaphysical." *The Word became flesh* "demythologizes" religious thinking preoccupied with the individual salvation of the soul out of the world or with an abstract "best being," a "beyond this world" that is not also a "*for* this world."[125] Tellingly, Bonhoeffer defines "this-worldliness" at one point as throwing oneself "completely into the arms of God" by "living fully in the midst of life's tasks, questions, successes and failures, experiences, and perplexities."[126] So even if the world (phenomenologically speaking) does not "belong" to the human (Heidegger), belonging to the world (as creation) is a way—*the* way—of belonging to God. As a result, Bonhoeffer suggests it is "a cardinal error" to regard Christianity as "a religion of redemption" rooted in an other-worldly "mythological hope."

Rather, Christian hope "refers people to their life on earth in a wholly new way ... to drink the cup of earthly life to the last drop."[127]

Living fully in the penultimate, then, is the *how* of receiving the gift of creation—not "the gift of Being" only but of "earthly happiness" as well. Bonhoeffer says of the hymn line "this poor earth / is not our home" that remembering this is "only the very last thing." But situated in the next to last, "we are to so love God in our *life* and in the good things God gives us ... that, when the time comes and is here—but truly only then!—we also go to God with love, trust, and joy ... One should find and love God in what God directly gives us; if it pleases God to allow us to enjoy an overwhelming earthly happiness, then one shouldn't be more pious than God and allow this happiness to be gnawed away through arrogant thoughts and challenges and wild religious fantasy that is never satisfied with what God gives."[128] Gratitude for *the* gift means at once faithfulness to God *and* a certain kind of worldliness (and in this sense: worldliness *is* faithfulness). In light of his question, "where in the world is Christ to be found?" Bonhoeffer does not point to the limits but answers: "as the center of our existence"[129]—for "Christ takes hold of human beings in the midst of their lives" not in "boundary-experiences."[130] As Bethge reiterates, even in his ecclesiology, which privileges the church as "Christ existing as community"[131] (and hence the place of divine-human encounter *par excellence*), even "in the *arcanum*" of the church's hidden confession and worship, Bonhoeffer maintains that "Christ takes everyone ... and turns them around to face other people and the world."[132]

To summarize, Bonhoeffer consistently affirms that world and earth are part of God's intentions for humanity. Of course, that is not to say we can therefore presume to experience God as an intentional object in the world.[133] But perhaps the conditions of this impossibility are precisely given by God, and perhaps not in order to be subverted.[134] In this case, the interposition of the world is neither that which must be effaced in order to stand before God nor that which facilitates the immediate experience of God, but that which has been taken up by God in Christ. These points indicate not only that there are other ways of coordinating the terms "world" and "creation" and "being-in-the-world" and "being-before-God" but, further, that if we do not draw creation into the discussion of incarnation, world, and humanity we are left with a truncated Christology, an unearthly eschatology, and no way to live before God in the world except tenuously.

Questions, Convergences, and the Cross

In conclusion, this initial pairing of Bonhoeffer and Lacoste undoubtedly raises more concerns than it settles. When brought to bear on Lacoste's liturgical reduction to kenotic existence, Bonhoeffer's inclinations help us articulate a range of important questions concerning the world-creation relationship: Can we dwell in the world *as* creation (Bonhoeffer), and how, or does living our creation now somehow mean voiding the world (Lacoste), and in what sense? What do we actually mean when we say "world"—cosmos, *imperium*, fallen creation, earth, *ens creatum*, *dilectio mundi*, Kingdom of God? What do the incarnation and resurrection mean for the world-creation relationship and, conversely, how do our assumptions about world and creation inform Christology? Does the eschaton entail a restoration of creational goodness or is it a qualitatively different kind of reconciliation—an elevation, a transfiguration? What would a "phenomenology of creation"[135] look like and how might it help us interpret not only the "thin sound of silence" (1 Kgs 19:12) met so often in prayer but also the concrete joys and sorrows of existence? What would it disclose about the lineaments of creational finitude and the conditions of human experience? How does God relate to the finitude of humanity—both "original" and fallen?

As this set of questions suggests, further dialogue between Bonhoeffer and Lacoste will continue to uncover ground that abounds with footholds for ecumenical thought. While their confessional commitments and resources are evident, at the same time, they make for a distinctly unstereotypical contrast: on the one hand, we have a Catholic philosopher emphasizing the individual soul before God, the disjunction between grace and the "natural" order, human incapacity for the experience of God, and the unpredictable and sovereign inbreaking of revelation—themes commonly associated with Reformed theology; on the other hand, we have a Lutheran theologian stressing the relationship between grace and creation fundamentally stabilized by the incarnation and, concomitantly, the connection between faith and righteous action in the world—which are more typically Catholic accents.[136] But this is precisely the sort of theological freedom and philosophical resourcefulness encouraged by Lacoste in his call for a move "from theology to *theological thinking*"[137]—a shift that perhaps heralds new possibilities not only for the integration of philosophy and theology but also for ecumenical convergence and cross-pollination.

Finally, although I have focused on the fact that the divergence in Bonhoeffer and Lacoste's answers concerning the *how* of facing God has something to do with the ambiguous relationship between "world" and "creation," thoroughly interlacing this problem are their different senses of what the cross means for the shape of reconciled existence in the penultimate. Is Christ crucified the center of earthly life as the one who concretely unites God and world in himself, as for Bonhoeffer, or is he a demonstration of the existential aporia between the rules of the world and the meaning of humanity, as for Lacoste?[138] We might finally inquire whether a certain Christology could maintain both, and in such a way that we win with Lacoste his critical phenomenological delimiting of the atheism native to experience, yet also glean from Bonhoeffer his leading back of the human to a more a more relational *imitatio Christi* and a more creational *imago dei*.

10

The Conversion of Social Life

Bonhoeffer's Mandates as Theological Dispositifs

MARKUS FRANZ

Bonhoeffer's *Ethics* remains one of the most studied and inspiring articulations of Christian ethics in the twentieth century.[1] This fact is particularly interesting given the unfinished nature of the project. What leads Christian thinkers, both Protestant and Catholic alike, to return so often to this incomplete and even sometimes contradictory work? This essay suggests that one central reason for this popularity is the insightfulness with which it attempts an articulation of a fundamental concern of Christian theology: how does a theological ethic take into account both the gospel of the Advent of God's reign in Christ, and the manifold "realities" of the world that demand ethical deliberation? In Bonhoeffer's own words the "subject matter of a Christian ethic is God's reality revealed in Christ becoming real [*Wirklichwerden*] among God's creatures."[2] Bonhoeffer's *Ethics* provides a sustained effort to hold ethical reflection together around this twofold center. While beginning always from the theological foundation of the gospel of God's becoming human (*Menschwerdung*) in Jesus Christ, Bonhoeffer tries to show how this foundation already provides for a *concrete* ethics—that is, one which takes into account both the materiality and sociality of human life within this world.[3]

However the concreteness of human social life itself is not a "brute fact"; rather, it is mediated through a variety of (contradictory and competing) discourses, which follow their own theoretical dispositions. In Bonhoeffer's own day, Nazi ideology functioned as the dominant discourse that tried to frame and govern social relations in a totalizing manner.[4] It is no surprise that Bonhoeffer saw the need for a "concrete theological ethics [*konkrete evangelische Ethik*]"[5] that is driven by the Gospel and thus able to resist all totalizing ideologies.[6] The *Ethics* fragments accordingly can be read as Bonhoeffer's initial attempt at such an articulation.

This essay contends that the contemporary predominance of a managerial approach to "social problems" in western societies has led towards an "economization of the social," which threatens to work in a similarly totalizing fashion. In this development some have even seen the "death of the social."[7] This situation provides an important reason to follow through on Bonhoeffer's insights today. All the more so, since sophisticated managerial approaches claim already to have mastered the task of including moral restraints and preferences in their systems. Economic calculus has long since discovered the market value of such "ethically-qualified" products. Given this development within capitalist managerialism itself, ethical reflection must take special cognizance of the danger of losing its critical distance. Our situation therefore demands renewed deliberation on the theoretical and practical foundation and disposition of ethical reflection itself.

Few in contemporary social theory have captured the managerial commodification of social life in more revealing ways than Michel Foucault. This paper thus seeks to create a dialogue between Bonhoeffer and Foucault on this point. In the following, I pursue this dialogue in three steps. *First*, I explore Foucault's analysis of *discursive practices* that subsume both sociality and individuality into what he called *dispositifs* (or "apparatuses," as the English translators of Foucault's work render the French term), i.e., mechanisms of managerial power.[8] I trace especially the ways these dispositives regulate but also subvert social relations. Here I also draw on Giorgio Agamben, who further develops important aspects of Foucault's thought. *Second*, I ask how the concept of dispositives compares to Bonhoeffer's articulation of the "mandates," which involve both given, ordered social relationships and their new re-ordering according to the commandment of God. In this regard I want to show that Bonhoeffer combines the concept of the "mandates" with the term "*Ausrichtung*,"[9] which refers to the way the commandment of God "disposes" the discursive and material elements of social life through human authority and power relations involved in the mandates. *Third*, I then ask more constructively: might we understand Bonhoeffer's articulation of the commandment of God within the mandates as enabling the "conversion" of modern dispositives, i.e., providing an alternative discursive formation of social life and social ethics which can resist the current economic commodification of both? In sum, might the mandates open a new possibility for redressing the concrete, contemporary obstacles to genuine sociopolitical life so clearly uncovered by Foucault and Agamben?

In pursuing this investigation, I will show that Agamben offers a particularly challenging depiction of the contributions of theology itself to the problems identified by Foucault. At the same time Agamben points to the necessary question for redressing the problem: How can current social structures be converted (Agamben uses the term "profaned") to allow the free subjectivity that both constitutes and sustains genuine forms of sociality? Yet, as we will see, for Agamben the actual possibility for renewal remains tenuous at best. I thus turn to Bonhoeffer's mandates, arguing that they offer a theological modality that can counter the problems identified by Agamben. Thus, they allow and sustain an alternative formation and foundation of social life. Within the mandates, hearing the commandment, human beings can recognize and experience the governing of God openly.[10] Therefore, they can recognize and experience themselves as *free* from the government of ideological management. This freedom is both individual and social, because it is constituted within the mandates as ordered social structures and relationships.[11]

Governing Social Relations through *Dispositifs*

What precisely does Foucault then name and criticize with the concept, "*dispositif*"? The term first begins to appear in Foucault's work in the mid-1970s, when he formulates it in relation to the problem of "*gouvernementalité*" (governmentality). Governmentality names the governing of humans through managerial structures and technologies of social control. Foucault claims that these structures and technologies take the form of a variety of different "dispositives of power." He cites, for instance, juridical and disciplinary structures, mechanisms that claim to defend the "security" of society, or even practices and conceptions of sexuality installed as "normal" and "normative."[12] In Foucault's historical descriptions, social life and practices seem to be increasingly formed and constrained by such dispositives.

In an interview from 1977, Foucault gives the most developed account of what he understands by *dispositif* and what the concept yields for his analysis.[13] Here Foucault claims that the concept names "a thoroughly heterogeneous ensemble, consisting of discourses, institutions, architectural forms, regulatory decisions, laws, administrative measures, scientific statements, philosophical, moral and philanthropic propositions—in short, the said as much as the unsaid."[14] That is, for Foucault, *dispositif* refers to a complex social reality consisting of *discursive* and *non-discursive* elements. Much of Foucault's work therefore traces how the combinations of *discourses* and specific *practices* always interweave power and knowledge in complex networks.

For Foucault the individual elements are not simply important in themselves; rather, their import also lies in the way in which they are ordered and connected. For, the "apparatus [*dispositif*] itself is the system of relations [*le réseau*, the network] that can be established between these elements."[15] Therefore, in his analysis of these specific ensembles or networks, Foucault intends to identify the particular "*nature* of the connections which can exist between these heterogeneous elements."[16] The specific ways these elements are ordered are of analytical importance because, "there is a sort of interplay of shifts of position and modifications of function which can also vary very widely."[17] Foucault observes that the way this interplay continually responds to concrete "historical urgencies" adds to their contingent character. This contingency makes it extremely difficult to clearly identify the exact functioning of dispositives within a given social structure. Therefore, it is possible that human persons within such networks are formed to perceive themselves as free and sovereign while they are actually being subjected to specific but hidden power relations. Thus, the person's perception and realization of their "freedom" can be the worst kind of delusion, insofar as it becomes the very vehicle of their continued subjection.[18] With personal freedom so deeply subverted, the problems of "governmentality" seem to take on the force of social fate.

Accordingly social programs, regulations or even social ethics must likewise appear intrinsically coercive and violent, since their disposing character always aims at and produces submission to the mechanism of managing social relations. Furthermore, this description of the dynamics of dispositives indicates that alternatives for social life cannot arise through simple appeal to a sovereign subject, since subjectivity itself might now simply function as one more dispositive within the managerial networks.[19]

To fully grasp the implications of Foucault's analysis requires a further exploration of the concept *dispositif* itself and his notion of the production of subjects. My claim is that the Italian philosopher Giorgio Agamben, who draws on Foucault throughout his work, offers one version of this exploration that is particularly necessary and helpful. In the following section, drawing especially on Agamben's essay "What is an apparatus?," I will demonstrate that Agamben takes Foucault's analysis further by providing a more robust analysis and genealogy of the term *dispositive*. Agamben thus applies Foucault's genealogical methodology to Foucault's own concept. He does so for two reasons. First, he wants to underscore the significance of Foucault's insight that subject formation as subjection in the negative sense at work in governmental activities is itself a contingent, historical development. Therefore, it is potentially reversible. Second, Agamben's analysis wants to go further than Foucault's by showing us how a *theological* articulation of the nature of social life stands behind this development. Attending to the specifics of this criticism will make clear in turn how Bonhoeffer's concept of the mandates can offer an alternative theology of social life.

The Historical Nature and Religious Roots of Dispositives

On the basic conceptual level, Agamben agrees with Foucault's critical analysis of the nature and function of dispositives in modern social life. He joins Foucault in claiming that these "pure activities of governance" exert a radically constraining force on living beings.[20] Like Foucault, he also finds that the dispositive tends to obfuscate what governs and who is governed. Dispositives are so insidious precisely because they gain their power by promising subjects the very control they cede by participating in the dispositional network. Yet, as indicated, Agamben also attempts to go further than Foucault by providing a deeper analysis and genealogy of the discursive and practical development of the notion of dispositives itself.

First, Agamben locates what he takes to be the most proximate source of Foucault's articulation of the dispositive. He points out that what Foucault came to call *dispositif* he first referred to as "*positivité*" in his "Archaeology of Knowledge."[21] Agamben traces the source of the latter term back to Hegel via a mediation through Foucault's teacher Jean Hyppolite.[22]

According to Hyppolite, *positivité* is the term used by the young Hegel to grasp the historical element of religion, "loaded as it is with rules, rites and institutions that are imposed on the individual."[23] For Agamben, Foucault's work brings out particularly well the *historical* dimension of this definition of dispositives. For him, the individual always exists within the "historical element"; thus she always exists within "a set of institutions, of processes of subjection and of rules in which power relations become concrete."[24] Accordingly, concepts like "subjectivity" or "power" are never to be understood as something abstract but always as something historically concrete. Foucault thus advances his notion of dispositives over against concepts such as the State, Sovereignty, Law, or Power that came to govern modern sociopolitical self-understanding. Foucault's revolutionary approach was to view these so-called "universals" as historically contingent and particular forms of *power relations*. Thus in Foucault's work, treating power in terms of dispositives makes the concrete nature and roots of power more transparent.[25]

Yet second, Agamben believes that Foucault did not pay close enough attention to the *religious* nature of the modern/Hegelian concept he appropriates. Thus, Agamben offers a genealogy which reaches back beyond Hegel to the source of this concept in early Christian theology.[26] He traces the French term *dispositif* back to the Latin *dispositio*, the term which the Fathers of the Western Church used to invoke *the providential governance of the world by God*. *Dispositio* in turn translates the Greek term *oikonomia* (economy), used by Christian theologians of the East operating in the second to sixth centuries.[27] Yet importantly, Agamben notes, more than mere translation occurred when the common Greek notion of "economy," which refers primarily to the practice of administering and leading the *oikos* (the household),[28] was merged into the notion of *providence*. Here all forms of governance became related to God's divine governing and administering of creation as the *oikos* of God. Thus, Agamben contends, the whole "complex semantic sphere"[29] already structuring the Christian depiction of God's own governance became operative in the general understanding of the governance of social life still at work in Western social and ethical theory.

Agamben then points out that the theological adoption and reconfiguration of the term "economy" in terms of God's providence occurs in the context of the developing formation of Trinitarian dogma. However–and this is the decisive point for Agamben–this dogma tries to conceptualize and articulate the nature of God through a strong principle of distinction between the "immanent," inner being of God "as such," and the three divine persons who appear and act in the "economy" (*oikonomia*) of salvation history. Agamben contends therefore that despite the intention of the dogma to relate God's saving action to God's being, it in fact seems to suggest that each element has an independent plausibility of its own. Consequently Trinitarian dogma introduces into theological discourse a split between the *being* of God and the saving *activity* of governance.

Likewise, following the argument above that broader Western theory derived its notion of governance from theological definition, Agamben argues that theological discourse thus offered Western theory the "schizophrenic legacy" of a similar division between being and action, i.e., between ontology and praxis. As a result, writes Agamben, "action (economy, but also politics) [now] has no foundation in being."[30] "Economic" governance, rather than being "a practical activity" *of someone* became "an epistemic paradigm" for discourses and practices that structure social reality, i.e., that administer and regulate social relations towards a specific end.[31] This shift seems like an ironic inversion of the original economic praxis: what used to have a concrete subject now has only a more or less specific object, the end of management itself.

The Production and Dissolution of Subjectivity in Modern Life

Agamben's additional analysis and genealogy also enables him to say more than Foucault regarding the sources, nature, and extent of the corruption of the place and function of subjectivity by modern dispositives.[32] As a result of the strong division between being and action just described, Agamben claims, "[There now exist] two large groups or classes: on the one hand, living beings (or substances) and on the other hand apparatuses, in which living beings are incessantly captured. On one side ... lies the ontology of creatures, and on the other side, the *oikonomia* of apparatuses that seek to govern and guide them toward the good."[33] Moreover,

Agamben claims, because dispositives have no foundation in being, "they *must* produce their subject" as one who has only a functional, "subjected" place in the managerial network.[34]

The quotations offer three important insights. First, the "must" in the latter quotation is important, for it indicates that an economy which has no foundation in being cannot but produce a formal subjectivity that *also* lacks being. This entails a second point, namely that, given the natural overlap between subjectivity and concrete living beings, the dispositives themselves are thereby divorced from the responsible and free actors, which opens the potential for the managerial form of power. Third, the divorce between subjectivity and managerial networks means that the degeneration of Western sociopolitical life is accelerating.

Agamben offers a further specification of the nature of this acceleration. He claims that, due to the growing number of modern dispositives by which it is captured in our time, the category of subjectivity "is losing its consistency."[35] Thus the problem is not that subjectivity is destroyed by modern dispositives, but rather that it is numerously multiplied. There exists, according to Agamben "not even a single instant in which the life of individuals is not modeled, contaminated, or controlled by some apparatuses" in this "extreme phase of capitalist development in which we live."[36] Agamben offers as evidence particularly the massive proliferation of technical devices and "virtual" realities which occupy and change our social relations.[37]

What then is the potential path to the renewal of Western societies and ethical theory, given these problems? Before turning to that question, it is worth underscoring the role Agamben gives to theology in establishing the problem. With the help of the genealogy of the term *dispositif*, Agamben suggested that the legacy of the theological articulation of *oikonomia* as divine *providence* stands behind the "eclipse of politics, which used to presuppose the existence of subjects and real identities . . . and the triumph of an oikonomia, that is to say of a pure activity of government that aims at nothing other than its own replication."[38] For Agamben it is this "governmental machine" in its "incessant though aimless motion [that] . . . in a sort of colossal parody of theological oikonomia, has assumed the legacy of the providential governance of the world."[39] In other words, it seems as if Christian theology itself is at least partly responsible for the epistemic basis of Western managerialism, or governmentality.

Finding the Path to Renewal

What then, according to Agamben and Foucault, might be the path to the renewal of social life in the midst of its thoroughgoing commodification in late modernity, if there is such a path? Moreover, does the Christian theology so clearly implicated in the underlying problem have any role to play in possible paths to renewal?

The early Foucault had focused on "processes of subjection" (*assejuttissement*) in a negative sense. However, reflecting on the importance of retrieving subjectivity, the later Foucault tried to articulate alternative "technologies of the self" which could be called processes of subjectification (*subjectivacion*) in a positive sense.[40] Significantly, the Christian act of penance functioned for Foucault as one historical example of such a practice. Agamben likewise suggests that penance is a dispositional practice in which "a new I is constituted through the simultaneous negation and assumption of the old I."[41] Implied in these treatments of penance seems to be some recognition that the problematic theoretical disposition of Christian theology did not always overtake more beneficial Christian practices. Nevertheless, Agamben and Foucault both largely pursue the goal of renewal in a clearly atheological way, developing practices that do not substantially depend on the *divine* action originally so central to the economy at work in Christian penance. Of course, given these thinkers' conception of their task and their philosophical commitments, this approach is no doubt unsurprising.

Among the various practices of renewal that these thinkers develop, Agamben's conception of "profanation" is perhaps most central for our concerns. Profanation is important both because it is the primary practice to which Agamben attends, and because it bears important similarities to aspects of the mandates I will develop in the latter half of this essay. The term "profanation" comes from Roman law, where it means restoring something to the "use and property of human beings,"[42] which had been separated for use in a "sacred" act. For Agamben these "processes of separation that define [more or less, all] religion"[43] are pushed to the extreme by contemporary dispositives, which therefore need just such a restoration to common use to overcome the separation of the living beings and pure action. Yet Agamben himself asks whether anyone actually can conduct this restoration, for the possibility of profanation seemingly "cannot be properly raised as long as those who are concerned with it are unable to intervene in their own processes of subjectification, any more than in their own apparatuses, in order to then bring to light the Ungovernable, which is the beginning and, at the same time, the vanishing point of every politics."[44] So again, Agamben seems to leave us with the impression that the modern, negatively-subjectifying disposition of life has the force of fate.

Yet what if theology could offer a more substantive redress of its own problematic contribution to the split between being and praxis that enabled these dispositives to take hold? What if, in so doing, it could "bring to light the Ungovernable" in a clearer and *more concrete* sense? Might it then re-open the possibility of a genuine politics that proceeds from a *different* freedom and governance?

This is the more fundamental possibility I wish to investigate in the final section of this essay. To do so, I return once more to the role of economic activity within Trinitarian discourse. One important Protestant approach to this activity has been through the notion of "orders of creation." The sad fact that this concept in one guise contributed to a theological justification of National Socialist ideology, including especially its efforts at social management,[45] seems to strengthen the criticism of Agamben. Yet contemporary Lutheran scholarship has begun to retrieve the way in which, for Luther, the "orders" stood, not for the endorsement of human categorizations of social life, but for the commitment to the possibility of experiencing the freedom of living as creatures of God— that is, the freedom of being attentive to the promises and good works of God the Creator.[46] One of the main features of Luther's theology is his understanding that the orders are essentially specific elementary forms of living instituted and ordered by the Word of this God.[47] How might we more fully develop this possibility today?

As the next sections will show, it was in fact the correlation of God's commanding Word with creaturely freedom that Bonhoeffer sought to revive with his still understudied concept of the orders as "mandates." I want to argue that this revival implies something quite different for social "economy" than an anonymous divine providence (as a pure activity of governance). With Bonhoeffer, I want to suggest that the mandates are thus best understood as concrete *discursive, social practices* in which humans encounter the good works *of God.*[48] This encounter provides a basic social structure in which humans are set free to live with God and each other.

God's Sanctification of Social Life within the Mandates

In this second half of the essay then, I will outline Bonhoeffer's understanding of the mandates, showing that they parallel Foucault's description of dispositives but with a decisive difference: Bonhoeffer's formulation of God's involvement in these dispositives resolves the problematic rift between being and action. This involvement thus has decisive effects on the "processes of subjectification" Agamben and Foucault identify. Overcoming what those thinkers call "governmentality," Bonhoeffer's mandates promote a freedom and a subjectivity which give them a genuine political character, while still being situated within concrete forms of power relations. On this basis, I want to show that it is possible to understand Bonhoeffer's mandates as "theological dispositives" that not only imitate the governmental dispositives Foucault and Agamben criticize but which reverse the inversion worked by the earlier Trinitarian dogma.[49]

Thus, I contend further, Bonhoeffer is able to "convert" and reclaim elements of power and authority Foucault and Agamben find ineliminably problematic. The idea of "conversion" thus intends to show that the action of God reflected in the *discursive practices* of the mandates claims social relationships already in motion. Thus, unlike Agamben's uncertain process of "profanation," God's *sanctification* succeeds in "restoring to common use" forms of personal and social life which are wrongly separated from their creaturely form. Living within the mandates is living together within common places of sanctification. Thus for Bonhoeffer, as well as for the Lutheran discourse he is adapting, the mandates constitute certain recognizable sites as *res publica*—public and concrete places where human beings act together and where they can understand and experience their action as cooperation with God in the light of the promises of God. This *res publica* involves ecclesial, familial, and economic life, as well as the activity of governing (carried out by "the State" in late modernity). Bonhoeffer accordingly identifies four mandates: Church, marriage and family, work or culture, and government.[50]

However, to understand the "conversion" provided by the mandates, it is most important to grasp first that the mandates refer beyond the particular forms of each mandate to how social reality is constituted as a differentiated but single unity in Christ. Centrally for our interests, *Ethics* here takes its cue from Bonhoeffer's awareness of a divorce in the epistemic foundation of our social reality essentially the same as that which

Agamben criticized in early Trinitarian dogma, i.e., the divorce between "God governing reality" and the "realities of the world." According to Bonhoeffer, immediately after New Testament times, the idea that came to dominate all Christian ethics, explicitly or implicitly, is that of "two realms bumping up against each other: one divine, holy, supernatural and Christian; the other worldly, profane, natural, and unchristian."[51] Bonhoeffer suggests this split introduces two dangers. First, "the concern of Christ becomes a partial, provincial affair within the whole of reality."[52] Second, the strong dichotomy between the realm of "being" in Christ and purely immanent "action" for earthly ends leaves humans with only two possibilities: either they choose one of these two elements and withdraw from the other, or they try to live in both realms simultaneously, claiming that living in ongoing conflict is the only genuine form for a Christian existence.[53]

According to Bonhoeffer, this separation is foreign to both biblical thinking and the Reformation, which claim instead that: "There are not two realities, but *only one reality*, and that is God's reality revealed in Christ in the reality of the world. The reality of Christ embraces the reality of the world in itself."[54] Bonhoeffer thus never situates our social reality outside the Christ-reality. Instead, this "unity of the reality of God and the reality of the world . . . realizes itself again and again in human beings."[55] This, I want to argue, is the foundation of the political character of Bonhoeffer's social ethics. Operating out of this unity, Bonhoeffer's ethical discourse intrinsically links economy to being itself, within Christology. As he summarizes, "Like all of creation, the world has been created through Christ and toward Christ and has its *existence* only in Christ (John 1:10; Col 1:16). To speak of the world without speaking of Christ is *pure abstraction*. The world stands in relationship to Christ whether the world knows it or not. This relation of the world to Christ becomes *concrete* in certain mandates of God in the world."[56] Importantly, this quotation reveals two sides to Bonhoeffer's depiction of the ontology of creation. On the one hand, the world exists only through God's continual gift of being that disposes reality through God's own governing Word. Yet on the other hand, this Word effectively preserves, sustains and forms social life within discursive practices. In other words, "actual being"—and not yet another abstraction—is given in Christ. Centrally for Bonhoeffer, these elements attain their concrete interrelation within the mandates.[57] For Bonhoeffer, this interrelation holds precisely because Christ provides a determinative *form of being* (*Gestalt*) that remains linked to God's being and acting.[58]

Understanding the twofold nature of Bonhoeffer's mandates is essential to grasping how this conception compares to the positive and negative forms of disposition and subjectification discussed by Foucault and Agamben. Consider the following, pivotal passage from the *Ethics*: "By 'mandate' we understand the concrete divine commission [*Auftrag*] grounded in the revelation of Christ and the testimony of Scripture. It is the [empowerment] and legitimization to *declare* [*Ausrichtung*] a particular divine commandment, the conferring of divine authority on an earthly institution. A mandate is to be understood simultaneously as the laying claim to, commandeering of, and formation of a certain earthly domain by the divine command."[59] On the one hand, this quotation makes clear that Bonhoeffer's theology does not intend to avoid such concepts as power, authority, and "institutional" legitimacy. The ongoing importance of these elements seems to subject Bonhoeffer's mandates to Foucault's criticism.[60] On the other hand, I want to argue that the element of the commission (*Auftrag*) to "declare" (*Ausrichtung*) the "commandment of God" provides a decisive difference. For, as we saw above, it is through this commanding Word that the gift of being comes again and again to renew creation.

This difference becomes clear by considering the role the divine *Auftrag* plays in Bonhoeffer's response to the kind of total *management* of social life he found in Nazi ideology. As noted, this management was theologically supported by a certain version of the doctrine of the orders of creation put forward by the "German Christians."[61] Thus, Bonhoeffer writes, "We speak of divine mandates rather than divine orders [so that] thereby their character as divine commission [*göttlicher Auftrag*], as opposed to a determination of being [*Seinsbestimmung*], becomes clearer."[62] With this discursive change, Bonhoeffer wants to preserve ethical and theological deliberation against historical, socio-empirical, or even theological arguments that claim to "manage" (determine) the "being" of creation independently of the Christ-reality. These arguments in fact do not participate in "being" at all, since they are divorced from God's creative gift. Precisely what makes them so insidious is that they name as "being" what in fact is only their own, immanent economy. In contrast, Bonhoeffer seeks to keep all discursive determinations of the "facts" of creation, and all practices of creaturely economy, linked to the *commission* concretely given through God's constitution of the world within his own economy of becoming human for the world in Christ.

Yet how does Bonhoeffer understand the operation of the commandment of God through the attendant use of immanent power and authority given through the commission? Three pivotal aspects of Bonhoeffer's theology of the mandates clearly distinguish them from the dispositives Foucault describes. Moreover, I claim, in these three elements Bonhoeffer points the way toward the "conversion" of social life constituted by free persons with real identities, subjecting themselves to the governing of God's Word.

First, in contrast to the way that a coercive dispositive hides its own influence over the subject, a mandate attains to manifestation, or *publicity*. In theological terminology, God's commandment, which continually forms the mandates as discursive practices, has the character of a *revelation*, a self-disclosure. Always appearing in concrete shape, it manifests in a recognizable way its relation to other discursive and non-discursive elements in the "nets of our *Lebenswelt*."[63] Yet it does not appear simply to "follow" from the nature of human social life or the logic of any worldly economy (i.e., as if they are functioning in-and-for-themselves). Thus, the commandment of God neither is absorbed into the dispositives nor becomes yet another dissimulating network that cloaks its own derivation of power.

This publicity also then operates *within* immanent authority itself, converting economic action toward unity with the living reality supplied by God. This becomes especially clear in Bonhoeffer's notion of ordering as *Ausrichtung*. In German, this term combines three elements: the operative execution of something, its adjustment or orientation, and its declaration to someone. Bonhoeffer's use of the term at times seems to draw on all three connotations. However, the element of *declaration* is particularly important for our purposes. For it is through this element of declaration that immanent authority points to and participates in the more primordial level of God's own being and determination, that is, the "divine commissioning grounded in the revelation of Christ and the testimony of Scripture."[64] Drawing on the divine commission, immanent authority likewise has to take on the open character of publicity, if it wants to claim legitimacy.

Second, Bonhoeffer also succeeds in further specifying *how* the commandment retains its critical distance over against immanent social structures. Precisely against a theology of orders that would simply identify the existence of a social structure with its "being commanded" and thus with divine legitimation, as in the "German Christian" theology, in Bonhoeffer's mandates the commandment of God retains a "superiority" over against extant social life. It does so on the grounds of its function to order "these authorities in a relationship of being with each other, beside each other, together with each other, and over against each other."[65] That is, the commandment of God disposes by working not only within the mandates but also outside and in between them. Here, ultimate authority remains in the hands of God, who never legitimizes any order nor relinquishes the power of governance itself to an economic technique, but continues to rule through his own Word and promises. The "governing reality" of God's own will and commandment therefore offers an alternative to the "governmental dispositives" of both Bonhoeffer's day and our own.[66]

Third, for Bonhoeffer God's commandment provides persons with precisely the genuine political agency and freedom Foucault and Agamben find missing in contemporary dispositives. This freedom comes through the commandment's demand for obedience, which summons the response of a subject who is *free*, over and beyond the subjectivity constituted by the immanent dispositives. Herein lies one of the main differences from authority as governmentality. For Bonhoeffer, the commandment of God as structuring "*Ausrichtung*" is never technical or abstract, and never just anonymous discourse. Instead, it is "always a concrete speaking *to* someone, and never an abstract speaking *about* something or someone. It always *addresses* and claims the hearer in such a comprehensive and at the same time definitive way that it no longer permits the freedom of interpretation and application, but only the freedom of obedience or disobedience . . . The commandment of God is permission to live before God as a human being. God's commandment is permission. It is distinguished from all human laws in that it commands freedom."[67] God's commandment is personal, and thus it gives—even commands—a freedom that is itself personal, the freedom that is the foundation of the political as well as the social. For Bonhoeffer, only this freedom generates the responsible and authoritative action that actualizes social renewal: "Only where freedom understands its origin, essence and goal to be grounded in God's own action, which means only where it is God who appears on the scene as an acting subject (through the free responsible action of a human being), can we speak about good in history."[68]

Bonhoeffer thus also clarifies the nature of freedom in a twofold way. First, it is evident that Bonhoeffer is not referring to freedom in the sense of being an innate feature of human nature nor as the option for independent choice. His paradigm makes clear that such references in fact attach freedom to an immanent economy divorced from being in Christ. In contrast, Christian freedom is "grounded in God's own action"; it is realized only "where it is God who appears on the scene as an acting subject." This marks the socio-political core of the mandates. Secondly, then, Bonhoeffer shows that political freedom appears and is realized within the paradigmatic activities of *beginning* and *cooperating*, as Hannah Arendt also has reminded us.[69] Of course the theological discourse of the mandates maintains that it is *God's beginning* and the *cooperatio cum Dei* through which all human beginning and cooperation can sustain their political and social character. Otherwise, even such apparently political human acts can fall prey to the power of the governmental dispositives described so clearly by Foucault and Agamben.

In what then does this political freedom consist, more specifically? Bonhoeffer uses the term "responsible action" to name the operation of the free subjectivity brought about through the continual conversion of social life by the commandment of God. Acting responsibly signifies precisely the human correspondence to God that "allows [human beings] to live and act with the certainty and confidence of being guided [governed] by the divine commandment."[70] This confidence leads to *co-creative* human deeds.[71] In obedience to the concrete commandment of God, human beings can explore how their social life can express the creaturely good of all. No longer trapped within an anonymous or obscure process of submission and desubjectivication, they find themselves in a cooperative and political encounter of creaturely "subjectification."

Toward Concrete Social Ethics

In sum, I have argued that the critical *"Aufklärung"* of Foucault and Agamben is right to warn us regarding the ways that even theological articulations of the economy of God constantly are in danger of becoming just another governmental disposition. Yet I also have argued that the "mandates" offer an alternative theological articulation of social life as it remains within the *oikonomia* of God. This articulation holds together both being and praxis, "inverting" the degenerative movement toward managerialism through the ongoing presence of the unifying commandment of God. Moreover, I claimed, that Bonhoeffer developed the mandates as concrete *discursives practices*, which offer precisely the kind "conversion" of the form of our social reality to allow the exercise of free and responsible subjectivity and personhood.

With his *theo-political* disposition ("*Ausrichtung*") of the mandates, Bonhoeffer thus articulates the kind of "concrete theological ethics" that can continue to guide social life today. Indeed, by encouraging theology to reclaim its distinctiveness as a careful attention to God's commandment, Bonhoeffer significantly enables a public speech and action not easily absorbed into the dominating discourses of our time. It is this theological "disposition" of speech and action that brings us out of our false economies and returns us to the economy of God's gracious being for the world in Christ.

11

Ethics beyond Biopower

Bonhoeffer, Foucault, and the Problem of Race

BRANDY DANIELS

"This is the first function of racism: to fragment, to create caesuras within the biological continuum addressed by biopower."

—MICHEL FOUCAULT

The exclusion of the weak and insignificant, the seemingly useless people, from everyday Christian life in community... may actually mean the exclusion of Christ; for in the poor sister or brother, Christ is knocking at the door."

—DIETRICH BONHOEFFER

IN HIS LECTURE SERIES *Society Must Be Defended*, Michel Foucault provides one of the clearest articulations of his groundbreaking theorizations of power, tracing the shifts from sovereign power to disciplinary power, and finally to biopower, that is, the "power of regularization," of "making live and letting die."[1] In these lectures in particular, he explicates specific technologies, or mechanisms, of biopower. Racism, he suggests, functions as *the* basic mechanism of biopower, operating through and as the construction of categories of difference, whether ethnic, social, linguistic, or otherwise—a "way of separating out the groups that exist in a population."[2] Nazi Germany functions for Foucault as a paradigmatic instance of these racial operations of biopower.

Foucault's analysis of racism is especially salient when read in conjunction with Dietrich Bonhoeffer, much of whose theological scholarship was produced during the ascendancy and reign of the Third Reich. Biographers like Eberhard Bethge and Ferdinand Schilingensiepen have indicated how Bonhoeffer's opposition to Nazism shaped his theology,[3] and scholars such as Charles Marsh and Clifford Green have done insightful work articulating the broad contours of Bonhoeffer's concept of social life.[4] This essay argues that Foucault provides one helpful lens through which we may see *why* Bonhoeffer's experience in a Nazi context gave rise to christological social concepts that continue to prove so valuable for addressing concrete social problems.[5] Foucault shows us how the thinking and discourse involved in Nazism as well as many more modern malformations of social power as biopower is "racial" at its core. Thus, in responding to the way elements of German thought involved in Nazi ascendancy performed the inscription of this power, Bonhoeffer forms a theological conception of community that presciently responds to racializing mechanisms more broadly. Specifically then, my argument is that Bonhoeffer's narration of Christ's mediation of our knowledge of the Other provides an alternative epistemological hermeneutic and correlative ethical vision that overcomes racialization, and thus biopower, at its core.

Foucault on Racism

Foucault grounds his discussion of biopower within his broader analysis of the determinative and motivating forces at work in human history. According to him, we often misconstrue what is most primal in giving shape to that history: "One's point of reference should not be to the great model of language *(langue)* and signs, but to that of war and battle. The history which bears and determines us has the form of war rather than that of a language: relations of power not relations of meaning."[6] For Foucault, in other words, different manifestations of power are simply "the continuation of war by other means."[7] On this basis, *Society Must Be Defended* argues for the centrality of concrete analyses of the operation of power. The question that accordingly guides his work is, "what are the rules of right that power implements to produce discourses of truth?"[8] Explaining that there are multiple "rules of right" utilized to establish the legitimacy of power relations and mask the reality of domination, Foucault nevertheless maintains that the most basic instance of power as a "relationship of force" requires the closest examination. To this end, he turns to an analysis of society itself.[9]

That analysis reveals that biopower is the contemporary manifestation of this relationship of force, which he also closely connects to the emergence of the modern nation-state. At the turn of the seventeenth century, when war itself was expelled to the limits of the state, the operations of power shifted from *sovereign rule*, or "the power over life and death," to *disciplinary power* marked by coercive control over the body, and finally to "a second seizure of power that is not individualizing but, if you like, massifying, that is directed not at man-as-body but at man-as-species."[10] Biopower, "an explosion of numerous and diverse techniques for achieving the subjugation of bodies and the control of populations," was employed by the state to secure stability through these two poles.[11] In this final form, power has "taken control of life in general—with the body as one pole and the population as the other."[12]

Foucault then explains how racism emerged as a primary mechanism for the dispersal of biopower. For Foucault, it is the norm, the power of regularization, that connects the individual body and the population, circulating between the two and cohering them. Racism ensures the establishment of a norm through delineating and demarcating groups within a community. "The appearance within the biological continuum of the human race of races, the distinction among races, the hierarchy of races," Foucault writes, "is a way of fragmenting the field of the biological that power controls."[13] The aim of war shifts from victory over the adversary to extermination of the "internal" threat. "The war that is going on," he explains, "is, basically, a race war."[14] "Race" becomes a way of delineating difference from the "norm," the creation of an other who can be identified as a threat. States then take their self-definition through creating and identifying some racialized body, some internal threat, against which they are "defending society." Nazi Germany for Foucault was "the paroxysmal development of [these] new power mechanisms," the successful management of society providing the justification of the termination of life.¹⁵

For Foucault, it is precisely modern discourse that undergirds the racist mechanisms of biopower—a form of discourse that operates through epistemological practices which intrinsically function to assert and attain power. Foucault's work on discourse thus offers a paradigm for understanding the deeper ramifications of Bonhoeffer's analysis of "scholarly questions," namely by providing an "archaeology of knowledge" that excavates the relationship between knowledge and power throughout the history of these questions.[16] Specifically, Foucault traces a formative element in the problems of biopower to the Kantian epistemological framework, which merges objective knowledge with experience in the effort "to articulate the possible objectivity of a knowledge."[17] In other words, Kant gave impetus to a movement to make the acquisition of categorical knowledge and the concrete fulfillment of human life the same basic project.

Foucault writes at length about the classificatory gestures of knowledge formation and production, pointing to its culturally constructed character as well as its function as a mode of control.[18] "Once knowledge can be analyzed in terms of region, domain, implantation, displacement, transposition," he explains, "one is able to capture the process by which knowledge functions as a form of power and disseminates the effects of power."[19] For him, this knowledge as a classifying system of control also then operates as a social code that punishes deviancy, ultimately creating subjects that conform—which are simultaneously persons who are coerced.[20] Foucault thus elucidates the inextricable connection between the desire for knowledge and the social production of racialized bodies, as these bodies are forced into the framework that has now become the only possible human fulfillment.

Knowledge as Social Praxis in Modern Germany

Sociologist Susanne Zantop and historian Claudia Koonz provide further evidence of the depth of the problems Foucault identifies so powerfully. In her book *Colonial Fantasies,* Zantop shows that the exercise of knowledge as power had come to form the German *ethos* long before the ascendancy of Nazism. She explains: "As critical, disinterested, "objective" observers, German commentators delighted in the role of intellectual arbiter... The aim was to "capture all observations systematically and to understand them critically," to reproduce the sum of all knowledge and to pass it on to the general public. There is a kind of imperial gesture, a sense that only those not directly involved can capture and sort the totality of lived reality "out there."[21] Zantop names this as a "totalizing classificatory impulse," and explains that, for most German scholars, "the impulse to 'objectify,' 'authenticate,' and to process information was coupled with a moral impulse."[22] Historian Claudia Koonz argues that this association between morality and systems of classification and order was precisely one of the elements of discourse that the Nazis drew on. Her work *The Nazi Conscience* describes in detail how the Third Reich drove their political program with a moral philosophy and worldview that emphasized the need for coherence and order as a stabilizing antidote to the political disorder of the Weimar Republic.[23]

Both Zantop and Koonz thus point to the imperializing impulse embedded within the modern intellectual project as expressed pre-eminently in German scholarship and political, ethical, and moral vision. Both also then show how the construction of categories of difference was central to this framework, as Foucault suggested. Naming the imperialist motives behind knowledge production as an "intellectual colonialism," Zantop points to how "racial" difference undergirded colonial fantasies in eighteenth- and nineteenth-century Germany.[24] Phenotypic, "ethnic" differences operated as both motivating force and justification in the pursuit of this colonial fantasy. Koonz likewise explores how this operated within Nazism itself, and explains that ethnicity was wielded as a tool to propagate Nazi power. The National Socialist Party garnered power, Koonz argues, by creating a moral framework based on ethnic purity and superiority. "Nazi theorists used the language of parasitology to describe a threat *within* the ethnic organism," the Jews being the outsiders lurking within that threatened the well-being of the German people, the *Volk*.[25] "The Nazi state was founded on ethnicity and race," she thus avers, "on self-love and other-hate."[26] Koonz's argument that the Jewish people were arbitrarily expelled from the German *Volk* aligns with Foucault's assessment of "the distinction among races" operating as a primary mechanism of biopower. Here the need to defend society from an internal threat served as the moral impetus to garner and justify power.[27]

Christ and the Mediation of Knowledge

How does this analysis relate to Dietrich Bonhoeffer? Notably, Bonhoeffer begins his 1933 lectures on Christology with an appraisal of the coercive potential in modern forms of epistemology that largely parallels the concerns of the foregoing thinkers and vindicates, in the midst of the Nazi rise to power, their later analysis of it.[28] First, he claims that scholarly questions of all kinds, in the natural sciences as well as the humanities, are classificatory: "[H]ow does this object X fit into the classification I already have at hand?"[29] Second, he thus interprets the act of classifying—the task of scholarship itself—to be one of mastery and self-affirmation: "The object is defined, recognized, and understood by means of its possibilities, by means of its 'how,' ... [it is thus] determined by the human logos."[30] Third, Bonhoeffer then summarizes the sentiment of asking "how" in a way that makes clear its intrinsically ethical dimensions: "Tell me *how* you exist, tell me *how* you think, and I'll tell you who you are."[31] The parallels to Foucault's description of the operation of power are striking: through the "scientific" power of categorizing, the knower here claims the authority to fully identify an embodied person—"*I'll* tell *you* who you are." Bonhoeffer acutely recognized how scholarly work, especially in Germany, operated as a tool of mastery and power.

After extrapolating on the destructive possibilities of scholarly questions, and acknowledging the way they stem from and ground knowledge in the assertion of the self, Bonhoeffer turns to Christology. Christ, he asserts, disrupts the discursive patterns that we establish: "Here is it no longer possible to fit the Word made flesh into the logos classification system."[32] Whereas, in our efforts to control and classify, to manage and master, we ask the question "how," Christ the Counter-Logos leaves us with only the question "*who* are you?" For Bonhoeffer, the question "who?" is "the question asked by horrified, dethroned human reason, and also the question of faith."[33] Bonhoeffer thus presents Christ as the One who disrupts our attempts at securing and objectifying knowledge. The counter Logos reconfigures our knowledge processes, calling into question our knowledge of God and ourselves. "With the 'who question," Bonhoeffer writes "the person asking is queried about the limits of his or her own being. If the person asking must hear, in reply, that his or her own logos has reached its limit, then the questioner has encountered the boundaries of his or her own existence."[34] Bonhoeffer's christological reflection therefore shifts the locus of knowledge and power from *what we* know to *who* knows.³⁵ The counter Logos effectively disrupts the imperial gestures of the knowing ego by disrupting its very ability to classify and thus to master. Bonhoeffer thus opens a path beyond the basic posture of modern epistemology.

For Bonhoeffer then, proximity to theology is therefore vital to the work of scholarship as such. As the one whose transcendence refuses our attempts to classify according to our own "immanent" values, Christ thus becomes "the center of the realm of scholarship itself."³⁶ The christological question becomes the foremost one, since "only from the question of transcendence does the human logos receive the rights peculiar to it, its necessity and also its limits . . . In this way, Christology as logology becomes that which makes all knowledge possible."³⁷

Furthermore, for Bonhoeffer, the theology that opens this alternative entails specific practices of its own. Especially, Bonhoeffer asserts, theology must begin in silence.³⁸ "To speak of Christ is to be silent," he exhorts; "the church's speech through silence is the right way to proclaim Christ."³⁹ Insofar as the transcendent Christ exceeds our understanding, theology's own first movement should not be to control and classify but rather to wait for the one who reveals himself to us. This practice of "waiting" thus guides particular acts of right knowing as well as forms agency more generally to release its hold on "knowing" in favor of "being known" by God in Christ.

Ethics beyond Biopower: Christ and Community

Bonhoeffer's *Christology* lectures thus speak to the problematic epistemology that undergirds an imperialist ethics, which he characterizes in terms of the question "how." At the same time, the lectures suggest that Christ, as the center of knowledge, transforms how we pursue and produce knowing itself. Not only does he reposition our approach to knowledge generally, he goes on to claim that the question "who is Christ?" leads also to relinquishing the claim to organize the bodies of others by telling them "who" they are on the basis of the "how." Through Christ, Bonhoeffer claims that we begin to ask also of the *human* other, "who are you?" This is "the question that asks about the other person, the other being, the other authority. It is the question about love for one's neighbor."⁴⁰ My claim is that Bonhoeffer's theological praxis of christological questioning thus opens new practices of Christian community as well. In this section,

I bolster that claim by turning to Bonhoeffer's *Life Together*, composed after his experiences as the director of the underground Preacher's Seminary of the Confessing Church at Finkenwalde. I argue that *Life Together* both specifies further how our mode of knowing affects our relationships with others and articulates a christological praxis of community formation that runs counter to the racializing and exclusionary discourses at work in modernity.

According to *Life Together*, what Finkenwalde taught Bonhoeffer is that in fact, "we belong to one another only through and in Jesus Christ."[41] Vice versa, "without Christ there is discord between God and humanity and between one human being and another . . . without Christ we would not know other Christians around us; nor could we approach them. The way to them is blocked by one's own ego."[42] Prefiguring Foucault's description of social forms as "war by other means," Bonhoeffer expresses how communities of "egos" attempting to relate directly to one another, through their own knowledge and power, simply produce a community structured by and on conflict. Foucault however shows perhaps more clearly than Bonhoeffer how threat of such conflict in turn justifies and bolsters the notion that society must be defended against division through the delineation and subsequent exclusion of the difference mapped on to the "racial" body. Biopower functions through this pledge to provide unity.

Centrally, Bonhoeffer specifically preempts this 'threat' by highlighting the givenness of unity in Christ's salvific act. Christ therefore simultaneously mediates genuine unity and access to one another through this givenness of relationship while foreclosing our attempts at classification and control: "Because Christ stands between me and an other, I must not long for unmediated community with that person . . . As only Christ was able to speak to me in such a way that I was helped, so others too can only be helped by Christ alone. However, this means that I must release other from all my attempts to control, coerce, and dominate them with my love." [43] Put in explicitly theological terms, since it is through Christ alone that we are justified, it is through Christ alone that we can relate to one another without trying to justify ourselves over against the other. Bonhoeffer summarizes these points in the following passage, worth quoting at length:

> God taught us to encounter one another as God has encountered us in Christ . . . I am a brother or sister to another person only through what Jesus Christ has done for me and to me;

others have become brothers and sisters to me through what Jesus Christ has done for them and to them. *The fact that we are brothers and sisters only through Christ is of immeasurable significance.* Therefore, the other who comes face to face with me earnestly and devoutly seeking community is not the brother or sister with whom I am to relate in the community. My brother or sister is instead that other person who has been redeemed by Christ, absolved from sin, and called to faith and eternal life.[44]

In place of the attempt to secure and determine community through our own social program, Christ's salvation mediates an alternative form of community stemming from the given acceptance of every other.[45]

Moreover, the redeeming work of the transcendent Christ leads not just to acceptance of one another but to a positive need for and dependence on one another, rooted in our experience of salvation *through others*. Bonhoeffer writes, "Help must come from the outside, and it has come and comes daily and anew in the Word of Jesus Christ . . . it is the Word of God in Jesus Christ that grants [us] salvation, blessedness, and righteousness."[46] If "God has put this Word into the mouth of human being so that it may be passed on to others," the Christian practice of hearing the word teaches them that "they need other Christians who speak God's Word to them." [47] This need for one another makes it imperative that we do not preclude who that other might be. Bonhoeffer speaks forcefully to the dangers of exclusion in community: "Every principle of selection and every division connected with it that is not necessitated quite objectively by common work, local conditions, or family connections is of greatest danger to a Christian community. The exclusion of the weak and insignificant, the seemingly useless people, from everyday Christian life in community [*Lebensgemeinschaft*] may actually mean the exclusion of Christ; for in the poor sister or bother, Christ is knocking at the door."[48] Because Christ confronts us through one another, we are unable to draw lines of demarcation, to determine in advance who the other might be. In *Life Together*, it thus becomes clear once more how Bonhoeffer's explicitly theological discourse and practices provide the key for wider practices of community that have the ability to overcome and replace the operations of biopower.

For Foucault, as pointed out above, the paradigmatic example of the racial machinations of biopower was the Nazi regime. There has been no other State, Foucault points out, "in which the biological was so tightly, so insistently, regulated."[49] The series of increasingly harsh and violent laws and actions against the Jews (as well as others) served to secure the purity of the German community. In the next section, I aim to show how Bonhoeffer not only articulated a conception of christological community, but already performed it—if imperfectly—by including European Jews in Christ.

Biopower, Bonhoeffer, and the "Jewish Question"

In his essay "The Church and the Jewish Question," first delivered as a lecture just three months after Adolf Hitler took power in 1933, and its subsequent memorandum "The Jewish-Christian Question as Status Confessionis," Bonhoeffer offers theological and pastoral remarks on the status of Jews within the church. As the German church moved closer to enforcing the already established Aryan paragraph which called for forced retirement of anyone of non-Aryan descent, and the government became more assertive in their actions with the boycotts of Jewish businesses, Bonhoeffer's vision of community mediated by Christ led him to challenge these actions directly.

Writing for a group of pastors, Bonhoeffer frames his essay with discussion on the relationship between the church and the state. Operating from a framework based on Luther's "two kingdoms" doctrine, Bonhoeffer explains that the church can, and must, "keep asking the government whether its actions can be justified as *legitimate state* actions, that is, actions that create law and order, not lack of rights and disorder."[50] The church can relate to the state in three possible ways—it can simply *question* the state regarding the legitimacy of its actions, it can serve the victims of those actions, or it can work to "not just to bind up the wounds of the victims beneath the wheel but to seize the wheel itself."[51] The third form of action is only justified for Bonhoeffer when the state fails in its function of fostering law and order, instituting either too little or too much. Bonhoeffer foresees evidence of the latter in the Nazi regime: "In the case of an attack, coming from the state, on the nature of the church and its proclamation, such as the obligatory exclusion of baptized Jews from our Christian congregations or a ban on missions to the Jews. In such a case, the church would find itself in *statu confessionis*, and the state would find itself in the act of self-negation."[52] For Bonhoeffer, the inclusion of Jewish Christians in the life of the church is a matter in which "the very truth of the gospel and Christian freedom are at stake."[53]

Ontology and Ethics

Bonhoeffer continues throughout the remainder of the essay and the following memorandum to argue forcibly against the exclusion of Jewish Christians from full participation in the life of the church—speaking not only to the differing responsibilities and authorities of the church and the State, but to the status of the Jews as a religious people and *the nature of Christian community itself*.[54] For Bonhoeffer, "it is the duty of Christian proclamation to say: here, where Jew and German together stand under God's word, is church," and that he who refuses to be in fellowship with Jewish Christians "is turning his back on the place where the church of Christ stands."[55] Bonhoeffer here performs in regard to German Jews the theology he later would articulate more explicitly at Finkenwalde, claiming that Christ has established the givenness of community with the Jews in a way that transcends any other actions, empirical relationships, or rational determinations.

Inversely, since the transcendent Christ mediates our relationships, confronting us through one another and thus precluding us from determining who that other might be, to exclude Jewish Christians from worship means the exclusion of Christ himself. Bonhoeffer makes this explicit in the memorandum, where he writes: "The exclusion of the Jewish Christian from our communion of worship would mean: The excluding Church is erecting a racial law as a prerequisite of a Christian communion. But in doing so, it loses Christ himself, who is the goal of even this human, purely temporal law. The Christian Church cannot deny to any Christian brother the Christian communion which he seeks."[56] Because our relationships are mediated by and bound up in Christ, the exclusion of the Jewish Christian calls our own status into question. "With the exclusion of the Jewish Christian from the communion of worship," Bonhoeffer writes, "he who realizes the nature of the Church must feel himself to be excluded also."[57] The nature of the Church, of life together, is founded on the mediating work of the transcendent Christ, which thus makes it "an ecclesiastical impossibility to exclude, as a matter of principle, Jewish Christian members from any office of the Church."[58]

It is important to acknowledge that scholars have rightly noted that this essay still remains problematic in many ways. First, Bonhoeffer speaks solely against the exclusion of Jewish *Christians*, so it is not immediately clear how far the reforming impulse of christological community extends. Moreover, he criticizes Jewish adherence to the law, blames the Jews for the crucifixion of Christ, and expresses the need for their conversion to Christianity in terms that still attest to an overt anti-Semitism.[59] Despite these shortcomings, however, this essay takes a radical and courageous stance in calling to church to stand in defense of the Jews. German theologian Heinz Eduard Tödt makes precisely this point. "In 1933 Bonhoeffer was almost alone in his opinions," he writes. "He was the only one who considered solidarity with the Jews . . . to be a matter of such importance as to obligate the Christian churches to risk a massive conflict with that state—a risk which could threaten their very existence."[60] For Bonhoeffer, the mediating work of the transcendent Christ compelled this inclusion in the church community.[61]

At the very least, we should then acknowledge the change of social direction that Bonhoeffer began to embody. Precisely as the Nazi regime reached "the paroxysmal point" of the racist mechanism of biopower, in delineating and excluding Jewish flesh, Bonhoeffer's rejection of this mechanism and his own positive vision of community re-enfleshed the christological movement toward an alternative ethics, beyond biopower.

Endnotes

Notes to Chapter 1—Clark and Mawson

1. We are indebted to Robin Lovin for the language of "three generations" of Bonhoeffer scholarship.

2. For example, see Kirkpatrick, *Attacks on Christendom in a World Come of Age*, and Gregor, *Cruciform Self*.

3. Heidegger paradigmatically asks whether most discussions of ontology are not in fact "ontotheologies," which collapse genuine Being into the discursive projects of historical actors, projects often secured through attribution of their scheme for existence to "God." See esp. his "The Onto-theo-logical Constitution of Metaphysics," in *Identity and Difference*. In his strong criticism of the phenomenological tradition leading to Heidegger, Emmanuel Levinas essentially asks whether the real problem is not the collapse of the transcendence of the Other, and thus of ethics into the same projects. See "Is Ontology Fundamental?," in *Emmanuel Levinas: Basic Philosophical Writings*. Jacques Derrida asks questions similar to Levinas, while providing a more positive assessment of "phenomenological" thinkers like Hegel, Husserl, and Heidegger. From post-Nietschean and/or post-Marxist perspectives, thinkers like Michel Foucault and Judith Butler ask whether discourse does not function to produce "reality" (ontology) in determinative ways that must be taken into account, whatever one's intellectual or ethical projects. See, in dialogue with Levinas and other thinkers mentioned above, Butler, *Giving an Account of Oneself* (2005). One could, of course, add numerous other thinkers and issues to this list, but these at least make clear the fraught nature of discussions of ontology and ethics today.

4. As indicated, many thinkers in this volume pursue the aim of elucidating questions of ontology and ethics in dialogue with Continental thought. Thus, their concerns stand in close conversation with essayists in the collection by Zimmerman and Gregor, *Bonhoeffer and Continental Thought*. However, the primary aim of that volume is to "introduce Bonhoeffer the philosophical theologian,"

who has important insights to offer regarding the philosophy of religion and especially the relationship of philosophy to theology (Introduction, 1–2). The primary aim of this volume is to elucidate the development of reflection on ontology and ethics per se, both across Bonhoeffer's own corpus and in subsequent Bonhoeffer scholarship.

5. More specifically, Bonhoeffer was initially arrested for his involvement in "Operation 7," in which fourteen Jews were smuggled out of Germany and into Switzerland. His participation in the plot against Hitler was confirmed subsequently. See Schliengensiepen, *Dietrich Bonhoeffer*, 314ff.

6. See Schliengensiepen's opening comment in the preface to his recent biography, *Dietrich Bonhoeffer*, xv: "I first heard the name Dietrich Bonhoeffer in 1948, when I was given the small volume *Zeugnis eines Boten* (Testimony of a Messenger), edited by W. A. Visser 't Hooft of the Netherlands, the first General Secretary of the World Council of Churches." It was through the portrayal of Hooft and others that Bonhoeffer eventually came to be revered as something of a Protestant martyr. The ascription "martyr" also appears in the subtitles of both Schliengensiepen's and Eric Metaxas's recent biographies.

7. Bonhoeffer's *Ethik* was published in 1949 and then translated into English in 1955. *Widerstand und Ergebung* appeared in 1951, and a selection of its documents were translated and published in English in 1953 as *Letters and Papers from Prison* (a popular republication in 1954 retitled the work, *Prisoner for God*, a title used in several subsequent publications). The interest provoked by these works led in turn to the republication of several of Bonhoeffer's early works, published during his lifetime, and eventually to the compilation and publication of a *Gesammelte Schriften* (between 1958 and 1974), first in four and then in six volumes. The *Gesammelte Schriften* made available a larger selection of Bonhoeffer's personal letters, essays and more occasional writings.

8. Feil, *The Theology of Dietrich Bonhoeffer*, 3. On the reception history of Bonhoeffer's *Letters and Papers*, see Marty's *Letters and Papers from Prison: A Biography*.

9. For more on Bethge, see de Gruchy's biography *Daring, Trusting Spirit*.

10. Thanks to Clifford Green for reminding us of the "shock effect" these works would have had in the context of their original publication.

11. See for instance: Müller, *Von Der Kirche Zur Welt* (1961); Robinson, *Honest to God* (1963); Cox, *The Secular City* (1965); and the work of "death-of-God" theologians, e.g., Altizer and Hamilton, *Radical Theology and the Death of God* (1966).

12. See particularly the exchanges edited by Gregor Smith in the *World Come of Age* series. These publications brought together articles by a wide array of prominent scholars, including Gerhard Ebeling and others, whose interpretations of Bonhoeffer continue to be appropriated and resisted today.

13. For Bonhoeffer's own description of the importance of Bethge as his constant companion, see DBWE 8, 475, 482. In the first of these, Bonhoeffer shifts without warning to questions of religionless Christianity, etc., as simply offering "a few more thoughts on our topic." Thus, he marks his collegial dependence on Bethge in an *ongoing process* of thinking through these questions.

14. The articles appeared in the fall edition of the *Union Seminary Quarterly Review* and Gregor Smith's *World Come of Age Series*, respectively. Christian Kaiser Verlag published Bethge's biography in 1967, and an abridged version appeared in English in 1970. The full version appeared in 2000.

15. Bonhoeffer cites these elements, and uses the term "religionlessness," in a letter to Bethge dated 30 April 1944 (see DBWE 8, 364). Bethge quotes this citation in making the argument above in "Bonhoeffer's Christology and his Religionless Christianity," 73.

16. See esp. Bethge, "Bonhoeffer's Christology," 71–77.

17. The quotation is from a letter from Bonhoeffer, dated July 21, 1941, the day after the attempt on Hitler's life failed. It comes from an earlier translation of *Letters and Papers*, cited by Bethge with commentary at the end of "Turning Points," 19ff.

18. See 16 July 1944 in DBWE 8, 473f.

19. See especially "The New Theology," 853–54, in Bethge's biography. See also DBWE 6, 169–70, 339–42 for Bonhoeffer's most explicit discussions of "unconscious Christianity."

20. Although it is clearly impossible to indicate all of the important works written on Bonhoeffer during this period, some examples include Godsey's *The Theology of Dietrich Bonhoeffer* (1960), Ott's *Wirklichkeit und Glaube* (1966), William Kuhns's *In Pursuit of Dietrich Bonhoeffer* (1967), Phillips's *Christ for Us in the Theology of Dietrich Bonhoeffer* (1967), Dumas's *Une théologie de la réalité: Dietrich Bonhoeffer* (1968), Mayer's *Christuswirklichkeit* (1969), Woefel's *Bonhoeffer's Theology* (1970), Feil's *Die Theologie Dietrich Bonhoeffers* (1971), and Green's *Bonhoeffer: A Theology of Sociality* (1972). In addition, there are many other scholars who were important for this generation of scholarship through their editorial work and their involvement in the International Bonhoeffer Society, including Heinz Eduard Tödt, Ilse Tödt, and Hans Pfeifer, in Germany, and Geffrey Kelly, James Patrick Kelley, Keith Clements, Martin Rumscheidt, and Michael Lukens, in America. This list is by no means complete.

21. Cf., e.g., Green's review of Ott and Dumas, in which he claims that their recognition of the centrality of Bonhoeffer's "christological ontology" was not yet determined enough by his specific anthropology, among other things. "Interpreting Bonhoeffer," 270–75.

22. As Green reflected in 1972, "almost all interpreters of Bonhoeffer's theology have repeatedly emphasized the close connection between Bonhoeffer's

Endnotes

theology and his life experience" (*Bonhoeffer: A Theology of Sociality*, 11).

23. See Green, *Bonhoeffer: A Theology of Sociality*, chap. 4. N.B., 105n1, which shows that Bonhoeffer himself attributed this turn more to his reading of the Bible in relation to these experiences, than to the experiences themselves.

24. See Moltmann, "The Lordship of Christ and Human Society," in Moltmann and Weissbach, eds., *Two Studies on Dietrich Bonhoeffer*, 56–57.

25. The International Bonhoeffer Society emerged out of discussions at the first international Bonhoeffer Congress held in 1971.

26. The material included in the seventeen volumes of the DBW series significantly exceeds that collected in the *Gesammelte Schriften* and other earlier publications. The editorial and translation work has also been much more rigorous.

27. The German editions of this series began in 1986 and were completed in 1999. Already in the early 1980s an editorial team working under Robin Lovin began working on English editions (and the celebration of the completion of the English editions took place in November 2011). It is difficult to overemphasize the importance of both the International Bonhoeffer Society and DBW series for research on Bonhoeffer.

28. Again, it is not possible to indicate all of the scholars and works of this second generation. Some prominent examples might include Floyd's *Theology and the Dialectics of Otherness* (1988), Pangritz's, *Karl Barth in der Theologie Dietrich Bonhoeffers* (1989), Soosten's *Die Sozialität der Kirche* (1992), Marsh's *Reclaiming Dietrich Bonhoeffer* (1994), Wüstenberg's *Glauben als Leben* (1996), Boomgaarden's *Das Verständnis der Wirklichkeit* (1999), and Tietz's *Bonhoeffers Kritik der verkrummten Vernunft* (1999).

29. To be sure, these scholars certainly hold convictions about such questions and the importance of Bonhoeffer to them, as will be shown below. However there is no longer the sense that a predominately sociopolitical horizon needed to inform nearly every study of Bonhoeffer's theology.

30. See Lovin, *Christian Faith and Public Choices* (1984), 126–155. See also Lovin's *Christian Realism and New Realities* (2008).

31. See respectively: von Soosten, Boomgaarden, Tietz, Wüstenberg, and Pangritz. For a more recent volume continuing the exploration of specific intellectual relationships, see Peter Frick's *Bonhoeffer Intellectual Formation* (2008).

32. Marsh, *Reclaiming Dietrich Bonhoeffer*, 143.

33. Tietz is clear that Bonhoeffer's account of the church fundamentally relies on a "theological premise," but is still willing to draw on the conceptuality of ontology to clarify how this is the case.

34. The turn in later generations to a more explicit and detailed explication of Bonhoeffer's ontology as ethical and political doubtless has been facilitated by a broader shift from political theology to theological politics. See A. Rasmussen,

Church as Polis (1986).

35. There will continue to be important work on Bonhoeffer that undertakes careful textual analysis and revisits and challenges the conclusions of earlier scholarship. Schliesser's *Everyone Who Acts Responsibly Becomes Guilty* (2008) and DeJonge's recent *Bonhoeffer's Theological Formation* (2012) provide examples of this. Our claim is not that the work of these earlier generations is somehow complete, but that there now exists a foundation for a new kind of Bonhoeffer scholarship.

36. The trends we are identifying with an emerging generation obviously extends beyond this collection. Other books that display some of what we are describing here include Muer's *Keeping God's Silence* (2004), Greggs's *Theology Against Religion* (2011), Burnell's *Poetry, Providence and Patriotism* (2010), McBride's *The Church for the World* (2012), and the essays in Gregor and Zimmerman, *Bonhoeffer and Continental Thought* (2009), and Zimmerman and Gregor, *Being Human Becoming Human* (2010). In addition, our account draws on the forty-nine proposals we received for the conference *New Conversations on Bonhoeffer's Theology* in late 2010. It was noteworthy how many of these proposals sought to mobilize Bonhoeffer's theology for constructive dialogues and projects and how few sought to address themes within his theology along more established lines.

37. These authors differ from the second generation on this score primarily in now having the opportunity to turn their attention to concepts (Nowers on Hegelian "objective spirit") and interlocutors (Phillips on Dilthey) whose importance is perhaps not as immediately obvious.

38. For instance, Jeremy K. Kessler works in legal studies while Brian Gregor is a philosopher.

39. Somewhat similar work can be found in the recent volume of essays edited by Jenkins and McBride, *Bonhoeffer and King* (2009).

40. See Stout, *Ethics after Babel* (2001), especially the discussion of bricolage in the postscript to the Princeton edition, 334–35; Derrida, "Structure, Sign, and Play in the Discourse of the Human Sciences" (1967); Deleuze and Guattari, *Anti-Oedipus: Capitalism and Schizophrenia* (1972). For these thinkers of course, engaging in *bricolage* is not really an "option" but simply belongs to the nature of discourse. Stout, for instance, claims that the inability to think otherwise than through the terms set by the concrete ethos of a given community's discourse means that "I am not so much proposing that moralists *should* engage in *bricolage* as I am saying that all moralists who are self-conscious about the concepts they are employing *are* engaging in it . . . Any ethical thinking or writing of any originality involves making decisions about which concepts to employ and how to work out the relations among those selected" (*Babel*, 336). See Derrida, "Structure," 286: "If one calls *bricolage* the necessity of borrowing one's concept from the text of a heritage which is more or less coherent or ruined, it must

be said that every discourse is *bricoleur*." Deleuze and Guattari's text, drawing on Levi-Strauss, focuses on the way capitalism does not distinguish between producing and product. That is, the rush to product eclipses the differences that make elements of the original material "fragmentary," or refractory, to one another (*Anti-Oedipus*, 7–8). Thus, it is capitalism, rather than some sort of intellectual choice and sifting as in Stout, that installs the mode of *bricolage*. Indeed, *Anti-Oedipus* would suggest that the description of "choice," when made by Stout and others, masks a more fundamental material determination of the whole process. Moreover, in Derrida, Deleuze, and Guattari, *bricolage* thus appears to be a process whose discursive givenness promises rather less in the way of progress than Stout's version. This is somewhat unsurprising, in that Stout explicitly sees his pragmatism as the American reformulation of aspects of Hegel, who of course "fathered" many historicist progressivisms. Arbitrating between these notions of *bricolage* is obviously beyond the task of this introduction. However, it is significant to note that the present authors assume that their appropriations will have some positive, constructive effect. Thus, they retain at least *something* of the Hegelian confidence. This confidence may be attributed to Bonhoeffer's parallel confidence that, while history is not progressing in Hegel's sense, a definitive "end" to history has appeared in Christ. Christ thus provides an ontological matrix through which concepts and concrete life can thus be reformed, if not "evolved."

41. An example is Kuhns's *In Pursuit of Dietrich Bonhoeffer*. Kuhns wants to identify Bonhoeffer's theology as "Catholic" in a much more programmatic sense.

42. This turn is also particularly evident in several of the essays in Gregor and Zimmerman's *Bonhoeffer and Continental Thought*.

43. NB: Lovin's essay thus could also fall at the end of the collection, insofar as it represents a constructive negotiation of the implications of Bonhoeffer's late ontological reflections for today's "global" context. We retain Lovin at the beginning of the collection, however, both for his continued resonances with the first generation of Bonhoeffer scholarship and for the helpfulness of his essay in setting out one framework for thinking about the task of Bonhoeffer studies today.

44. See his *Christian Realism and the New Realities* (2008). On the importance of "christological wholeness" to these dialogues, see especially chapter 6.

45. Ott, *Reality and Faith*, 65–66.

Notes to Chapter 2—Lovin

1. DBWE 6, 369.

2. Schlingensiepen, *Dietrich Bonhoeffer*, xvi.

3. DBWE 6, 388–94.

4. DBWE 3, 139–40.

5. DBWE 4, 225.

6. DBWE 6, 100–101.

7. Bethge, *Dietrich Bonhoeffer*, 104–6.

8. DBWE 6, 130.

9. Ibid.,163.

10. Schlingensiepen, *Dietrich Bonhoeffer*, 265–69, 301–03.

11. DBWE 6, 69.

12. DBWE 6, 262.

13. See especially the paragraphs on "civil courage" and "immanent justice" in the essay "After Ten Years" in Bonhoeffer, DBWE 8, 40–41, 45–46.

14. DBWE 16, 605.

15. DBWE 6, 73.

16. Ibid., 88–90.

17. Ibid., 130. See above at n8.

18. DBWE 15, 210.

Notes to Chapter 3—Tietz

1. Feil, *Theology*.

2. E.g., DBWE 1, 121.

3. DBWE 8, 362.

4. I here refer to the results of my dissertation *Bonhoeffers Kritik der verkrümmten Vernunft* (*Bonhoeffer's Critique of Incurved Reason*). Those interested in this topic further may also want to look at deJonge's *Bonhoeffer's Theological Formation* and the standard work by Green, *Bonhoeffer: A Theology of Sociality*.

5. DBWE 1, 21.

6. See ibid.: There is a "social intention of all the basic Christian concepts. 'Person,' 'primal state,' 'sin,' and 'revelation' can be fully comprehended only in reference to sociality. If genuinely theological concepts can only be recognized as established and fulfilled in a special social context [German: "eigenen sozialen Sphäre," DBW 1, 13; it should better be translated as: "in a social sphere of its own"], then it becomes evident that a sociological study of the church has a specifically theological character" [German: "so läßt sich von hier aus der spezifisch theologische Charakter einer Untersuchung zur Soziologie der Kirche wahren";

Endnotes

it should be translated as: "from here on the specifically theological character of a sociology of the church can be protected"].

7. DBWE 1, 126.

8. DBW 1, 79.

9. DBWE 1, 125 (my emphasis).

10. Bonhoeffer explains this by quoting "You did not choose me, but I chose you" from John 15. DBWE 1, 125.

11. DBWE 1, 125.

12. Cf. DBWE 1, 126–27: "The new ontic basic-relations are the foundation of a social entity that, viewed from the outside, can only be called a 'religious community.' . . . [T]he claim of the church to be God's church [has to be taken] . . . seriously . . . One premise . . . will not have to be justified further, namely that we take the claim of the church seriously, i.e., not as being historically comprehensible, but as being grounded in the reality of God." Bonhoeffer distinguishes between the *essential* and the *empirical* church. With this he changes the traditional pair of the invisible and the visible church, because the "concept of the invisibility of the church is dangerous mainly because it implies that the visible, i.e., the empirical church, is not church." Bonhoeffer instead wants to say that the "'essential' church becomes literally visible in the empirical church. Its members are very concretely visible, but only faith sees them in their capacity as members" (DBWE 1, 221); only faith sees them as members of the essential church which is set up by God.

13. Cf. DBWE 1, 125–26.

14. DBWE 1, 126.

15. Ibid.

16. DBWE 1, 127.

17. DBWE 2, 76.

18. DBWE 2, 110.

19. DBWE 10, 453.

20. DBWE 2, 94.

21. DBWE 2, 89.

22. This self-enclosure of reason is so fundamental that reason is unable to recognize its self-enclosure. For recognizing it would mean to recognize at least some truth (cf. DBWE 2, 80). But then sin would not be an existential category shaping a human being's whole existence: "For it would mean that human beings could place themselves into the truth, that they could somehow withdraw to a deeper being of their own, apart from their being sinners, their 'not being in the truth'" (DBWE 2, 136). In philosophy, that thinking tries to understand

itself out of itself "really means, however, that it basically does not understand itself. Indeed it does not understand itself until this I has been encountered and overwhelmed in its existence by an other" (DBWE 2, 45).

23. DBWE 2, 110 (translation altered).

24. DBWE 1, 202.

25. DBWE 1, 127.

26. DBWE 2, 82. Cf. Barth, *Die christliche Dogmatik*, 295, quoted in DBWE 2, 82–83: "The relation between God and human beings, in which God's revelation to me, to a human being, is truly imparted, would have to be free and not static in the sense that its constancy could never mean anything other than the constancy of an action that is not only continuous but in every instance beginning, in all seriousness, at the beginning."

27. DBWE 2, 82 (translation altered).

28. DBWE 2, 90–91 (second emphasis is mine).

29. Letter of Bultmann to Barth, February 16, 1930, in Barth and Bultmann, *Briefwechsel 1911–1966*, 102 (my translation).

30. DBWE 2, 78n89 (my emphases).

31. DBWE 1, 126 (my emphasis).

32. Bonhoeffer explains that all actions of the mind at least could be communicated with others—e.g., we use language, when we think. Yet: "The phenomenon of language would be meaningless . . . were not the understanding of the listener or reader potentially correlated to each word. Thus, with language, a *system of social spirit* has been built into human beings" (DBWE 1, 69–70).

33. Cf. DBWE 1, 67.

34. DBWE 1, 72.

35. Ibid.

36. DBWE 1, 75.

37. DBWE 2, 94.

38. DBWE 2, 89.

39. DBWE 1, 47.

40. DBWE 1, 49.

41. Cf. DBWE 1, 51.

42. Cf. DBWE 1, 52.

43. Ibid.

44. Ibid.

45. Cf. DBWE 1, 49: "It is a Christian insight that the person as conscious

Endnotes

being is created in the moment of being moved–in the situation of responsibility, passionate ethical struggle, confrontation by an overwhelming claim; thus the real person grows out of the concrete situation."

46. DBWE 1, 55. Cf. DBWE 8, 501: "The transcendent is . . . the neighbor within reach in any given situation."

47. DBWE 2, 127 (my emphases). Cf. DBWE 2, 126: It is only the "encounter . . . by the person of Christ in judgment or in the incorporation into the community of faith," which really comes from the outside.

48. DBWE 10, 403 (my emphases).

49. DBWE 2, 45.

50. E.g., DBWE 1, 121.

51. DBWE 1, 190 (emphasis in the original).

52. DBWE 2, 114 (my emphases).

53. Cf. DBWE 10, 456. This can also be deduced from Bonhoeffer's concept of ethical responsibility which creates a person: to be ethically responsible you need to be free and unique.

54. Cf. ibid.

55. Cf. DBWE 2, 110–11. Cf. the trenchant wording in ibid.: The Christian revelation "for those human beings living in the church, in each present, this once-and-for-all occurrence is qualified as future" ["dies einmalig Geschehene [ist] qualifiziert . . . als Zukunft für den je in Gegenwart lebenden Menschen in der Kirche"] (DBW 2, 107–8).

56. DBWE 1, 140.

57. DBWE 2, 112n39.

58. Cf. DBWE 1, 178, my translation of the phrases "strukturelles Miteinander" and "tätiges Füreinander" (DBW 1, 117).

59. DBWE 1, 181 (emphasis in the original).

60. DBWE 1, 178.

61. DBWE 1, 184 (emphasis in the original).

62. DBWE 1, 183.

63. Cf. DBWE 1, 182.

64. Cf. DBWE 1, 56.

65. DBWE 1, 213.

66. DBWE 1, 54.

67. DBWE 1, 190.

68. DBWE 1, 78.

69. Cf. DBWE 1, 140.

70. DBWE 2, 112.

71. Cf. DBWE 2, 111.

72. DBWE 2, 113.

73. DBWE 2, 112.

74. DBWE 2, 113.

75. Cf. DBWE 2, 129.

76. There is also continuity on the side of the hearer of the sermon. As it is not mainly the individual who hears, but the church that hears (even in the person of the preacher himself) the proclamation is always heard. It is not me as a hearer who has to guarantee that the revelation always reaches people; it is the church that guarantees the continuity of the hearer as well; cf. DBWE 2, 113–14.

77. Cf. DBWE 2, 114.

78. DBWE 2, 113.

79. DBWE 2, 114.

80. DBWE 2, 115 (= DBW 2, 111: "Schwebe zwischen Seiendem und Nichtseiendem").

81. DBWE 2, 122 (translation altered).

82. DBWE 2, 114–15.

83. Cf. DBWE 2, 115.

84. DBWE 2, 115.

85. DBWE 2, 112 (translation altered).

86. DBWE 2, 114.

87. DBWE 2, 117.

88. This happens very concretely: only when you believe in Christ will you then believe that the church is established by God and thus will understand what the church is about; cf. DBWE 2, 116.

89. DBWE 2, 117.

90. Cf. ibid.: "To believe means much the same as to find God, God's grace, the community of faith of Christ already present."

91. DBWE 2, 118.

92. DBWE 2, 120.

93. Cf. ibid.

94. Ibid.

95. Ibid.

96. DBWE 2, 119–20, my emphases (= DBW 2, 117).

97. DBWE 2, 115 / DBW 2, 111: "Schwebe zwischen Seiendem und Nichtseiendem."

98. DBWE 1, 127.

99. Cf. ibid.: "[T]he church can be understood fully only from within, on the basis of its own claim; only on this basis can we develop appropriately critical criteria for judging it."

100. DBWE 1, 277.

Notes to Chapter 4—Nowers

1. Part of the specter surrounding the term *Geist*, both generally and more specifically in the context of Hegel's philosophy, is the challenge of translating the word into English. Some have opted for "mind," others for "spirit." Both attempts, however, are ultimately deficient. The former runs the risk, at least on a superficial level, of reducing *Geist* to individual brains; the latter tends to conjure up visions of ethereal mysticism. My own decision to leave *Geist* untranslated is intended to highlight the complexity of the term and to allow the nuances of its meaning to emerge without the *a priori* imposition of *prima facie* English equivalents.

2. Kotsko, "Objective Spirit and Continuity in the Theology of Bonhoeffer," 19.

3. DBWE 1, 21.

4. Stace, *Philosophy of Hegel*, 321.

5. On Hegel's trinitarian theology, see his *Lectures on the Philosophy of Religion*, 185–247, 275–347.

6. DBWE 1, 146.

7. DBWE 1, 115.

8. On the matter of Bonhoeffer's anti-Judaism and its ramifications, see Haynes, *Bonhoeffer Legacy*.

9. DBWE 1, 150.

10. DBWE 1, 152.

11. DBWE 1, 121. This key phrase is a reworking of Hegel's formula—"God existing as *Gemeinde*" (*Lectures on the Philosophy of Religion*, 331). Bonhoeffer was alerted to the significance of this formula by his *Doktorvater* Reinhold Seeberg (see Floyd, "Encounter with an Other," 98n57; Green, *Bonhoeffer: A Theology of Sociality*, 23, 26). The meaning of the term *Gemeinde*, for Bonhoeffer, is not exactly "church" or "community," but rather "church-community"; it is

Bonhoeffer's "christological term for defining *Kirche* [church]" (Green, "Editor's Introduction," DBWE 1, 16).

12. DBWE 1, 157, emphasis added.

13. DBWE 1, 124.

14. DBWE 1, 157.

15. DBWE 1, 165.

16. DBWE 1, 167.

17. DBWE 1, 173.

18. DBWE 1, 178.

19. DBWE 1, 213–14.

20. DBWE 1, 66.

21. DBWE 1, 67.

22. In an important footnote, Bonhoeffer distinguishes between "structure" and "intention": "The structure of the whole certainly only becomes visible in the individual intentions to action, but in principle it is independent of them" (DBWE 1, 67n3). That is, *being* is revealed in *act*, yet *being* remains categorically distinct from *act*. "Structure" thus relates to the ontological; "intention," to the empirical. Here the former is Bonhoeffer's concern.

23. DBWE 1, 74.

24. DBWE 1, 73.

25. Ibid.

26. DBWE 1, 98.

27. DBWE 1, 98–99.

28. DBWE 1, 105.

29. DBWE 1, 78.

30. DBWE 1, 90.

31. DBWE 1, 100.

32. DBWE 1, 93.

33. DBWE 1, 72.

34. DBWE 1, 165.

35. Cf. Hegel's *Philosophy of Right*, §156.

36. DBWE 1, 288.

37. Hodgson, *Hegel: Theologian of the Spirit*. This is, of course, not to suggest that Bonhoeffer is a "theologian of the spirit" in precisely the same way that Hegel is, or that he conforms to Hodgson's reading of Hegel. Rather, if Bonhoeffer is a

Endnotes

"theologian of the spirit," he is such by virtue of his *own* theological recrafting of objective *Geist*.

Notes to Chapter 5—Phillips

1. There are two conflicting dates for the end of the lectures. Bonhoeffer's students Hilde Pfeiffer et al. recorded July 22 1933 as the last lecture (cf. L. Rasmussen's note, DBWE 12, 299n1). Bethge, however, gives an alternative date in *Dietrich Bonhoeffer: A Biography*, 293.

2. Rasmussen, DBWE 12, 299 n1.

3. Dudzus in Bethge, *Bonhoeffer*, 164.

4. DBWE 2, 29n18, 46n29, 54n26.

5. Wüstenberg, *Theology of Life*, cf. particularly 112–13.

6. For Luther, see DBWE 12, 303n12; 320n55; 321n59; 326n69; 357n176; Barth is not directly referenced in the lectures, but cf. Green, *Theology of Sociality* 277–78, who states that these lectures were the work of a "Barthian in Berlin."

7. Cf. Tietz-Steiding, 31–32; Green, *Theology of Sociality*, 277–78; Janz, *God the Mind's Desire*, 117.

8. The claim made in this paper, that Bonhoeffer dispossesses his hearers of the sort of scientific approach and the sort of subject inscribed by early twentieth-century, hermeneutic philosophy, does not need an explicit influence between Bonhoeffer and Dilthey to be established in order to be valid. The claim would be equally valid if the influence were found to be more implicit than explicit.

9. For example, DBWE 2, 54n26: "Dilthey's inquiry into the reality of the external world . . . attempts fundamentally to overcome the whole of the idealistic theory of knowledge in favor of a philosophy of life shaper by history. [It] is of decisive significance." I would also suggest that Bonhoeffer's decision not to include Dilthey in the "ontological attempt" of "an autonomous understanding of *Dasein* in philosophy" (ibid., 59–60) suggests that he considers Dilthey's philosophy not subject to quite the same errors as the contemporaries of Dilthey he discusses there.

10. Cf. Bonhoeffer's use of *Sinnzusammenhang* in DBWE 12, 301 / DBW 12, 281, with Dilthey's use of *Sinnvoll Zusammenhang* in Dilthey, *Selected Works*, 3:23 / *Gesammelte Schriften* 7:3; cf. *Struktur* in DBWE 12, 314, 315, 352 / DBW 12, 295, with Dilthey, *Selected Works*, 3:34–38, 344–48 / *Gesammelte Schriften*, 7:13–18; cf. *Für-mich-sein* in DBWE 12, 315 / DBW 12, 296, with Dilthey, *Selected Works*, 3:47 / *Gesammelte Schriften*, 7:26.

11. Dilthey, *Selected Works*, 3:104. Cf. ibid., 3:8, 95, 140, 191–92.

12. Bowie, *Introduction to German Philosophy*, 19.

Endnotes

13. Dilthey, *Selected Works*, 3:9–32.

14. Ibid., 3:8.

15. Ibid., 3:95, 252–56 / *Gesammelte Schriften*, 7:73–74, 232–37.

16. Dilthey, *Selected Works*, 3:95.

17. Ibid., 3:23 / *Gesammelte Schriften*, 7:3.

18. Dilthey, *Selected Works*, 3:104, 111.

19. Dilthey, *Selected Works*, 1:198–99.

20. Dilthey, *Selected Works*, 3:142.

21. Hodges's translation of Dilthey, *Gesammelte Schriften*, 5:175, 196; Hodges, *The Philosophy of Wilhelm Dilthey*, 207.

22. Cf. Dilthey, *Selected Works*, 3:104, 111.

23. Ibid., 3:23–24, 140.

24. Ibid., 3:23.

25. Ibid., 3:45–46 / *Gesammelte Schriften*, 7:24.

26. Dilthey, *Selected Works*, 3:38, 43, 140.

27. Ibid., 3:140 / *Gesammelte Schriften*, 7:118; cf. Dilthey, *Selected Works*, 1:198–99.

28. Dilthey, *Selected Works*, 3:47–48, 140.

29. Ibid., 3:36.

30. Dilthey, *Selected Works*, 3:37, 344.

31. Rodi, "Dilthey's Concept of 'Structure,'" 107.

32. Ibid., 111 (Rodi's translation of the Dilthey quote is originally in Dilthey, *Gesammelte Schriften*, 19:101)

33. The draft is the 1887 *Poetics*, found in Dilthey, *Selected Works*, 5:96–97.

34. Rodi, "Dilthey's Concept of 'Structure,'" 115.

35. Ibid, 36–37.

36. Dilthey, *Selected Works*, 3:39 / *Gesammelte Schriften*, 7:19 (cf. *Selected Works*, 4:235 / *Gesammelte Schriften*, 5:317)

37. Dilthey, *Selected Works*, 3:4–5, 176, 277.

38. Ibid., 3:253.

39. Ibid., 3:256 / Dilthey, *Gesammelte Schriften*, 7:236.

40. Dilthey, *Selected Works*, 3:267–68.

41. Cf. Hodges, 207.

Endnotes

42. Bonhoeffer, DBWE 12, 305.

43. DBWE 12, 301.

44. DBWE 12, 301–2.

45. DBWE 12, 302–3 / DBW 12, 283.

46. DBWE 12, 304 / DBW 12, 284. I have altered the DBWE translation of *die gegebene Frage* slightly from "understanding the question as it is given" to the more straightforward "understanding the given question."

47. DBWE 12, 303.

48. All quotes in this paragraph from DBW 12, 304.

49. DBWE 12, 302.

50. DBWE 12, 301, 304 / DBW, 280.

51. DBWE 12, 314–5 / DBW 12, 296–97. Bonhoeffer's concept of "being-for-me" is primarily derived from Luther (cf. particularly Luther, *Luther's Works* 51:190–91), but this does not necessarily preclude other valuable sub-textual lines of investigation, in this case: the epistemological. In an epistemological investigation of the concept, the use of the same phrase (with a very similar meaning) by Dilthey is significant.

52. DBWE 12, 314–15 / DBW 12, 296–97.

53. DBWE 12, 315 / DBW 12, 296; and Dilthey, *Selected Works*, 3:47 / *Gesammelte Schriften*, 7:26.

54. DBWE 12, 324.

55. DBW 12, 308.

56. DBWE 12, 324–6.

57. DBWE 12, 301.

58. DBWE 12, 325.

59. Ibid.

60. The suggestion that this constitutes an appropriation of the category of meaning is given further weight in that at the outset of his lectures, Bonhoeffer delineates Christology in relation to the other sciences as "the center of knowledge," soon after defining the *Geisteswissenschaften* as an asking after meaning. Cf. DBWE 12, 301; 305 / DBW 12, 286.

61. DBWE 12, 324–25.

62. Ibid.

Notes to Chapter 6—Gregor

1. For an excellent and illuminating study of this topic, see Moyn's *Origins of the Other*.

2. Levinas, *On Escape*, 49–50.

3. Ibid., 50.

4. See Levinas, *Is it Righteous to Be?*, 220, 251,

5. Levinas, *On Escape*, 50–51.

6. Ibid., 52.

7. Ibid., 53.

8. Ibid., 54.

9. Ibid., 55.

10. Ibid., 71.

11. Ibid., 58–59.

12. Ibid., 61–62.

13. Ibid., 62–63 (italics mine).

14. Ibid., 63.

15. Ibid.

16. Ibid., 64.

17. Ibid., 67.

18. Ibid., 64.

19. Ibid., 65.

20. DBWE 6, 303.

21. DBWE 3, 86–87.

22. DBWE 3, 97–99.

23. DBWE 3, 122.

24. DBWE 3, 123.

25. DBWE 3, 124.

26. DBWE 6, 303.

27. DBWE 3, 101.

28. DBWE 3, 124.

29. DBWE 3, 113.

30. DBWE 3, 90–91.

Endnotes

31. DBWE 3, 135.
32. DBWE 3, 90.
33. DBWE 3, 90–91.
34. DBWE 3, 143.
35. DBWE 3, 142–43.
36. Levinas, "Reflections on the Philosophy of Hitlerism," 66.
37. Levinas, *Existence and Existents*, 31–32.
38. Ibid., 31.
39. DBWE 6, 304.
40. DBWE 8, 215.
41. DBWE 3, 92.
42. DBWE 6, 306.
43. DBWE 3, 139.
44. DWBE 3, 139–40.
45. See Editor's Introduction to DBWE 3, 12. Also see Green, *Bonhoeffer: A Theology of Sociality*, 128–29; 203.
46. Levinas, *On Escape*, 73.
47. Levinas, "Reflections on the Philosophy of Hitlerism," 69.
48. Ibid., 70.
49. Ibid., 71.
50. Elshtain, "Shame and Public Life," 18.
51. Levinas, "Reflections on the Philosophy of Hitlerism," 63.
52. Levinas, *Existence and Existents*, 17.
53. Ibid., 95–96.
54. Ibid., 98.
55. Ibid., 102.
56. Cf. Robert Bernasconi's Foreword to *Existence and Existents*, xiv. For instance, see Levinas, *Time and the Other*, 112–13.
57. Levinas, *Totality and Infinity*, 22.
58. Levinas, *Humanism of the Other*, 4; cf. Levinas, *Is it Righteous to Be?*, 173, 186.
59. DBWE 1, 48–50.
60. DBWE 1, 54.

61. Like Levinas, Bonhoeffer contends that this limit is not simply epistemological; ethical transcendence is quite another thing than epistemological transcendence. It involves the encounter with the concrete other person. I cannot subsume this person under a universal, nor can I render him an object for myself as subject. According to Bonhoeffer, one point of continuity in the philosophical tradition is the concept of the spirit as *immanent*, which precludes any possibility of a genuine understanding of community (DBWE 1, 43). Otherness always succumbs to the schematics of sameness and unity. Consequently, the only possibility for genuine sociality arises when the dominance of the intellect is "*confronted by some fundamental barrier* [Schranke]" (DBWE 1, 45–46). This barrier, then, is the concrete, existing, other person.

62. DBWE 1, 54.

63. DBWE 1, 50.

64. DBWE 1, 51.

65. DBWE 1, 52.

66. DBWE 6, 306–7.

67. DBWE 3, 139–40.

68. DBWE 6, 63ff.

69. DWWE 12, 286.

70. DBWE 6, 155.

71. DBWE 12, 292.

72. "The earth wants us to take it seriously. It will not let us escape, not into the salvation of otherworldly piety nor into the utopia of this-worldly secularism" (DBWE 12, 290).

73. By contrast, the created goodness of being is at best a point of ambiguity in Levinas. Didier Franck suggests that there is a certain violence evident in Levinas' thought: "To equate being with evil, to say that you are guilty of being—that's colossal. It isn't even biblical, besides, since Creation is good. I don't see how we can affirm such a position." Quoted by Malka in *Emmanuel Levinas: His Life and Legacy*, 278.

Notes to Chapter 7—Kirkpatrick

1. Kirkpatrick, *Attacks on Christendom*, 1–8.

2. Cf. Mackey, "Loss of the World"; MacIntyre, *After Virtue*, 39–45; and Roberts, "Thinking Subjectively."

3. Feil, *Theology*, xix.

4. Feil, *Theologie*, 277n39; Hopper, "Metanoia," 72–74; cf. Hopper, "Love of the World." Part of Feil's discussion of Kierkegaard appears in footnotes that, sadly, were dropped from the English version of the book.

5. Law, "Anti-Ecclesiology," and "Cheap Grace." Kierkegaard was himself aware of the potential charge of being considered either acosmic or Gnostic. However, he dismisses these charges as merely the interpretation of "busy thinkers." Kierkegaard, *Postscript*, 341.

6. Kant, *Conflict*, 115.

7. Cf. Blanshard, "Kierkegaard on Faith," 118.

8. Plant, *Bonhoeffer*, 49. Plant is right to raise the issue of where the encounter of Christian ethics takes place. Plant here draws on Bonhoeffer's criticisms of Kierkegaard in *Sanctorum Communio* (DBWE 1, 57). However, this paper will argue that the simplistic separation between the duties to God and those to the neighbor ascribed to Kierkegaard is a stereotype that Bonhoeffer himself overcame.

9. Kirkpatrick, *Attacks on Christendom*.

10. This essay will describe Kierkegaard as the author of *Fear and Trembling*. This does not take into account the significance of Kierkegaard's use of pseudonymity in general, nor the persona of Johannes de Silentio in particular. An article-length essay does not afford the opportunity to expand on these themes. However, as the aim of the essay is to discuss Bonhoeffer's interpretation of *Fear and Trembling* and his relationship to Kierkegaard (rather than offer an objective account of both) the author considers this inaccuracy a justifiable one.

11. Kierkegaard, *Fear and Trembling*, 57.

12. Kierkegaard, *Postscript*, 1:158, 395; cf. DBWE 10, 473.

13. Kierkegaard, *Fear and Trembling*, 83.

14. Ibid., 83, 89, 96.

15. Ibid., 77.

16. Ibid., 75.

17. Ibid., 96.

18. Ibid., 105.

19. Kierkegaard, *Postscript*, 1:137.

20. There have been various attempts to classify the periods of Bonhoeffer's authorship. Bethge offers a convincing account, defining this first period as lasting from his first doctoral dissertation, *Sanctorum Communio*, through to his lectures at Friedrich-Wilhelm University, Berlin, including "Creation and Sin" and "Christology." Bethge, "Challenge," 26–43.

21. Bonhoeffer's own copies of these works are filled with underlinings and

annotations, and played a significant role in Bonhoeffer's early authorship.

22. DBWE 4, 97.

23. DBWE 4, 98.

24. Kierkegaard, *Fear and Trembling*, 99–100.

25. In both *Postscript* and *Concept of Anxiety* Kierkegaard argues that all systematic thought failed since all thinking is enclosed within itself and so cannot conceive of its own beginning. Bonhoeffer's similarity with Kierkegaard is particularly clear in *Creation and Fall* (DBWE 3, 25ff).

26. cf. Kierkegaard, *Postscript*, 1:314; DBWE 1, 53; DBWE 10, 471–72.

27. DBWE 2, 39.

28. DBWE 10, 368.

29. DBWE 10, 360.

30. DBWE 3, 107.

31. DBWE 6, 311.

32. DBWE 6, 301.

33. DBWE 6, 311.

34. DBWE 3, 98n11.

35. DBWE 4, 135.

36. DBWE 6, 81.

37. This again is described most forcefully in Bonhoeffer's Barcelona lecture, "Basic Questions of a Christian Ethic" (DBWE 10, 359ff), and in the essay, "Ethics as Formation" (DBWE 6, 81–82).

38. Cf. Kirkpatrick, *Attacks on Christendom*, 109–10, 216–19.

39. DBWE 1, 162.

40. This can be seen most significantly in *Life Together* and *Discipleship*.

41. Kierkegaard, *Fear and Trembling*, 101.

42. DBWE 4, 96.

43. Mooney, *Knights of Faith*, 31.

44. Ibid., 59.

45. Vogel, "Christus," 297ff.

46. Kelly, "Revelation in Christ," Appendix II, 33–34; cf. 309nn63, 64.

47. Kierkegaard, *Einzelne*, §148; *Journals*, §600; *Papirer*, 10/4:A 246.

48. Kierkegaard, *Einzelne*, §94; *Journals*, §2952; *Papirer*, 10/2:A 390.

49. DBWE 6, 81

50. Kelly, *Testament to Freedom*, 347.

51. DBWE 6, 82.

52. Fletcher, *Situation Ethics*, 28.

53. DBWE 6, 321.

54. DBWE 6, 271. Heinz Tödt describes these as "laws that are inherent in life and indispensable for its preservation." Tödt, *Authentic Faith*, 166.

55. Cf. Paul Ramsey, *Deeds and Rules in Christian Ethics*.

56. Kierkegaard, *Fear and Trembling*, 98.

Notes to Chapter 8—Kessler

1. For the dating of the relevant *Ethics* manuscripts, see "Editors Afterward to the German Edition," DBWE 6, 421–26; 440–49.

2. DBWE 6, 378.

3. See L. Rasmussen with R. Bethge, *Dietrich Bonhoeffer*, 111–43.

4. Müller, *Von der Kirche zur Welt*, 288–89.

5. Rasmussen, "Question of Method," 105.

6. Ibid 135.

7. See, inter alia, DBWE 1, 138.

8. Green, *Dietrich Bonhoeffer*, 64. Green goes on to note the always-essential caveat with Bonhoeffer's intimate christology: "To be sure, Bonhoeffer is never in danger of identifying God and humanity, any more than of confusing Christ and the church" (ibid.).

9. DBWE 2, 91.

10. DBWE 12, 324.

11. DBWE 4, 285.

12. L. Rasmussen, "Question of Method," 113. Similarly, Feil points to a letter that Bonhoeffer wrote to Theodor Litt on January 22, 1939, shortly before beginning his work on *Ethics*, as marking the transition from "the 'Christ for us,' which still governed *The Cost of Discipleship* . . . to the *Christus pro aliis* . . . from here on christology and the understanding of the world will be inseparably related one to the other" (Feil, *Theology of Dietrich Bonhoeffer*, 138). More recently, Gregersen has echoed this assessment: "[In the *Ethics*,] Christ is existing not only as community . . . but Christ is also existing in the world *as* the mediator between God and world" (Gregersen, "The Mysteries of Christ and Creation," 154).

13. L. Rasmussen, "Question of Method," 114.

14. DBWE 6, 67.

15. See DBWE 6, 68; for the dating, see the "Editors Afterward to the German Edition," ibid., 426.

16. DBWE 6, 68.

17. DBWE 6, 69.

18. DBWE 6, 70.

19. Bonhoeffer, "On the Theological Basis of the Work of the World Alliance," DBWE 11, 98-99.

20. Quoted in L. Rasmussen, "A Question of Method," 119.

21. Ibid.

22. Ibid., 126.

23. See Wüstenberg, *Theology of Life*, 199n95.

24. L. Rasmussen, "Question of Method," 110.

25. DBWE 6, 247.

26. DBWE 6, 272-73.

27. DBWE 6, 274.

28. DBWE 6, 274-75.

29. DBWE 6, 296.

30. DBWE 6, 296-97.

31. DBWE 6, 297.

32. DBWE 6, 284.

33. Ibid.

34. DBWE 6, 297.

35. He did so after reading the proofs of Karl Barth's *Church Dogmatics* 2/2, which treated, among other things, the command of God. See DBWE 6, 415, where the editors write that "[c]onversations with Karl Barth in Basel and access to the galley proofs of Barth's *Church Dogmatics* 2/2 helped give Bonhoeffer's *Ethics* manuscripts of 1942 the freshness of a new beginning." The editors specifically point to the manuscripts "God's Love and the Disintegration of the World" and "The 'Ethical' and the 'Christian' as a Topic" as evidence of this "freshness." L. Rasmussen has detailed the extent to which Bonhoeffer relied on Barth's treatment of the command of God, but he also notes what distinguishes Bonhoeffer's account: "Bonhoeffer's strongest emphasis is not Barth's—Barth's theme is of constant accountability before God. Bonhoeffer's, rather, is God's permission of man to live 'as man, and not merely as a taker of ethical decisions'" (L. Rasmussen, "Question of Method," 125, quoting Bonhoeffer).

Endnotes

36. DBWE 6, 366.
37. Ibid., emphasis added.
38. DBWE 6, 367.
39. See DBWE 6, 367n16.
40. For this term, see DBWE 6, 178.
41. DBWE 6, 367.
42. DBWE 6, 367–68.
43. DBWE 6, 373.
44. DBWE 6, 274.
45. DBWE 6, 378.
46. Ibid.
47. L. Rasmussen, "A Question of Method," 128.
48. DBWE 6, 297.
49. DBWE 6, 380.
50. DBWE 6, 384.
51. DBWE 6, 381.
52. See his discussion of marriage and adultery in DBWE 6, 382.
53. DBWE 6, 386.
54. DBWE 6, 384.
55. DBWE 6, 385.
56. DBWE 6, 386.
57. DBWE 6, 385.
58. I am indebted to Matthew Puffer for this insight. Indeed, Bonhoeffer's last use of the word "guilt" in the *Ethics* manuscripts occurs on page 297 of the English edition, at the end of "History and Good [2]."
59. Bonhoeffer makes a similar distinction in a letter to Eberhard Bethge on 5 May, 1944, when he asks: "Hasn't the individualistic question of saving our personal souls almost faded away for most of us? Isn't it our impression that there are really more important things than this question (perhaps not more important than this *matter*, but certainly more important than the *question*!?[sic])?" (DBWE 8, 372). The *matter* of guilt is still almost certainly crucial for Bonhoeffer. But the *question* of guilt has been set aside.
60. See, e.g., DBWE 8, 515.
61. DBWE 6, 400, emphases added.
62. DBWE 6, 401.

63. Ibid.

64. L. Rasmussen, "A Question of Method," 131.

65. Ibid.

66. DBWE 16, 633–634.

67. Already in 1941, Bonhoeffer had spoken of a "providential correspondence . . . between the contents of the second table and the law inherent in historical life itself" (DBWE 16, 515). Similarly in the post-"History" *Ethics* manuscript, "Church and World I," Bonhoeffer discussed this correspondence (DBWE 6, 339–41).

68. For bibliographic analysis of Bonhoeffer's historical study in this area, see Wüstenberg, "The Influence of Wilhelm Dilthey on Bonhoeffer's *Letters and Papers from Prison*," 167–73; Wüstenberg, *Theology of Life*, 101–12, 140–44; Feil, *Theology of Dietrich Bonhoeffer*, 178–85.

69. See, e.g., "Editor's Introduction to the English Edition," DBWE 8, 15; Feil, *Theology of Dietrich Bonhoeffer*, 160.

70. DBWE 8, 362.

71. Feil, *Theology of Dietrich Bonhoeffer*, 174. The other two phenomena that Feil identifies as the core concepts of Bonhoeffer's negative understanding of religion are "metaphysics" and "inwardness."

72. DBWE 8, 482 (emphases added).

73. Wüstenberg argues that Bonhoeffer develops "a 'nonreligious' triad of faith, participation (in suffering), and life (as a totality), formulating this contra the 'religious triad' of unbelief, nonparticipation (in suffering), and non-living religious partiality" (*Theology of Life*, 132).

74. DBWE 8, 364.

75. DBWE 8, 366.

76. Wüstenberg, *Theology of Life*, 127.

77. DBWE 8, 427.

78. Bonhoeffer writes that the apologetic critique of worldliness is "like trying to put a person who has become an adult back into puberty, that is, to make people dependent on a lot of things on which they in fact no longer depend, to shove them into problems that in fact are no longer problems for them" (DBWE 8, 427).

79. I understand Bonhoeffer's criticism of Barth's "positivism of revelation" (DBWE 6, 429) as part of this attempt to distance himself from the divisive tendency of the language of law-giving. As Heinz Tödt writes, Bonhoeffer's objection to Barth's account of revelation, as he understood it, was that its "significance . . . would be unintelligible for a religionless human being." For Bonhoeffer, on

the other hand, revelation is "an event that concerns the human being *wholly* and not—like the religious act—only *partially*" (Tödt, *Authentic Faith*, 32, emphasis added).

80. L. Rasmussen, "Question of Method," 110.

81. See n68 above for helpful accounts of Bonhoeffer's reception of Dilthey.

82. DBWE 8, 425.

83. Quoted in Wüstenberg, *Theology of Life*, 143.

84. DBWE 8, 425.

85. DBWE 8, 476. For fuller discussion of Bonhoeffer's use of Grotius' phrase, see ibid., 476n23; Wüstenberg, *Theology of Life*, 140–44; Feil, *Theology of Dietrich Bonhoeffer*, 187–90.

86. DBWE 8, 479.

87. DBWE 8, 478.

88. DBWE 8, 501.

89. Of course Bonhoeffer may have intended modifications. Indeed, his call for the church "to give away all its property to those in need" reflects a changed understanding of the exact nature of the relationship of the church to the world (DBWE 8, 503). But, in general, the idea of a reality structured—christologically—by relationships with others had been, and clearly remained, the core of Bonhoeffer's ethical thought.

90. Feil, *Theology of Dietrich Bonhoeffer*, 189.

91. DBWE 6, 178.

Notes to Chapter 9—Cox

1. In its phenomenological use, "reduction, with the Latin root *re-ducere*, is a leading back, a withholding or withdrawal." Reduction is twofold, concerning both the subject (or noetic structures) and object (or noematic structures) of thought and experience—as one's "attitude" is restricted and purged (in the "transcendental" reduction), this increases one's ability to see the essence of things (through "eidetic" reduction). For a clarification of terms, see Sokolowski, *Introduction to Phenomenology*, 49, 61, 184.

2. Lacoste uses "liturgy" in a certain way. It is not to be confused with its common meaning ("the order of worship") or any particular religious activity. Most basically, it stands for the divine-human encounter or the posture of turning-toward-God. In his essay "Liturgy and Coaffection" in *The Experience of God: A Postmodern Response*, he defines it as "what people do *coram Deo*" (93). The definition will be clarified in what follows.

3. Bonhoeffer, DBWE 8, 479.

4. DBWE 8, 478.

5. In his dissertation *Sanctorum Communio*, DBWE 1, Bonhoeffer explores a "specifically Christian phenomenology of sociality" but rejects Husserl's sense of phenomenology as "presuppositionless science" (Gregor and Zimmerman, "Dietrich Bonhoeffer and Cruciform Philosophy," in *Bonhoeffer and Continental Thought*, 3–4).

6. In DBWE 2, Bonhoeffer engages Heidegger's analysis of Dasein in *Being and Time*. He prefers Heidegger to Husserl because Heidegger attempts to think "being itself" in terms of concrete existence (67–68).

7. Lacoste, *Experience and the Absolute*, 2–3.

8. Ibid., 194.

9. Ibid., 171, 173.

10. Ibid., 174, 167, my emphasis.

11. Ibid., 161.

12. Although Lacoste begins the work by saying it is not an "anthropology," quoting Heidegger—"Anthropology is an interpretation of man that already knows at bottom what man is, and cannot therefore ask what he is" (1)—he does conclude with an "anthropology of the cross" (192).

13. Ibid., 7. Deformalizing the "there" of the world as Heidegger does is a matter of understanding "place" not as "space" but as that which *takes place*, as the outcome of human temporalization.

14. Ibid., 8. Lacoste goes on to say that, "ipseity and corporeality are indissociable."

15. Ibid., 9, 16.

16. Inherence is a "mode of immanence that amounts to perpetually coming up against the limit that encloses it, while recognizing this limit to be inaccessible" (ibid., 10).

17. Ibid., 11–12.

18. As Heidegger says in his 1924 lecture "The Concept of Time," the question "What is time?" morphs into the question "Who is time?"—"Am I my own time?" *Becoming Heidegger*, 213.

19. Heidegger, *Ontology: The Hermeneutics of Facticity*, 5

20. Heidegger, *Being and Time*, 310.

21. Caputo, "Shedding Tears Beyond Being," 103.

22. "*Coram*" having, as Hannah Arendt points out, the threefold sense of returning to the beginning, referring to the end, and being in the presence of.

Endnotes

Augustine uses "*ante Deum*" interchangeably with "*coram deo*." Arendt, *Love and Saint Augustine*, 85. See Augustine, *Confessions*, 69.

23. Heidegger, *Being and Time*, 289.

24. Ibid., 294, 307, 310.

25. Ibid., 289, 294, 307, 310.

26. Lacoste, 13–14.

27. Ibid., 16.

28. Ibid., 17–18.

29. Ibid., 20.

30. In his early *Speeches*, Schleiermacher describes the immediate feeling (*Gefühl*) of the infinite (or "the feeling of absolute dependence") as an essential human possibility and the basis of religion. However, in his later dogmatic work, *The Christian Faith*, it is clear that revelation precedes and grounds experience and that all religious experience is fundamentally traditioned. Though usually overlooked by his critics, the priority of reception over affection is already intimated in his *Speeches*. Heidegger did not miss this. See Heidegger's notes on Schleiermacher's proto-phenomenology of religious experience and its order of events: reception—affection—action. Non-thetically, passivity precedes feeling for Schleiermacher; thetically, God is always already named in advance as the God revealed in Christ. "On Schleiermacher's Second Speech 'On the Essence of Religion,'" in *Becoming Heidegger*, 91.

31. Lacoste, 2.

32. Ibid., 23.

33. Ibid., 25.

34. As eccentric dwellers such as the recluse and the pilgrim teach us, it is possible to transfigure the logic of place—not in the sense that being before God could mean being nowhere (which is obviously absurd), but in the sense that one can decide on a particular relationship to a location by subordinating the *there* to the *toward which*. That is to say, vocation can govern facticity, even if only symbolically.

35. Ibid., 45. Thus far, bracketing the Incarnation. The encounter with God is not only not inevitable or necessary. Lacoste says, the human "has not existed immemorially face-to-face with the Absolute"—but, further, it is (assuming a certain sense of "experience") *impossible*. Prayer is a common example of this.

36. Ibid., 30, 41.

37. Ibid., 78.

38. Ibid., 45.

39. Yet ethics, like liturgy, helps declare the definitive over against the

provisional. Together, the daytime work of ethics and nighttime work of liturgy form the "fundamental rhythm" of the "Kingdom" (the kingdom being a "third term" intersecting and overlaying the dialectic of world and earth as "the eschatological place that the [one] who exists before God claims to represent") (ibid., 74, 76).

40. Ibid., 79. See Eberhard Jüngel, *God as the Mystery of the World*, 14–15.

41. Heidegger, *History of the Concept of Time*, 244.

42. Ibid., 88–89.

43. Hegel, *Phenomenology of Spirit*, 493. Hegel is disapproving of the theology and faith of his day, reproaching, on the one hand, the self-imposed ignorance of Enlightenment religion (which he associates with Kant) and the irrational immediacy of religious feeling on the other (which he attributes to Schleiermacher). In contrast to both, Hegel claims that the *History* (appearance) of the Absolute coincides with the *Science* (knowledge) of the Absolute.

44. Lacoste, *Experience and the Absolute*, 114; Hegel, *Phenomenology of the Spirit*, 346–347. The German translation of the Greek *nous* is "reason" rather than, as in English, "understanding." Hegel would agree that the peace of God passes "the understanding," as he uses that term, but he would not concede that God or the peace of God is other than Reason. The "peace of unity," of reconciled existence, Hegel says, "does not 'surpass all reason' but is rather the peace that *through* reason is first known and thought and is recognized as what is true."

45. Hegel, *Phenomenology of Spirit*, 475.

46. Lacoste, *Experience and the Absolute*, 115. Humanity is already reconciled with God in Christ, but fails (or at least failed for eighteen hundred years, until Hegel) to grasp this, to think this, and therefore remains within the realm of religious immediacy or (at best) representation and recollection. During this cognitive delay, we have the time of the "Unhappy Consciousness" in which the finite is divided. Consciousness is "unhappy" because it only "knows itself to be a duality" (finite separate from infinite) and not a unity (reconciled) (Hegel, *Phenomenology of Spirit*, 126–27).

47. Lacoste, *Experience and the Absolute*, 128–29, 119. Yet this realized eschaton cannot actually challenge the logic of being-in-the-world-toward-death. First, death cannot *not* be an issue for Hegel since his theoretical "end of history" is capable of abolishing neither the logic of facticity—"the empirical absolute future represented by death"—nor the possibility of seeing in death "the collapse of all meaning" (ibid., 128–29). Further, Hegel's assertion that God is no longer hidden (which amounts to an equation of Absolute Knowledge and the beatific vision), is called into question both by the ongoing veiling of God in the "chiaroscuro" of the world and by the fact that humans do not cease to question.

48. Ibid., 138.

49. Bonhoeffer, *Ethics*, DBWE 6, 120–21. For Lacoste, this is neither the

provisional (for the logic of the definitive is "already at work") nor the definitive (for the logic of the provisional persists). But, importantly, this is not the already/not-yet of inaugurated eschatology: the eschaton is not only *not* realized, it is not even inchoate this side of death and can only be *symbolically* represented by a (kenotic) liturgical identity.

50. Moreover, knowledge is neither absolute now—given the preeschatological chiaroscuro of the world—nor ever will be—God is always more.

51. Lacoste, *Experience and the Absolute*, 143.

52. Ibid., 145.

53. Ibid., 146–47. Lacoste uses knowledge and faith almost synonymously here and in several other places.

54. Ibid., 153. For Lacoste, it is of utmost significance here that we "dissociate two destinies, that of the subject and that of the [one] confronted by the Absolute," that is, "the soul." In sharp contrast to the tendency to interiorize the soul, Lacoste describes it as an extreme exteriority or carnality (155).

55. Ibid., 151–152, 155.

56. Ibid., 152.

57. Ibid., 163.

58. Ibid., 164.

59. Ibid., 175.

60. Ibid., 179.

61. Ibid., 1, 192.

62. The silence between God and God, as Hans Urs von Balthasar describes it in *Mysterium Paschale*.

63. Ibid. 191–92, 194. The joy of Easter has a place here, too, but only "paradoxically," as the eschatological reason for the strength and patience of the one who accepts the effacement and negation of their being-in-fact. Good Friday, however, is the secret of the present, the secret of humanity.

64. Ibid., 139, 145.

65. Ibid., 189.

66. Ibid., 194.

67. Of course, "creation" normally falls within the purview of theology, not phenomenology, and can hardly be considered an oversight in that sense. However, the frequency and freedom with which Lacoste avails himself theological categories (namely revelation and the cross) demonstrates his lack of regard for any strict division between philosophy and theology. It may be the case that he is so interested in a "Christological theory of experience" which legitimizes inexperience over against consciousness that he must downplay the idea of a trace

of the Creator in the creation (however this could be thought—*imago Dei, analogia entis*, the gift, general revelation, etc.). He insists that "God must be named beforehand for the heavens to sing his glory." *Only* a "secondary immediacy" enables the recognition of the Creator in creation (ibid., 102–4).

68. Lacoste contrasts the terms "beginning," "start," "initial," and "native" (i.e., the rules of factical existence) with "origin" (i.e., the extra-temporal source of being).

69. Bloechl, "A Response to Jean-Yves Lacoste," 106.

70. Ibid., 94, my emphasis.

71. Eph 2:12: "Remember that you were at that time separate from Christ, excluded from the commonwealth of Israel, and strangers to the covenants of promise, having no hope and without God (*atheios*) in the world (*kosmos*)." Cf. Gal 4:8.

72. Lacoste, *Experience and the Absolute*, 41. Importantly, the world is further defined as the place of "past pacts" with violence and "a native compromise with evil." Hence the claim that the Kingdom is not of this world and can only be represented here "asymptotically" (ibid., 93–94).

73. Arendt, *Love and Saint Augustine*, 66n80.

74. Bound up with this reduction of world is Heidegger's misunderstanding of biblical creation as product or effect, an objectified thing present at hand, the "handiwork" of a Maker. See Heidegger, *The Essence of Reasons*, 113; and *On the Way to Language*, 23–24.

75. While Heidegger's name predominates here, the obvious disjunction between the adjective "neutral" and Lacoste's description of the world in terms of "past pacts with evil" more closely resembles Kant's construal of the "principle" of or human "propensity" to "radical evil" which originarily (though not more originarily than "good") and inexplicably "posits" itself in the world. See Kant, *Religion within the Boundaries of Mere Reason*.

76. Yet the theological definition of the "world" still remains ambiguous. Is it *kosmos, imperium*, Nature, Augustine's *dilectio mundi*? And why not *ens creatum*? Can "world" be a reduction to "Kingdom," as Kevin Hart argues? How might Kingdom overlap with world, for Lacoste, when he recognizes neither the beginning of the Kingdom in Christ (as *autobasileia*, in Origen's sense) nor its inauguration in history but treats it as wholly eschatological?

77. In Lacoste's interpretation. Of course, Paul does not say here that "the world" as such (*kosmos*) is passing away, but the world "in its present form" or "mode"(*schema*)—and he does not say that it "must" but simply that it "is" or "will."

78. Lacoste, *Experience and the Absolute*, 90, 92, 98.

79. For Lacoste, we are born into a world that differs from and denies creation

not on account of fallenness from some original blessedness, but precisely on account of the logic of the gift which always contains its own forgetting. The worldly denial of the gift as gift is an *a priori* judgment the human (or Dasein) has always already made. A discussion of the fall could help clarify the relationship between world and creation. If its own denial is inscribed in the gift of creation—not simply as a possibility, but as an inevitability—then creatureliness looks like a sort of original fallenness (forgetfulness) from which we have to recover. The lack of clarity on this point raises many questions. Is the fall accidental/historical or essential/original/ontological? Does it have anything to do with the character of the world now? Is the world a perversion of creation? Is Lacoste able to maintain the goodness of "original" creation or does he risk equating creation with fallenness—as in a Gnostic fall into creation? Is it a happy fall since what really matters is eschatological consummation? Does death amount to salvation from facticity?

80. Ibid., 159.

81. My emphasis. Heidegger, "Phenomenological Interpretations with Respect to Aristotle" in *Becoming Heidegger*, 161.

82. Lacoste, *Experience and the Absolute*, 160.

83. Ibid., 158.

84. See Tillich, *Love, Power, and Justice*.

85. In Jacques Derrida and Jean-Luc Marion's conversations about the logic of the gift, it is *the giver* that must be bracketed (at least temporarily) for the gift to be received.

86. Lacoste, *Experience and the Absolute*, 193.

87. Ibid, 185–86.

88. Bonhoeffer, *Letters and Papers from Prison*, DBWE 8, 478.

89. Lacoste, *Experience and the Absolute*, 160.

90. Bonhoeffer, *Creation and Fall*, DBWE 3, 34, 36, 46, 68, 82. These associations are primarily made in the context of reflections on Genesis 1–2. When Bonhoeffer explicates Genesis 3 and "the fall," he does speak of the destruction of "God's work" (the world) and even the loss of creatureliness. Yet, even here "fallen creation" is simply "destroyed world," confirming the prelapsarian nonopposition of creation and world (ibid., 132).

91. See Feil, *Theology of Dietrich Bonhoeffer*, 108–10.

92. Nietzsche, *Thus Spoke Zarathustra*, in *The Portable Nietzsche*, 142–45.

93. Bonhoeffer, DBWE 3, 76.

94. Baptismal address, October 1932; quoted in the "Afterword" of DBWE 3, 163n67.

95. Bonhoeffer's use of "the natural" in *Ethics* differs from his use in

Discipleship and *Creation and Fall*.

96. Bonhoeffer, DBWE 6, 172–73. The primary difference between creation as such and "nature" (or fallen creation) is that, "The unmediated relation to God of the true creation becomes the relative freedom of natural life" (ibid., 173).

97. Bonhoeffer, DBWE 3, 47.

98. Bonhoeffer, DBWE 6, 63.

99. Bonhoeffer, DBWE 6, 258.

100. Bonhoeffer, DBWE 8, 228.

101. Ibid., 501.

102. Lacoste does address the "we" of prayer or collective "liturgical experience" in "Liturgy and Coaffection," 93–103.

103. Green, *Bonhoeffer: A Theology of Sociality*, 273.

104. Bonhoeffer, *Letters and Papers from Prison*, DBWE 8, 501.

105. On Levinas, see Lacoste, *Experience and the Absolute*, 50, 71–72. For Lacoste ethics and liturgy are related circularly; for Bonhoeffer the encounter with God always takes a relational or ethical (and therefore worldly) form.

106. Lacoste, too, understands ethics as a "call" (ibid., 75), but it is derivative of and secondary to liturgical identity or the vocation of prayer. On the relationship between ethics and liturgy see ibid., 70–76.

107. Of course, it is clear at this point that Lacoste and Bonhoeffer relate act and being differently—a contrast worth drawing out but not within the scope of this paper. Where Bonhoeffer appreciates that Heidegger maintains the unity of act and being (see *Act and Being*, DBWE 2, 67–68), Lacoste specifically attempts to undo the Heideggerian collapse of *existentia* and *essentia* in order to claim an identity that exceeds existence.

108. DBWE 8, 501. Bonhoeffer says, "Our relationship to God is a new life in 'being there for others,' through participation in the being of Jesus." Think too of Bonhoeffer's statement that "we can be Christian today in only two ways, through prayer and in doing justice among human beings" (ibid., 389). The neighbor mediates our prayer and God our righteous action. They are not hierarchically or contiguously related, but integral to one another.

109. In Irenaeus's interpretation of Paul, "the Redeemer gathers together, includes, or comprises the whole of reality in himself, the human race being included." Kelly, *Early Christian Doctrines*, 172. See Irenaeus, *Adversus Haereses* 5.14.2, 5.16.3.

110. See, e.g., DBWE 8, 230; DBWE 16, 543.

111. Bonhoeffer, DBWE 3, 21.

112. Lacoste, *Experience and the Absolute*, 185–86.

Endnotes

113. Bonhoeffer, DBWE 8, 393–94, 397. Although Bonhoeffer, like Lacoste, is critical of the Cartesian cogito and its legacy, he does not seem concerned that receiving the gift of ourselves might reinstantiate the self-privileging of appropriation. Perhaps this is because, as Charles Marsh points out, for Bonhoeffer, the "subject" that is always already de-centered is re-centered in Christ: the self is transformed into "a new creation" and, as such, is "always more than I" (rather than less) (Marsh, *Reclaiming Dietrich Bonhoeffer*, 108–9; 2 Cor 5:17).

114. DBWE 6, 146–47.

115. DBWE 3, 22. Without rehashing the long-standing debate over whether and to what extent the "now" is present in the "not-yet," these comments minimally show that for Bonhoeffer living before God in the world cannot be all eschatological deferral in light of the reality of Christ.

116. Bonhoeffer, DBWE 6, 58.

117. Bonhoeffer, DBWE 6, 198.

118. Bonhoeffer, DBWE 16, 543.

119. Bonhoeffer, DBWE 6, 193–94.

120. DBWE 8, 229. Bonhoeffer quotes Gerhardt's lines: "Calm your hearts, dear friends; / whatever plagues you, / whatever fails you, / I will restore it all."

121. Bonhoeffer speaks of non-religious and worldly Christianity in multiple places and especially throughout DBWE 8. A few illuminating passages can be found in his letters to Bethge on April 30, May 5 and July 16, 1944 in DBWE 8, 361–67, 371–74, 473–82.

122. DBWE 6, 58. He continues, "or to wish to be worldly without seeing and recognizing the world in Christ" (ibid.).

123. See, e.g., DBWE 8, 366, 475, 479.

124. DBWE 8, 373. Cf. ibid., 447.

125. DBWE 8, 372, 501. "Mythological" is opposed to the earthly and refers alternately to 1) the "Christian" but, as Bonhoeffer sees it, unbiblical obsession salvation of the disembodied soul and 2) confused divine-worldly configurations such as are found in what he calls the "Greek" deification of the human and "oriental" animism or pantheism (see ibid., 501). "Metaphysical" is opposed to the historical (to the biblical story); it refers to an abstract transcendent or "beyond" and ignores the worldliness of God in Christ.

126. DBWE 8, 486.

127. DBWE 8, 447–48.

128. DBWE 8, 228.

129. DBWE 12, 324.

130. Bonhoeffer, *Letters and Papers from Prison*, DBWE 8, 448. On the theme

of "strength" see ibid., 451, 457.

131. Bonhoeffer, *Sanctorum Communio*, DBWE 1, 121, 141, etc.

132. Bethge, *Dietrich Bonhoeffer: A Biography*, 787.

133. Bonhoeffer is just as skeptical as Lacoste is of the early Schleiermacher's description of "religion" as a "sense and taste for the Infinite" (Schleiermacher, *Speeches*, 278).

134. In *Creation and Fall*, Bonhoeffer comments on Genesis 2:28–31, when God beholds God's work as "very good" and blesses it saying, "be fruitful and multiply:" "It is humankind's whole *empirical* existence that is blessed here, its creatureliness, its worldliness, its earthliness" (DBWE 3, 69; my emphasis).

135. Given the so-called "theological turn" of recent phenomenology, with works like Jean-Louis Chretien's *The Call and the Response*, Jean-Luc Marion's *Being Given*, and Michel Henry's *I am the Truth*, it is by no means self-evident that there can be no phenomenology of creation.

136. Bonhoeffer's thoughts on grace, nature, and creation prefigure in some ways the position developed by Kathryn Tanner in *Christ the Key*. Particularly in chapters two and three, Tanner navigates the traditional divide between Protestants and Catholics on this point and constructs an alternate theology of grace that draws on but distinguishes itself from both lines of thought.

137. My emphasis. "From Theology to Theological Thinking" is the title of Lacoste's three-part paper delivered for the 2010 James W. Richards lectures at the University of Virginia. He argues against a sharp distinction between philosophy and theology as independent disciplines.

138. Much depends upon whether, when Lacoste says, "the limits of the existential are not the limits of . . . humanity," he means these limits are not essentially or meaningfully linked to being human or merely that they are not the *only* limits of humanity (Lacoste, *Experience and the Absolute*, 105).

Notes to Chapter 10—Franz

1. Dietrich Bonhoeffer, *Ethics*, DBWE 6. I thank especially Adam C. Clark and Mike Mawson for assisting with my English and for making many insightful and helpful suggestions throughout the editorial process.

2. DBWE 6, 49.

3. Bonhoeffer does not divide individual from social ethics. He regarded the so-called "social ethics" of his time as an "ethical aporia." He discards both this division (as in Reinhold Niebuhr's, *Moral Man and Immoral Society*, for example) as well as an understanding of the "social" formed by National Socialist ideas of society. Furthermore, although Bonhoeffer's ethics have their foundation in the

Endnotes

gospel of Jesus Christ, they are no "absolute ethics of the gospel," as Weber criticized Christian ethics. Weber differentiated *"Gesinnungsethik"* (ethics of [pure] intention) as apolitical in opposition to *"Verantwortungsethik"* (ethics of responsibility) which for him is the only adequate ethics for the professional political and public realm. Cf. Weber's talk "Politics as a Vocation" from 1919. As will be shown the notion of responsibility is central in *Ethics*.

4. As most disastrously put into effect through the Nazi biopolitics that distinguished "life worth living" from "life unworthy of living" (*lebenswertem und lebensunwertem Leben*). Bonhoeffer opposes this distinction in the section on "The Right to Bodily Life" in the Ethics fragment "The Natural Life," DBWE 6, 185-96.

5. The translation "concrete theological ethics" points to the content and grammar of Bonhoeffer's ethics, whereas "protestant" or "evangelical" would add an unintended confessional feature.

6. In the section "Ethics as Formation" Bonhoeffer writes, "Thereby we are turned away from any abstract ethic and toward a concrete ethic" (DBWE 6, 99). I want to argue that this is a fundamental characteristic of Bonhoeffer's *Ethics*. Cf. also Bonhoeffer's remarks in a letter from the year 1943 to defend his own case, which he wrote among others in Tegel prison (*"Wehruntersuchungsgefängnis Tegel"*) addressing the Judge Advocate (*"Oberkriegsgerichtsrat"*) Dr. Manfred Roeder (DBW 16, 410).

7. Cf. Rose, "Death of the Social?," 327-56.

8. Foucault restricts the analysis of discursive practices in the beginning to what he calls "archaeology." Later he opens analysis further through the method of "genealogy," which reflects on the operations of specific social forms across history. Cf. esp. Michel Foucault, *The Archaeology of Knowledge and The Discourse on Language*.

9. As will be shown below, the German verb *"ausrichten"* can have several meanings—the most basic ones might be rendered by the English verbs *to orient, to declare, to execute*.

10. Taking Christian worship as the paradigmatic place for hearing the commandment of God, it becomes clear that even this is a *public* event.

11. Cf. Martin Luther, *Freedom of a Christian* (LW 31:327ff [WA 7:20-38, 49-73]). For a discussion of contemporary Lutheran Ethics, see also Hütter's "The Twofold Center of Christian Ethics: Christian Freedom and God's commandments," 31-54.

12. Cf. esp. Foucault, *Discipline & Punish: The Birth of the Prison* and idem, *The History of Sexuality*, vol. 1. The French originals were first published in 1975 and 1976.

13. Foucault, "The Confession of the Flesh," 194-228.

14. Ibid., 194.

15. Ibid.

16. Ibid., my emphasis.

17. Ibid., 195.

18. For instance, in *History of Sexuality*, Foucault tries to show how a simple "repression theory," which holds that during the eighteenth and nineteenth centuries individual sexuality was not free but rather constantly repressed on a societal scale, misses the point. On the contrary Foucault points to the fact that a growing number of discourses regarding sexuality appeared at that time. This "dispositive of sexuality" functioned not by restricting sexuality, but rather in such a way that it demanded constant attention to sexuality by oneself and society. Demanding constant attention meant providing for a healthy sexuality, controlling it at childhood, medically analyzing its perversions, etc. For the twenty-first century we could probably add "making sure sexuality is *free*." Thus it becomes clear how "freedom" might be an element of a dispositive that is actually working coercively.

19. It is therefore not surprising that "being free" and "being sovereign" are predominant features of the individualism that seems to be one of the main driving forces of the economic system we are living in right now.

20. Agamben, "What is an apparatus?," 11.

21. This text was written in the late 1960s and provides Foucault's most concentrated methodological reflections on the early period of his work.

22. Hyppolite, *Introduction à la philosophie de l'histoire de Hegel*. Hegel in turn develops this concept in his "Die Positititivität der christlichen Religion."

23. Agamben, "What is an apparatus?," 5. Agamben goes on to stress Hegel's insight that, while positivities thus seem to be imposed externally, they "become . . . internalized in the system of beliefs and feelings." Therefore *positivité* refers not only to normative elements in-and-for-themselves; rather, it addresses the specific, subjectively-assimilated relations in which they are ordered toward each other.

24. Ibid.

25. How do we know that this definition of dispositives remains practically in effect in modern discourse and practice? Agamben's exploration of the definition of *dispositif* in the French standard dictionary "*Le Petit Robert*" offers one supporting example. As other Foucault scholars have also pointed out, this entry shows that *dispositif* reflects everyday French discourse and practice and not just purely academic reflection. According to this entry, *dispositif* is inherently juridical; it is "the part of a judgment that contains the decision separate from the opinion . . . the section of a sentence, that decides, or the enacting clause of a law." Moreover, it denotes the formation of identity according to conformity to

the good prescribed by "Law." Yet *dispositif* has also a technological connotation; it is the "way in which the parts of a machine (*appareil*) or of a mechanism and, by extension, the mechanism itself are arranged." And finally, this mechanical form of governance entails a strategic, "military" implementation as power: a *dispositif* involves a "set of [such] means arranged in conformity with a plan." The practical field that this dictionary entry captures clearly reinforces juridical, legal, technological, and strategic aspects that implement managerial subjection. Cf. "What is an apparatus?," 7–8. For a similar account in other thinkers, see Link, "Dispositiv," 237–42.

26. Agamben conducts this genealogy in greater detail in his recently published *The Kingdom and the Glory: For a Theological Genealogy of Economy and Government*. Interestingly enough the title is an appeal to the Lords prayer, "For thine is the *kingdom* and the power and the *glory*, for ever and ever. Amen." For reasons of brevity I will give his arguments mostly from his essay, "What is an apparatus?"

27. Cf. Richter, *Oikonomia*.

28. Cf. Aristotle, *Politics*, 1253b ff.

29. Agamben, "What is an Apparatus?," 11.

30. Ibid., 10. Agamben of course is not the first one who recognizes such a split. Theologians also have identified the the split between God's being and God's saving action as a fundamental and structural problem plaguing modern dogmatics. Cf. Mildenberger, "Die Verhältnisbestimmung von Theologie und Ökonomie als grundlegendes Strukturproblem einer modernen Dogmatik," 340–58.

31. Agamben, "What is an Apparatus?," 9. Note how oikonomia in this sense becomes merely a technical strategy.

32. The following quotations will mostly use the term "apparatus." I continue to use the term "dispositive" or "modern dispositive" to keep the connection to Foucault's concept.

33. Ibid., 13.

34. Ibid., 11, my emphasis.

35. Ibid., 15.

36. Ibid.

37. Agamben himself names the cell phone. I want to add virtual realities like "social networks." Of course, these technologies have their merits, but at the same time they are also changing our ways we communicate and interact. Thus, they do change the form of our social and political relations.

38. Ibid., 22.

39. Ibid.

Endnotes

40. Cf. esp. Foucault's *History of Sexuality*, vol. 3, *The Care of the Self* (1984), and the lecture he gave at the Collège de France in 1981–1982: *The Hermeneutics of the Subject*.

41. Agamben, "What is an Apparatus?," 32.

42. Ibid., 18.

43. Ibid., 19.

44. Ibid., 24.

45. Although the concept of the "orders of creation" was never fully homogeneous within the Lutheran tradition itself, it must be confessed that the mainstream of German Lutheran Theology in the 1930s and 1940s advanced a highly problematic understanding and application of the concept. For some, e.g., it served as legitimization of dubious "orders" invoked by the Nazis, like that of a pure *Volkstum* (people) and *Rasse* (race).

46. Regarding this eschatological and exploratory logic of "living in the becoming of created beings," cf. Ulrich, *Wie Geschöpfe leben. Konturen evangelischer Ethik*.

47. Cf. Wannenwetsch, "Wovon handelt die materiale Ethik? Oder warum die Ethik der elementaren Lebensformen ('Stände') einer 'Bereichsethik' vorzuziehen ist," 95–136. Wannenwetsch understands Luther's "three estates" (*Stände*) as "*rudimentary forms of living*" (*elementare Lebensformen*).

48. Cf. Eph 2,10.

49. I thank Hans G. Ulrich for helpful remarks regarding this point in suggesting that the mandates are not simply to be identified with the Foucauldian dispositives, but rather can be understood as their "*inversions*."

50. Bonhoeffer, DBWE 6, 380.

51. DBWE 6, 56.

52. DBWE 6, 57.

53. For Bonhoeffer, the personifications of these paradigmatic antipodes are the figures of the *monk* and that of the nineteenth-century "*Kulturprotestant*." Regarding "*Kulturprotestantismus*," cf. DBWE 6, 57, footnote 40.

54. DBWE 6, 58.

55. Ibid.

56. DBWE 6, 68, my emphasis.

57. In *Act and Being* (DBWE 2) Bonhoeffer tries to overcome the difference between a transcendental and an ontological approach in understanding the Church as a unity of act and being, "*Akt-Seinseinheit*." Both approaches on their own are not able to free the *cor curvum in se*, are not able to sustain a real "from the outside," a real transcendence and lead to an "I enclosed system"

Endnotes

(*ichbeschlossenes System*). Cf. the exposition of the "Problem in Bonhoeffer" by Feil, *The Theology of Dietrich Bonhoeffer*, 9ff. The Church is one of the mandates. Yet this raises the question, do the other mandates constitute unities of act and being as well? How does language, the Word, the political relate to act and being? Bonhoeffer is exploring just these questions in his later *Ethics*.

58. Cf. Bonhoeffer's reflections on "*Gestaltwerden Jesu Christi*" in the section "Ethics as formation" (*Ethik als Gestaltung*).

59. DBWE 6, 389.

60. Admittedly in Bonhoeffer's discourse of the mandates there seems to be always an inherent power relation through an ordering of "above" and "below" as a hierarchical structure. This characteristic feature of the mandates, as well as of Luther's "orders" (or "hierarchies" as he also refers to them) has to be analyzed in greater detail.

61. Cf. esp. Bonhoeffer's reflections on "euthanasia" in the *Ethics* section "The Right to Bodily Lilfe," 190ff. This rigorous form of social management shows to what extreme it can be realized what Foucault describes as governmentality

62. Bonhoeffer, DBWE 6, 68–69, modified translation.

63. This formulation resembles a title of a book by the German philosopher Waldenfels, *In den Netzen der Lebenswelt*. There Waldenfels picks up a controversy between Habermas and Foucault regarding the rationality and/or the positivity of existing orders.

64. Bonhoeffer, DBWE 6, 389. Bonhoeffer claims that this presence of Christ creates a "polemical unity" by which the mandates correct one another.

65. DBWE 6, 380.

66. Cf. Luther's exegesis of Gal 5:18, "But if you are [governed] by the Spirit, you are not under the Law" (*Regiert euch aber der Geist, so seid ihr frei vom Gesetz*), and his "Temporal Authority: To what extent it should be obeyed."

67. Bonhoeffer, DBWE 6, 381–82, my emphasis.

68. DBWE 6, 226.

69. Cf. esp. Hannah Arendt, "What is Freedom?," 143–71.

70. Bonhoeffer, DBWE 6, 385.

71. DBWE 6, 70–71.

Notes to Chapter 11—Daniels

1. Foucault, *Society Must Be Defended*, 247.

2. Ibid., 255.

3. See Bethge, *Dietrich Bonhoeffer: A Biography*, 620ff, 796ff; Schlingensiepen, *Dietrich Bonhoeffer 1906–1945*, 94ff, 127ff.

4. Marsh, *Reclaiming Dietrich Bonhoeffer* Green, *Bonhoeffer: A Theology of Sociality*.

5. For further analysis of Bonhoeffer and race, see Young, *No Difference in the Fare*; Jenkins and McBride, eds., *Bonhoeffer and King*.

6. Foucault, *Power/Knowledge*, 114–15.

7. Foucault, *Society Must Be Defended*, 15.

8. Ibid., 24, 23.

9. Ibid., 15. Power is a central, recurring theme in Foucault's oeuvre. In the first lecture, delivered on January 7, 1979, Foucault narrates the shift he is undergoing here from a local critique made possible by "the insurrection of subjugated knowledge's" through which his work on psychiatry, prisons, and sexuality can be understood (ibid., 7). "Perhaps the battle no longer looks the same," he suggests, and thus makes the move to examining power as a relation of force within the strictures of society as a whole (ibid., 11).

10. Ibid., 241, 248.

11. Foucault, *History of Sexuality*, 1:140. Whereas biopower is a major theme in the lectures that comprise idem, *Society Must Be Defended*, it first emerges as a topic in this text.

12. Foucault, *Society Must Be Defended*, 248.

13. Ibid, 255.

14. Ibid, 60.

15. Ibid, 259.

16. See Foucault, *Archaeology of Knowledge & the Discourse on Language*. The relationship between power and knowledge is a central theme in Foucault's work.

17. Foucault, *Order of Things*, 350.

18. Discussions of classification are dispersed through Foucault's texts. On the one hand, classifications serve as keys for understanding the construction of subjectivity in the development of what he calls the human sciences, new schemas for classifying information elucidating underlying conceptual shifts. Classifications also operate as the tools that produce those shifts, functioning as instruments of power. Foucault's historical analyses—of mental health: *Madness and Civilization*; prisons: *Discipline & Punish*; and sexuality: *The History of Sexuality*, vol. 1—all examine how classifications operate in these ways. *Archaeology of Knowledge*, as well as *The Order of Things*, offer deeper examination of the role of classifications in Foucault's methodology.

19. Foucault, *Power/Knowledge*, 69.

Endnotes

20. Foucault's discussion of discourse can be found primarily in *Archaeology of Knowledge*. See also his essay "Subject and Power," in Foucault, *Power/Knowledge*, 326–48.

21. Zantop, *Colonial Fantasies*, 38–39.

22. Ibid., 39. Zantop explicitly acknowledges the relationship between the colonial fantasies and scholarship, noting how the German intellectual project in this context "recognizes and theorizes the affinity between knowledge acquisition and colonial appropriation"(ibid., 41). Zantop references Immanuel Kant's *Critique of Pure Reason* as a paradigmatic example of this affinity, explaining that "Kant's narrative of exploring the island of truth and securing its possession against opposing claims defines the search for 'truth' as a colonial takeover . . . Even though Kant is speaking only about mental conquests and intellectual terrain, his choice of metaphor reveals the pervasiveness of the island fantasy in late eighteenth-century discourse and the extent to which theory has become complicitous with practical colonialism through discursive practices" (ibid., 42).

23. Koonz, *The Nazi Conscience*, 2ff.

24. Zantop, *Colonial Fantasies*, 41. Zantop explains that, though Germany did not become a colonial power until relatively later than other European nations, their drive for colonial conquest was of deep significance. This is what she names as Germany's "colonial fantasies," a "kind of colonialism without colonies." While I point to Zantop's recognition of the "racial" differences undergirding colonial endeavors, a main argument in Zantop's text is that the colonial fantasies of German culture were not solely or perhaps even primarily based on "racial" difference, but on gender and sexual difference. This critique is also applicable to Foucault's analysis of race. See, for instance, Stoler, *Race and the Education of Desire*. For more on "racial" difference underpinning the colonial fantasy, see Bhabha, *Location of Culture*; Said, *Orientalism*.

25. Koonz, *The Nazi Conscience*, 8. Koonz argues that a Nazi conscience stemmed from this notion of *Volk*, which "held out an egalitarian and ecumenical promise to members of a so-called community of fate"(ibid., 10). The language of *Volk* does appear in some of Bonhoeffer's earlier writings. In the introduction to DBWE 10, Clifford Green explains that "those who first read these words knowing Bonhoeffer the 'pacifist,' the antinationalist ecumenist, and the anti-Nazi resister are rightly shocked and embarrassed by this *völkisch* lebenstraum theology," and he notes that "three years later, we hear very different assertions" (ibid., 11). Green cites Eberhard Bethge and explains that "Bonhoeffer never spoke in this 'titanic' manner again" (*Bonhoeffer: A Theology of Sociality*, 128). In the afterword of *Ethics*, Bonhoeffer himself acknowledges the problematic relationship between *völkisch* thinking and German supremacy (DBWE 6, 416ff).

26. Koonz, *Nazi Conscience*, 10.

27. Foucault, *Society Must Be Defended*, 255.

28. Whereas Foucault's work is focused on addressing the particular predicament of post-Kantian subjectivity, Bonhoeffer is concerned with the overarching problem of (sinful) subjectivity, though—as my argument suggests—he does seem to see the post-Kantian subject as especially symptomatic of sinful self-assertion.

29. DBWE 12, 301.

30. DBWE 12, 302. Even the act of self-negation, for Bonhoeffer, is an act of self-affirmation.

31. DBWE 12, 303.

32. DBWE 12, 302.

33. Ibid.

34. DBWE 12, 303.

35. I am indebted to Willie Jennings' unpublished essay, "In the Form of the Aryan," for this turn of phrase. Jennings argues that, while Bonhoeffer's critique of knowledge speaks to the problematic, dominating impulses of epistemology that undergird a colonialist agenda, it does not adequately take into account the gendered contours of modern knowledge projects. This essay explores his claim that "Bonhoeffer gestured toward a way that might free *theological* knowledge from the process of objectification and commodification but not the fantasies of knowledge accumulation within gender ecologies" (24).

36. DBWE 12, 301.

37. DBWE 12, 304–5.

38. For a detailed account of the significance of silence in theology, see Muers, *Keeping God's Silence*.

39. DBWE 12, 300–301.

40. DBWE 12, 303.

41. DBWE 5, 31.

42. DBWE 5, 33.

43. DBWE 5, 44.

44. DBWE 5, 34, my emphasis.

45. Bonhoeffer also addresses the importance of the mediating work of Christ in relationships in his essay "Discipleship and the Individual" in DBWE 4. Here, Bonhoeffer explains that "people called by Jesus learn that they had lived an illusion in their relationship to the world. The illusion is immediacy" (94). Jesus as the mediator means that "there are no longer natural, historical, or experiential unmediated relationships . . . [that] there is no way from us to other than the path through Christ, his word, and our following him" (ibid., 95). *All* knowledge, including knowledge of another person, is a "God-given reality" that exists "only

Endnotes

through Jesus Christ" (ibid., 96, 95).

46. DBWE 5, 32.

47. Ibid.

48. Ibid, 45–46.

49. Foucault, *Society Must Be Defended*, 259.

50. DBWE 12, 364.

51. DBWE 12, 365.

52. DBWE 12, 366.

53. Ibid., n14. The editor of DBWE 12 cites the above quote from the Lutheran confessions (Formula of Concord, Epitome, Article X/6, *Book of Concord*, 516), explaining that "in *statu confessionis*" refers to "a state of confessional protest in which matters such as church membership and rules are no longer matters of convenience and doctrinal indifference (*adiaphora*)," but rather central to the Christian faith.

54. Bonhoeffer's discussion of the status of the Jews as a religious as opposed to racial people is particularly interesting, and speaks to Bonhoeffer's rejection of the racialization of biopower. Bonhoeffer calls the biologically-determined category of race into question, exploring instead the theological, covenantal nature of Jewish identity. "From the point of view of Christ's church," Bonhoeffer explains, "Judaism is never a racial concept but rather a religious one. Rather than the biologically dubious entity of the Jewish race, it means the "people Israel" (DBWE 12, 368).

55. DBWE 12, 370.

56. DBWE 12, 372.

57. DBWE 12, 373.

58. DBWE 12, 372–73.

59. That is, "The church of Christ has never lost sight of the thought that the "chosen people," which hung the Redeemer of the world on the cross, must endure the curse of its action in long-drawn-out suffering" (DBWE 12, 367); "The conversion of Israel is to be the end of its people's suffering" (ibid.). In "Dietrich Bonhoeffer: A Jewish View," Rosenbaum suggests that Bonhoeffer is merely the least of the offenders of an unequivocally anti-Semitic German intelligentsia.

60. Bethge, "Dietrich Bonhoeffer and the Jews," in Godsey & Kelly, eds., *Ethical Responsibility*, 63. Another document of particular significance and relevance here is the August revision of the Bethel Confession, co-written by Bonhoeffer with Wilhelm Vische: "For the same reason we reject the false doctrine that recognizes the Old Testament only as the Bible of Jesus, that is, of the original Christian church, and recognizes its validity only in that context (religious anti-Semitism)" (DBWE 12, 379). The editor remarks on the significance of this

passage, noting that Bonhoeffer "seems to draw an explicit connection between traditional Christian theological prejudices against Judaism with Nazi anti-Semitism" (ibid., 380n12). The editor also suggests that "That the Bethel confession addresses race, when it is not a subject "in either the Bible or the Lutheran confessions," is Bonhoeffer's rejection of Nazi racial ideology" (ibid., 388n26). The Bethel Confession speaks to the relationship between Judaism and Christianity at the interstices of race and the State. For an in-depth exploration of this intersection, including an examination of Foucault's work on the racial technologies of biopower, see the first chapter, "The Drama of Race: Toward a Theological Account of Modernity," of Carter, *Race: A Theological Account*, 39–77.

61. It is also worth noting that *Life Together* was written in the vacant home of Bonhoeffer's Jewish-Christian brother-in-law whose escape Bonhoeffer had helped to coordinate. Several passages in the text accordingly show that the inclusion of the Jews in genuine community, and an appreciation of Judaism more broadly, remained at the forefront of Bonhoeffer's mind as he continued to develop his understanding of christological community. See, for instance, DBWE 5, 53–54 and 71, along with the editors' notes. Cf. also the Editor's Introduction, ibid., 3–4, for the historical setting.

Bibliography

Agamben, Giorgio. *The Kingdom and the Glory: For a Theological Genealogy of Economy and Government*. Translated by Lorenzo Chiesa and Matteo Mandarini. Stanford, CA: Stanford University Press, 2011.
———. *What is an Apparatus? And Other Essays*. Translated by David Kishik and Stefan Pedatella. Stanford, CA: Stanford University Press, 2009.
Altizer, Thomas, and William Hamilton. *Radical Theology and the Death of God*. Indianapolis: Bobbs-Merrill, 1966.
Arendt, Hannah. *Love and Saint Augustine*. Edited by Janna Vecchiarelli Scott and Judith Chelius Stark. Chicago: University of Chicago Press, 1996.
———. "What is Freedom?" In *Between Past and Future*, 143–171. New York: Penguin, 1993.
Aristotle. *The Politics and the Constitution of Athens*. Edited by Stephen Everson. New York: Cambridge University Press, 1996.
Augustine. *The Confessions of Saint Augustine*. Translated by Francis Joseph Sheed. New York: Continuum, 1944.
Barth, Karl. *Die christliche Dogmatik im Entwurf, vol. 1: Die Lehre vom Worte Gottes. Prolegomena zur christlichen Dogmatik*. Munich: Kaiser, 1927.
———. *Der Römerbrief*. Zurich: TVZ, 1940.
Barth, Karl, and Rudolf Bultmann. *Briefwechsel 1911–1966*. Edited by Bernd Jaspert. Zurich: TVZ, 1994.
Bethge, Eberhard. "Bonhoeffer's Christology and his 'Religionless Christianity.'" *Union Seminary Quarterly Review* 23 (1967) 60–77.
———. "The Challenge of Dietrich Bonhoeffer's Life and Theology." In *World Come of Age*, edited by Ronald Gregor Smith, 22–88. London: Collins, 1967.
———. *Dietrich Bonhoeffer: A Biography*. Edited by Victoria Barnett. Rev. ed. Minneapolis: Fortress, 2000.
Biggar, Nigel, and Rufus Black, editors. *The Revival of Natural Law: Philosophical Theological and Ethical Responses to the Finnis-Grisez School*. London: Asghate, 2001.
Blanshard, Brand. "Kierkegaard on Faith." In *Essays on Kierkegaard*, edited by Jerry H. Gill, 113–26. Minneapolis: Burgess, 1969.
Bloechl, Jefferey. "A Response to Jean-Yves Lacoste." In *The Experience of God: A Postmodern Response*, edited by Kevin Hart and Barbara Wall, 104–12. Perspectives in Continental Philosophy. New York: Fordham University Press, 2005.

Bibliography

Bonhoeffer, Dietrich. *Dietrich Bonhoeffer Werke*. Edited by Eberhard Bethge et al. 17 Bände und 2 Ergänzungsbände. Gütersloh: Gütersloher, 1986–1999.
———. *Dietrich Bonhoeffer Works*. Edited by Victoria J. Barnett, Wayne Whitson Floyd Jr., and Barbara Wojhoski. 16 vols. Minneapolis: Fortress, 1996–.
———. *Gesammelte Schriften*. 5 vols. Münich: Kaiser, 1958.
Boomgaarden, Jürgen. *Das Verständnis der Wirklichkeit*. Münich: Gutersloher, 1999.
Bowie, Andrew. *Introduction to German Philosophy*, Cambridge: Polity, 2003.
Boyd, Craig A. *A Shared Morality: A Narrative Defense of Natural Law Ethics*. Grand Rapids: Brazos, 2007.
Browning, Don. *Marriage and Modernization: How Globalization Threatens Marriages and What to Do about it*. Grand Rapids: Eerdmans, 2003.
Burnell, Joel. *Poetry, Providence and Patriotism*. Eugene, OR: Pickwick, 2010.
Burtness, James. *Shaping the Future The Ethics of Dietrich Bonhoeffer*. Philadelphia: Fortress, 1985.
Butler, Judith. *Giving an Account of Oneself*. New York: Fordham University Press, 2005.
Caputo, John. "Shedding Tears Beyond Being: Derrida's Confession of Prayer." In *Augustine and Postmodernism: Confessions and Circumfession*, edited by John D. Caputo and Michael J. Scanlon, 95–114. Bloomington, IN: Indiana University Press, 2005.
Carter J. Kameron. *Race: A Theological Account*. New York: Oxford University Press, 2008.
Cox, Harvey. *The Secular City*. New York: Macmillan, 1965.
Cromartie, Michael, editor. *A Preserving Grace: Protestants, Catholics, and Natural Law*, Grand Rapids: Eerdmans, 1997.
Davies, Oliver. *A Theology of Compassion*. Grand Rapids: Eerdmans, 2001.
De Gruchy, John. *Daring, Trusting Spirit: Bonhoeffer's Friend Eberhard Bethge*. Minneapolis, Fortress, 2005.
DeJonge, Michael. *Bonhoeffer's Theological Formation: Berlin, Barth and Protestant Theology*. Oxford: Oxford University Press, 2012.
Delaney, C. F., editor. *The Liberalism-Communitarianism Debate*. Lanham, MD: Rowman & Littlefield, 1994.
Deleuze, Gilles, and Félix Guattari. *Anti-Oedipus: Capitalism and Schizophrenia*. Translated by Robert Hurley, Mark Seem, and Helen R. Lane. London: Continuum, 2004.
Derrida, Jacques. "Structure, Sign, and Play in the Discourse of the Human Sciences." In *Writing and Difference*, translated by Alan Bass, 278–94. London: Routledge, 1967.
Dilthey, Wilhelm. *Selected Works*. 5 vols. Edited by Rudolf A. Makkreel and Fritjof Rodi. Princeton: Princeton University Press, 1989–2002.
———. *Gesammelte Schriften*. 26 vols. Göttingen: Vandenhoeck & Ruprecht, 1914–.
Dumas, André. *Dietrich Bonhoeffer: Theologian of Reality*. Translated by Robert McAfee Brown. New York: Macmillan, 1971.
———. *Une théologie de la réalité: Dietrich Bonhoeffer*. Geneva: Labor et Fides 1968.
Ebeling, Gehard. *Word and Faith*. Translated by James W. Leitch. London: SCM, 1963.
Elshtain, Jean Bethke. "Shame and Public Life." *Dialog* 34/1 (1995) 18–22.
———. *Who are We? Critical Reflections and Hopeful Possibilities*. Grand Rapids: Eerdmans, 2000.
Feil, Ernst. *Die Theologie Dietrich Bonhoeffers*. Münich: Kaiser, 1971.

———. *The Theology of Dietrich Bonhoeffer.* Translated by Martin Rumscheidt. Philadelphia: Fortress, 1985.
Finnis, John. *Natural Law and Natural Rights.* New York: Oxford University Press, 1980.
Fletcher, Joseph. *Situation Ethics.* London: SCM, 1966.
Floyd, Wayne. "Encounter with an Other: Immanuel Kant and G. W. F. Hegel in the Theology of Dietrich Bonhoeffer." In *Bonhoeffer's Intellectual Formation*, edited by Peter Frick, 83–119. Tübingen: Mohr/Siebeck, 2008.
———. *Theology and the Dialectics of Otherness.* Lanham, MD: University Press of America, 1988.
Ford, David. *Self and Salvation: Being Transformed.* Cambridge: Cambridge University Press, 1999.
Foucault, Michel. *The Archaeology of Knowledge and The Discourse on Language.* New York: Vintage, 2010.
———. *Discipline & Punish: The Birth of the Prison.* New York: Vintage, 1995.
———. *The Hermeneutics of the Subject: Lectures at the Collège de France 1981–1982.* Edited by Arnold I. Davidson. Translated by Graham Burchell. New York: Picador 2005.
———. *The History of Sexuality.* Translated by Robert Hurley. 3 vols. New York: Vintage, 1990–1998.
———. *The Order of Things: An Archaeology of the Human Sciences.* New York: Routledge, 2002.
———. *Power/Knowledge: Selected Interviews and Other Writings.* Edited by Colin Gordon. New York: Pantheon, 1980.
———. *Society Must Be Defended: Lectures at the Collège de France, 1975–1976.* Translated by David Macey. New York: Picador, 2003.
Frick, Peter, editor. *Bonhoeffer's Intellectual Formation.* Tübingen: Mohr/Siebeck, 2008.
George, Robert P., editor. *Natural Law Theory: Contemporary Essays.* New York: Oxford University Press, 1992.
Godsey, John. *The Theology of Dietrich Bonhoeffer.* Philadelphia: Westminster, 1960.
Godsey, John D., and Geffrey B. Kelly, editors. *Ethical Responsibility: Bonhoeffer's Legacy to the Churches.* Toronto: Mellen, 1981.
Gregersen, Niels Henrik. "The Mysteries of Christ and Creation: 'Center' and 'Limit' in Bonhoeffer's *Creation and Fall* and *Christology* Lectures." In *Mysteries in the Theology of Dietrich Bonhoeffer*, edited by Kirsten Busch Nielsen, Ulrik Nissen, and Christiane Tietz. Göttingen: Vandenhoeck & Ruprecht, 2007.
Green, Clifford. *Bonhoeffer: A Theology of Sociality.* Rev. ed. Grand Rapids: Eerdmans, 1999.
———. "Interpreting Bonhoeffer: Reality or Phraseology?" *Journal of Religion* 55/2 (1975) 270–75.
Greggs, Tom. *Theology Against Religion.* London: T. & T. Clark, 2011.
Gregor, Brian. "Dietrich Bonhoeffer and Cruciform Philosophy." In *Bonhoeffer and Continental Thought: Cruciform Philosophy*, edited by Brian Gregor and Jens Zimmerman, 201–25. Bloomington, IN: Indiana University Press, 2009.
Gregor, Brian, and Jens Zimmerman, *Bonhoeffer and Continental Thought: Cruciform Philosophy.* Bloomington, IN: Indiana University Press, 2009.
———. *The Cruciform Self: A Philosophical Anthropology of the Cross.* Bloomington, IN: Indiana University Press, 2012.
Gregor Smith, Ronald, editor. *World Come of Age.* London: Collins, 1967.

Bibliography

Gustafson, James. *Christ and the Moral Life*. New York: Harper & Row, 1968.

Hart, Kevin. "Bonhoeffer's 'Religious Clothes': The Naked Man, the Secret, and What we Hear." In *Bonhoeffer and Continental Thought: Cruciform Philosophy*, edited by Brian Gregor and Jens Zimmerman, 177–97. Bloomington, IN: Indiana University Press, 2009.

———. "The Experience of the Kingdom of God." *The Experience of God: A Postmodern Response*, edited by Kevin Hart and Barbara Wall, 71–86. Perspectives in Continental Philosophy. New York: Fordham University Press, 2005.

Hauerwas, Stanley. *Performing the Faith*. Grand Rapids: Brazos, 2004.

Haynes, Stephen R. *The Bonhoeffer Legacy: Post-Holocaust Perspectives*. Minneapolis: Fortress, 2006.

Hegel, Georg Wilhelm Friedrich. "Die Positivität der christlichen Religion." In *Werke*, 1:104–89. Frankfurt: Suhrkamp, 1986.

———. *Lectures on the Philosophy of Religion*. Vol. 3, *The Consummate Religion*. Edited by Peter C. Hodgson. Translated by R. F. Brown, P. C. Hodgson, and J. M. Stewart, with H. S. Harris. Berkeley, CA: University of California Press, 1985.

———. *Phenomenology of Spirit*. Translated by A. V. Miller. Oxford: Oxford University Press, 1977.

———. *Philosophy of Mind*. Translated by W. Wallace and A. V. Miller. Revised by M. J. Inwood. Oxford: Oxford University Press, 2007.

Heidegger, Martin. *Becoming Heidegger: On the Trail of His Early Occasional Writings, 1910–1927*. Translated by Michael Bauer. Edited by Theodore Kisiel and Thomas Sheehan. Evanston: Northwestern University Press, 2007.

———. *Being and Time*. Translated by John Macquarrie and Edward Robinson. Oxford: Blackwell, 1962.

———. *The Essence of Reasons*. Translated by Terence Malick. Evanston: Northwestern University Press, 1969.

———. *History of the Concept of Time*. Translated by Theodore Kisiel. Chichester, UK: Wiley & Sons, 1992.

———. *Ontology: The Hermeneutics of Facticity*. Translated by John van Buren. Bloomington: Indiana University Press, 1999.

———. *Identity and Difference*. Translated by Joan Stambaugh. New York: Harper & Row, 1969.

———. *On the Way to Language*. Translated by Peter D. Hertz. New York: Harper & Row, 1971.

Hodgson, Peter C., editor. *G. W. F. Hegel: Theologian of the Spirit*. Minneapolis: Fortress, 1997.

Hopper, David H. "Bonhoeffer's 'Love of the World,' 'the Dangers of that Book,' and the Kierkegaard Question." Paper presented to the Bonhoeffer Group, American Academy of Religion Annual Meeting, 1989.

Hopper, David H. "Metanoia: Bonhoeffer on Kierkegaard." *Metanoia* [Prague] 2/3 (1991) 70–75.

Hütter, Reinhard. "The Twofold Center of Christian Ethics: Christian Freedom and God's commandments," In *The Promise of Lutheran Ethics*, edited by Karen L. Bloomquist and John R. Stumme, 31–54. Minneapolis: Fortress, 1998.

Hyppolite, Jean. *Introduction to Hegel's Philosophy of History*. Translated by B. Harris and J. B. Spurlock. Gainesville, FL: University Press of Florida, 1996.

Janz, Paul D. *The Command of Grace: A New Theological Apologetics*. London: T. & T. Clark, 2009.
Jenkins, Willis, and Jennifer McBride, editors. *Bonhoeffer and King: Their Legacies and Import for Social Thought*. Minneapolis: Fortress, 2010.
Jüngel, Eberhard. *God as the Mystery of the World: On the Foundation of the Theology of the Crucified One in the Dispute between Theism and Atheism*. Translated by Darrell L. Guder. Grand Rapids: Eerdmans, 1983.
Kant, Immanuel. *The Conflict of the Faculties*. Translated by Mary J. Gregor. New York: Abaris, 1979.
———. *Religion within the Boundaries of Mere Reason: And Other Writings*. Edited and translated by Allen Wood and George Di Giovanni. Cambridge: Cambridge University Press, 1998.
Kelly, Geffrey B. "Revelation in Christ: A Study of Dietrich Bonhoeffer's Theology of Revelation." PhD diss., Université Catholique de Louvain, 1972.
Kelly, Geffrey B., and F. Burton Nelson, editors. *A Testament to Freedom: The Essential Writings of Dietrich Bonhoeffer*. San Francisco: HarperSanFrancisco, 1990.
Kelly, J. N. D. *Early Christian Doctrines*. New York: Harper, 1977.
Kierkegaard, Søren. *Concluding Unscientific Postscript to Philosophical Fragments*. Vol. 1. Translated and edited by Howard V. Hong, Edna H. Hong. Princeton: Princeton University Press, 1992.
———. *Der Einzelne und die Kirche*. Translated and edited by Wilhelm Kütemeyer. Berlin: Wolff, 1934.
———. *Fear and Trembling*. Translated by Alastair Hannay. London: Penguin, 1985.
———. *Papirer*. Edited by P. A. Heiberg, V. Kuhr, and E. Torsting. 11 vols. Kiøbenhaven: Gyldendal, 1909–1948.
———. *Søren Kierkegaard's Journals and Papers*. Translated and edited by Howard V. Hong and Edna H. Hong. 7 vols. Bloomington IL: Indiana University Press, 1967–1978.
Kirkpatrick, Matthew D. *Attacks on Christendom in a World Come of Age: Kierkegaard, Bonhoeffer, and the Question of a Religionless Christianity*. Eugene, OR: Pickwick, 2011.
Koonz, Claudia. *The Nazi Conscience*. Cambridge, MA: Belknap, 1997.
Kotsko, Adam. "Objective Spirit and Continuity in the Theology of Dietrich Bonhoeffer." *Philosophy and Theology* 17 (2005) 17–31.
Kuhns, William. *In Pursuit of Dietrich Bonhoeffer*. Burns & Oates, 1967.
Lacoste, Jean-Yves. *Experience and the Absolute: Disputed Questions on the Humanity of Man*. Translated by Mark Raftery-Skehan. New York: Fordham University Press, 2004.
———. "Liturgy and Coaffection." *The Experience of God: A Postmodern Response*. Edited by Kevin Hart and Barbara Wall, 93–103. Perspectives in Continental Philosophy. New York: Fordham University Press, 2005.
Law, David. "Cheap Grace and the Cost of Discipleship in Kierkegaard's *For Self-Examination*." In *International Kierkegaard Commentary: For Self-Examination and Judge For Yourself!*, edited by Robert L. Perkins, 111–42. Macon, GA: Mercer University Press, 2002.
———. "Kierkegaard's Anti-Ecclesiology: the Attack on 'Christendom,' 1854–1855." *International Journal for the Study of the Christian Church* 7/2 (2007) 86–108.

Bibliography

Levinas, Emmanuel. *Existence and Existents*. Translated by Alphonso Lingis. Pittsburgh: Duquesne University Press, 1978.

———. *Humanism of the Other*. Translated by Nidra Poller. Urbana, IL: University of Illinois Press, 2003.

———. *Is it Righteous to Be? Interviews with Emmanuel Levinas*. Edited by Jill Robbins. Stanford, CA: Stanford University Press, 2001.

———. "Is Ontology Fundamental?" In *Emmanuel Levinas: Basic Philosophical Writings*, edited and translated by Simon Critchley and Robert Bernasconi, 1–10. Bloomington, IN: Indiana University Press, 1996.

———. *On Escape*. Translated by Bettina Bergo. Stanford, CA: Stanford University Press, 2003.

———. *Otherwise than Being*. Translated by Alphonso Lingis. Pittsburgh: Duquesne Univ. Press, 1998.

———. "Reflections on the Philosophy of Hitlerism." Translated by Seán Hand. *Critical Inquiry* 17/1 (1990) 62–71.

———. *Time and the Other*. Translated by Richard A. Cohen. Pittsburgh: Duquesne University Press, 1987.

Link, Jürgen. "Dispositiv." In *Foucault Handbuch. Leben-Wirken-Wirkung*, edited by Clemens Kammler, Rolf Parr, and Ulrich Johannes Schneider, 237–41. Stuttgart: Metzler, 2008.

Lovin, Robin. *Christian Faith and Public Choices*. Minneapolis: Fortress, 1984.

———. *Christian Realism and the New Realities*. Cambridge: Cambridge University Press, 2008.

Luther, Martin. *Career of the Reformer I*. Vol. 31 of *Luther's Works*, edited by Jaroslav Pelikan and Helmut T. Lehmann. St. Louis: Concordia, 1957.

———. *Lectures on Galatians 1–4*. Vol. 27 of *Luther's Works*, edited by Jaroslav Pelikan and Walter A. Hansen. St. Louis: Concordia, 1964.

———. *Sermons I*. Vol. 51 of *Luther's Works*. Edited and Translated by John W. Doberstein. Philadelphia: Fortress, 1959.

———. "Temporal Authority: To what extent it Should it be Obeyed." In *Luther's Works*, edited by Walter Brandt, 45:81–129. Philadelphia: Fortress, 1965.

MacIntyre, Alasdair. *After Virtue*. 2nd ed. Notre Dame: University of Notre Dame Press, 1984.

Malka, Salomon. *Emmanuel Levinas: His Life and Legacy*. Translated by Michael Kigel and Sonja M. Embree. Pittsburgh: Duquesne University Press, 2006.

Marsh, Charles. *Reclaiming Dietrich Bonhoeffer: The Promise of His Theology*. Oxford: Oxford University Press, 1994.

Marty, Martin. *Letters and Papers from Prison: A Biography*. Princeton: Princeton University Press, 2011.

McBride, Jennifer. *The Church for the World: A Theology of Public Witness*. New York: Oxford University Press, 2012.

Metaxas, Eric. *Bonhoeffer: Pastor, Martyr, Prophet, Spy*. Nashville: Nelson, 2010.

Mayer, Rainer. *Christuswirklichkeit: Grundlagen, Entwicklung und Konsequenzen der Theologie Dietrich Bonhoeffers*. Stuttgart: Calwer, 1969.

Mildenberger, Friedrich. "Die Verhältnisbestimmung von Theologie und Ökonomie als grundlegendes Strukturproblem einer modernen Dogmatik." *Zeitschrift für Theologie und Kirche* [ZThK] 87 (1990) 340–58.

Bibliography

Moltmann, Jürgen, and Jürgen Weissbach. *Two Studies in the Theology of Dietrich Bonhoeffer*. Translated by Reginald Fuller. New York: Scribner's Sons, 1967.

Moyn, Samuel. *Origins of the Other: Emmanuel Levinas Between Revelation and Ethics*. Ithaca, NY: Cornell University Press, 2005.

Muers, Rachel. *Keeping God's Silence: Towards a Theological Ethics of Communication*. Malden, MA: Blackwell, 2004.

Müller, Hanfried. *Von der Kirche zur Welt*. Hamburg-Bergstedt: Reich, 1961.

Niebuhr, Reinhold. *Moral Man and Immoral Society*. New York: Scribner's Sons, 1932.

———. *The Nature and Destiny of Man*. Vol. 1. Louisville: Westminster John Knox, 1964.

Nietzsche, Friedrich Wilhelm. *Thus Spoke Zarathustra*. In *The Portable Nietzsche*, translated by Walter Kaufman, 103–439. New York: Viking, 1954.

Ott, Heinrich. *Wirklichkeit und Glaube*. Zurich: Vandenhoeck & Ruprecht, 1966.

Pangritz, Andreas. *Karl Barth in der Theologie Dietrich Bonhoeffers*. Berlin: Alektor, 1989.

Phillips, John. *Christ for Us in the Theology of Dietrich Bonhoeffer*. New York: Harper & Row, 1967.

Porter, Jean. *Ministers of the Law: A Natural Law Theory of Legal Authority*. Grand Rapids: Eerdmans, 2010.

———. *Nature as Reason: A Thomistic Theory of the Natural Law*. Grand Rapids: Eerdmans, 2005.

Rasmussen, Arne. *The Church as Polis: From Political Theology to Theological Politics as Exemplified by Jürgen Moltmann and Stanley Hauweras*. Notre Dame: University of Notre Dame Press, 1986.

Rasmussen, Larry. *Dietrich Bonhoeffer: Reality and Resistance*. Louisville: Westminster John Knox, 2005.

———. "A Question of Method." In *New Studies in Bonhoeffer's Ethics*, edited by William J. Peck, 103–138. Lewiston: Mellen, 1987.

Rasmussen, Larry, with Renate Bethge. *Dietrich Bonhoeffer: His Significance for North Americans*. Philadelphia: Fortress, 1990.

Richter, Gerhard. *Oikonomia. Der Gebrauch des Wortes Oikonomia im Neuen Testament, bei den Kirchenvätern und in der theologischen Literatur bis ins 20. Jahrhundert*. Berlin: de Gruyter, 2005.

Robinson, John A.T. *Honest to God*. London: SCM, 1963.

Rodi, Fritjof. "Dilthey's 'Concept of 'Structure' Within the Context of Nineteenth Century Science and Philosophy." In *Dilthey and Phenomenology*, edited by Rudolf A. Makkreel and John Scanlon, 106–18. Washington, DC: University Press of America, 1987.

Rose, Nikolas. "The Death of the Social? Re-figuring the Territory of Government." In *Economy and Society* 25/3 (1996) 327–56.

Schleiermacher, Friedrich. *The Christian Faith*. Edited by H. R. Mackintosh and J. R. Stewart. London: T. & T. Clark, 2008.

———. *On Religion: Speeches to its Cultured Despisers*. Translated by Richard Crouter. Cambridge: Cambridge University Press, 2008.

Schliesser, Christine. *Everyone Who Acts Responsibly Becomes Guilty: Bonhoeffer's Concept of Accepting Guilt*. Louisville: Westminster John Know, 2008.

Schlingensiepen, Ferdinand. *Dietrich Bonhoeffer, 1906–1945*. Translated by Isabel Best. London: T. & T. Clark, 2010.

Bibliography

Sokolowski, Robert. *Introduction to Phenomenology*. New York: Cambridge University Press, 2000.
Soosten, Joachim von. *Die Sozialität der Kirche: Die Theologie und Theorie der Kirche in Dietrich Bonhoeffers "Sanctorum Communio."* Münich: Kaiser, 1992.
Stace, W. T. *The Philosophy of Hegel: A Systematic Exposition*. New York: Dover, 1955.
Stewart, Jon. *Kierkegaard's Relation to Hegel Reconsidered*. Cambridge: Cambridge University Press, 2003.
Stout, Jeffrey. *Ethics after Babel: the Languages of Morals and Their Discontents*. Princeton: Princeton University Press, 2001.
Tanner, Kathryn. *Christ the Key*. Cambridge: Cambridge University Press, 2010.
Tietz-Steiding, Christiane. *Bonhoeffers Kritik der verkrümmten Vernunft: Eine erkenntnistheoretische Untersuchung*. Tübingen: Mohr/Siebeck, 1999.
Tödt, Heinz Eduard. *Authentic Faith: Bonhoeffer's Theological Ethics in Context*. Edited by Glen Harold Stasssen. Translated by David Stassen and Ilse Tödt. Grand Rapids: Eerdmans, 2007.
Ulrich, Hans G. *Wie Geschöpfe Leben. Konturen Evangelischer Ethik: Ethik im Theologischen Diskurs*. Vol. 2. 2nd ed. Münster: LIT, 2007.
Visser 't Hooft, W. A., editor. *Das Zeugnis eines Boten*. Geneva, 1945.
Waldenfels, Bernhard. *In den Netzen der Lebenswelt*. Frankfurt: Suhrkamp, 1985.
Wannenwetsch, Bernd. *Political Worship: Ethics for Christian Citizens*. New York: Oxford University Press, 2004.
Wannenwetsch, Bernd. "Wovon handelt die materiale Ethik? Oder warum die Ethik der elementaren Lebensformen ("Stände") einer "Bereichsethik" vorzuziehen ist. Oswald Bayer zum sechzigsten Geburtstag," In *Kirche(n) und Gesellschaft*. Ed. Manfred Kwiran. Münich: Bernward bei Don Bosco, 2000.
Weber, Max. "Politics as a Vocation" In *From Max Weber: Essays in Sociology*, edited by H. H. Gerth and C. Wright Mills, 77–128. New York: Routledge, 1998.
Wüstenberg, Ralf. *Glauben als Leben: Dietrich Bonhoeffer und die nichtereligiöse Interpretation biblischer Begriffe*. Frankfurt: Lang, 1996.
Woefel, James. *Bonhoeffer's Theology: Classical and Revolutionary*. Nashville: Abingdon, 1970.
Wüstenberg, Ralf K. *Glauben als Leben: Dietrich Bonhoeffer and die nichtreligiöse Interpretation biblischer Begriffe*. Frankfurt: Lang, 1996.
———. "The Influence of Wilhelm Dilthey on Bonhoeffer's *Letters and Papers from Prison*." In *Bonhoeffer's Intellectual Formation: Theology and Philosophy in His Thought*, edited by Peter Frick, 167–73. Tübingen: Mohr/Siebeck, 2008.
———. *A Theology of Life: Dietrich Bonhoeffer's Religionless Christianity*. Translated by Doug Stott. Grand Rapids: Eerdmans, 1998.
Zantop, Susanne. *Colonial Fantasies: Conquest, Family, and Nation in Precolonial Germany, 1770–1870*. Durham, NC: Duke University Press, 1997.
Zimmerman, Jens, and Brian Gregor. *Being Human Becoming Human: Dietrich Bonhoeffer and Social Thought*. Eugene, OR: Pickwick, 2010.

www.ingramcontent.com/pod-product-compliance
Lightning Source LLC
Chambersburg PA
CBHW062022220426
43662CB00010B/1429

In this ethnographic contextual study of prosperity – *mafanikio* – theology, Tamie Davis achieves a whole lot. First, she centres Tanzania, a country that is historically underrepresented in missiological and world Christianity studies. Second, she narrates a grassroots story of women whose social positions identify their middle class status, yet whose contribution to spiritual insight is overlooked. This is an important trajectory in the emerging perspectives on the demographic transition of the continent in the twenty-first century, the place of Christian faith in shaping that transformation, and therefore the agency of African Christians in determining the future of the continent. Third, Tamie foregrounds the student movement of TAFES, which has had an exponential role in evangelization and the discipleship of students across Africa. Peter's words to the Sanhedrin in Acts 5:32 come to mind, Tamie is a "witness to these things, and so is the Holy Spirit, who, God has given to all who obey him." Let the story of what God is doing in Tanzania, among students, through women, and in the whole continent, be broadcast far and wide.

Wanjiru Gitau, PhD
Assistant Professor of World Christianity and Practical Theology,
Palm Beach Atlantic University, Florida, USA

There is a growing need for critical engagement with the prosperity gospel, particularly regarding its impact on the lives of African Christians – both on the continent and across the diaspora. Here, Tamie Davis offers a significant contribution to this discourse by illuminating a crucial dimension of African Christian experience: the interconnectedness of life and the holistic nature of God's blessings. Drawing from a local Tanzanian *mafanikio* theology, Davis presents a contextual understanding of a God who is deeply involved in the everyday lives of people, desiring their well-being and success. This work is a valuable resource for anyone interested in African Christianity, African theology, prosperity gospel studies, and African womanist theology.

Harvey Kwiyani, PhD
Executive Director, Missio Africanus
Lead, African Christianity Programme and Diaspora Centre,
Church Mission Society

What kind of *mafanikio* theology? This is Tamie Davis's key question as she carefully explores the dimensions of prosperity theology in Tanzania. Through ethnographic study and interviews with Tanzanian women, Tamie's attentive listening discloses a new understanding of and approach to what we have commonly called prosperity theology. Tamie's work is ground-breaking, as she explores it within its own context so we hear the perspectives of locals or insiders. Moreover, we hear the voices of women who are often overlooked in studies of this kind. She offers a theological approach, with which the women themselves resonate, as this is how they understand their living out of *mafanikio* theology. I warmly recommend Tamie's work not only for the new understanding it offers but also for how this is rooted in the lived experience of Tanzanian women seeking to be faithful to God.

Cathy Ross, PhD
Lead, Pioneer Mission Leadership Training Centre,
Church Mission Society
Canon Theologian, Leicester Cathedral, UK

Tamie Davis's work is a fascinating invitation to learn with Tanzanian women about the true nature of prosperity in everyday life. Davis has approached Tanzanian women leaders, all graduates of TAFES, with honour, respect, and humility, thus enabling the wider missions community to learn from their wisdom. With ethnographic rigour and theological depth, Davis has enabled the voices and practices of Tanzanian women to be heard in their *mafanikio* theology, which critiques the profligate prosperity gospel and offers a constructive alternative. *Mafanikio* theology embraces faithful discipleship, patient endurance, and holistic well-being within a Tanzanian worldview. Don't read this book to learn about Tanzanian women; read it to learn from them.

Rev. David Williams, PhD
Director of Training and Development,
Church Missionary Society Australia